School of QUILTING

The Definitive Guide

JESSICA AHLSTRAND KWAN

LUCKY SPOOL

Published in 2025
by Lucky Spool Media, LLC
www.luckyspool.com
5424 Sunol Blvd., Suite 10-118
Pleasanton, CA 94566
info@luckyspool.com

Editor: Teresa Stroin
Technical Editors: Teresa Stroin, Mary Flynn, and Sarah Ruiz
Designers: Page & Pixel and Sarah Rose
Illustrator: Teresa Stroin
Styling: Page & Pixel
Photography: Page & Pixel and Sarah Rose
Color Correction: Sarah Rose

9 8 7 6 5 4 3 2 1
First Edition
Printed in China
Library of Congress Cataloging-in-Publication
Data available upon request
978-1-940655-50-5
LSID0059

DEDICATED TO SUSANNE WOODS

who tirelessly supported women
and the art of quilting.
Your inspiration and influence live on.
We miss you.

TABLE OF CONTENTS

T-Shirt Quilts, 172

Small Projects, 180

Sashing and Borders, 188

The Quilt Sandwich, 200

Types of Quilting, 216

Finishing: Binding, Facing and More, 232

Quilt Storage and Care, 256

ACKNOWLEDGEMENTS

First and foremost, I want thank my husband Tony and my son Cameron. Your unwavering support has been a true blessing in this process. Tony, having you as a partner makes life a grand adventure, and you have encouraged me every step of the way. Cam, you give the best hugs and are the sweetest kiddo in the world. I love you both. Thank you to my parents for encouraging my creativity and always supporting what I wanted to do with my life. To my wonderful friends and family, thank you for checking in with me while I was working on this book, and thank you for the enthusiasm you've shown about a quilting book when none of you are quilters. To the awesome friends (you know who you are) who helped with childcare over the many months – you've helped so immensely and I appreciate you. Knowing I had your support made it easier to keep going. To my quilting friends, I appreciate the creativity we share, the laughs we have, and the time we spend together. Knowing I can check in with you anytime with an issue or idea has been a huge blessing. To Kristy, Nissa, and Teresa who worked their butts off to achieve my vision – we actually did it! And to Bruce who thought this was all possible in the first place, I appreciate that you saw something in me I hadn't known was there.

FOREWORD

I've always said that anyone who can sew a straight line can make a quilt. I said it to welcome beginners into the quilting universe which can be both overwhelming and intimidating. As an experienced quilter, I know it's a bit more complicated than that. Being self-taught, I turned to the internet for information after making errors or looking for techniques to help me make what I envisioned. It took years for me to find techniques and information to make my journey easier and probably quicker. As I scanned the Table of Contents of *School of Quilting*, I thought, "There it all is: the basics, the techniques, the fundamentals of quilting and finishing, and even projects for practice." What a gift.

Jessica and I connected through our relationships with Susanne Woods, my publisher and Jessica's guildmate and friend. We shared our joy and passion for making and finishing quilts. I'm thrilled that Jessica translated her passion into a practical guide for both the beginner and the experienced quilter. Her book is packed with valuable information, techniques, and tips that will make anyone's quilting experience easier and more successful; when that happens, we make more quilts.

With Jessica's *School of Quilting* in your library you will have a comprehensive resource to unleash your creativity and tackle whatever challenges you meet on your quilting journey.

Enjoy the journey,
Jacquie Gering

INTRODUCTION

Quilting isn't a straightforward proposition; there is much to learn. As a newcomer to quilting, we not only need to learn about quilting techniques, but also products, tools, and complicated sewing machines. (They're expensive, too!) How do we learn about the best fabrics to use? How do we figure out how to use new tools? How do we thread a sewing machine for goodness sakes?!?! The good news is: The information is out there, you just have to look. The bad news is: You have to look. I don't know about you, but when I'm really wanting to get going on a project, I want to go-go-go. Taking the time to search and sift through videos or tutorials to find what I need takes more time than I want to give it.

Now, there are plenty of quilting books out there. One simple internet search sends you down the rabbit hole of instructional publications. There are lots of amazing quilters showcasing their considerable talents through pictures and written instructions. These can be fantastic sources of information, but what I found I really needed as a beginner—and still sometimes as a seasoned quilter—is a simple, straightforward resource that gives me all the information I need. Most books on quilting focus on a single technique or style, so important information is often left out. This book gives you a clear path to understanding the supplies you'll need and why you'll need them, to mastering different techniques, along with instructions on completing a variety of projects.

LET'S DO THIS!

JANOME
START
STOP

EQUIPMENT & MATERIALS

SEWING MACHINES

Your sewing machine is the single most important investment you'll make for quilting. It will not only be your largest financial investment, but the machine you choose will basically be your trusty sidekick. Think of it this way: you and your machine will be creating *together*. It sounds silly to say, but over time you and your machine will become true partners. You'll learn how your machine works, how to get the best performance from it, you'll know which setting to use and when, and you'll learn to take care of your machine. When you have a sewing machine you love, working on projects will be easier and more fun.

COST

Let's be honest: sewing machines aren't cheap. While there are inexpensive machines out there, it is worth it to spend a bit of money on a decent one. Don't fall into the trap of buying the cheapest machine you can find; it will not last and will be poor quality. The most important feature to look for in a sewing machine is a good straight stitch with an even tension. (Refer to Piecing Basics: *Tension*, page 63.) In quilting, the straight stitch is pretty much the only stitch you can't do without. While decorative stitches are fun, they are considered a luxury rather than a necessity.

WHERE TO BUY

Buying a sewing machine can be daunting; there are so many choices! When buying a machine, your best bet is to "test drive" them. Yup, you can test drive sewing machines! Head on over to your local sewing machine shop and talk to the folks there about the machines that would work best for your needs. I highly (highly!) recommend patronizing an independently owned sewing machine shop; the employees will be knowledgeable about sewing in general and have experience with a variety of different manufacturers and machines at varying prices. They will be able to recommend machines based on your sewing needs and budget, and you'll be able to test drive any machine you are interested in.

While it may be tempting to try and find the cheapest machine online or at a big-box store, you will be sacrificing personalized service from people who really know sewing, and you won't be able to test out a machine before purchasing. Local sewing machine shops may also carry previously owned machines, which are a great option for the budget-conscious shopper.

SEWING MACHINE SUPPORT AND SERVICE: WHERE DO I GO?

At some point your sewing machine will need servicing. Whether you simply need a yearly cleaning and tune-up, or have a more serious issue that requires attention, the best place for support and service is your local sewing machine shop. They will provide service you won't receive from a big-box store or online retailer. Your local shop will be able to diagnose and fix any problems in order to get you sewing again. Having a local, trustworthy place to take your sewing machine is invaluable.

TYPES OF SEWING MACHINES

Although there are many types of sewing machines out there, we'll focus on those best for making quilts. From simple to complex, inexpensive to pricey, there are a variety of machines that can work for you. Most of us start out with less expensive models. A machine is a big investment, and it may be difficult to justify the cost when you're a beginning quilter.

Domestic Sewing Machines

Domestic sewing machines are the traditional, sit-down machines used by the home sewist. They come in variety of sizes and offer an array of features. While quilters use domestic sewing machines for piecing, quilting, and binding, they can also be used for a variety of other sewing projects. Inexpensive, small machines might have basic stitch options while larger, sophisticated machines provide hundreds of choices.

ANATOMY OF A SEWING MACHINE

Sewing machines are incredible pieces of technology! While every sewing machine is different, they all have the same basic mechanics. Below are some of the features you'll find on a modern, domestic machine.

1. Stitch width selector—Adjusts the stitch width (narrower or wider)

2. Stitch length selector—Adjusts the stitch length (shorter or longer)

3. Bobbin winder spindle—Holds the bobbin in place while winding it

4. Thread spool pin—Holds the spool of thread in place

5. Handwheel—Turning this wheel manually raises or lowers the needle

6. Stitch selector and function buttons—Buttons to choose a stitch or specialty machine setting

7. Thread cutter—Sharp blade mounted to the side of the machine to manually cut thread after sewing

8. Foot pressure dial—Adjusts the pressure of the presser foot on the fabric

9. Thread tension selector/dial—Adjusts the amount of tension applied to the top thread as it's being pulled through the tension discs

10. Needle screw—Holds the sewing machine needle in place

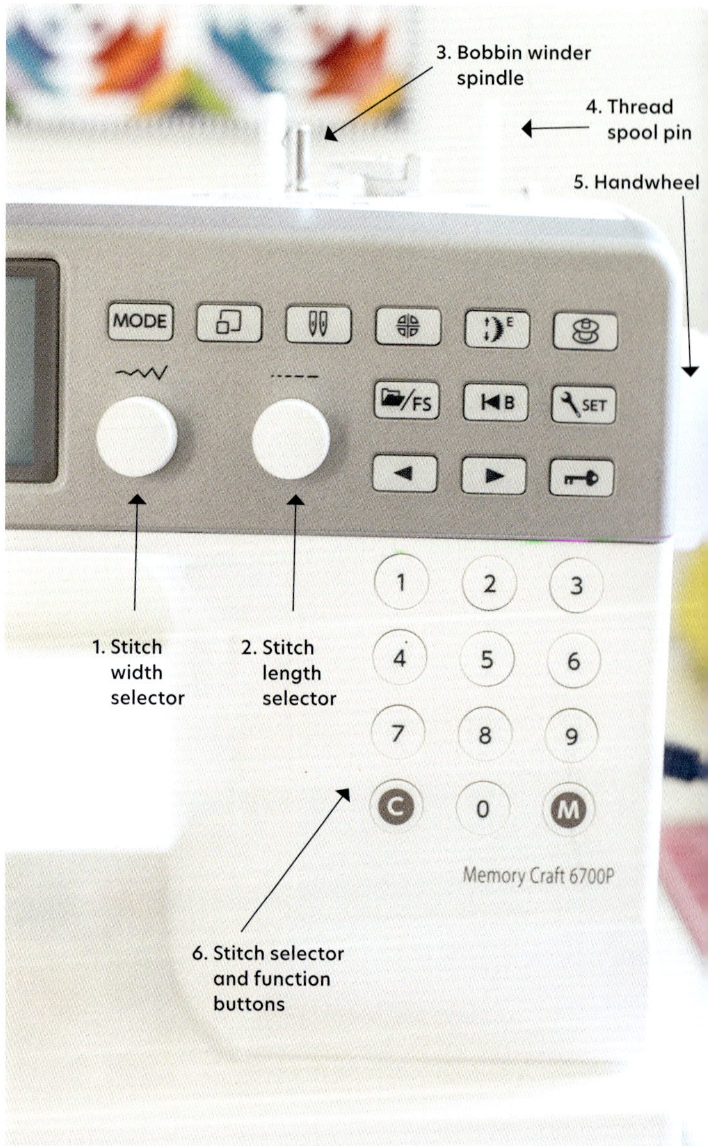

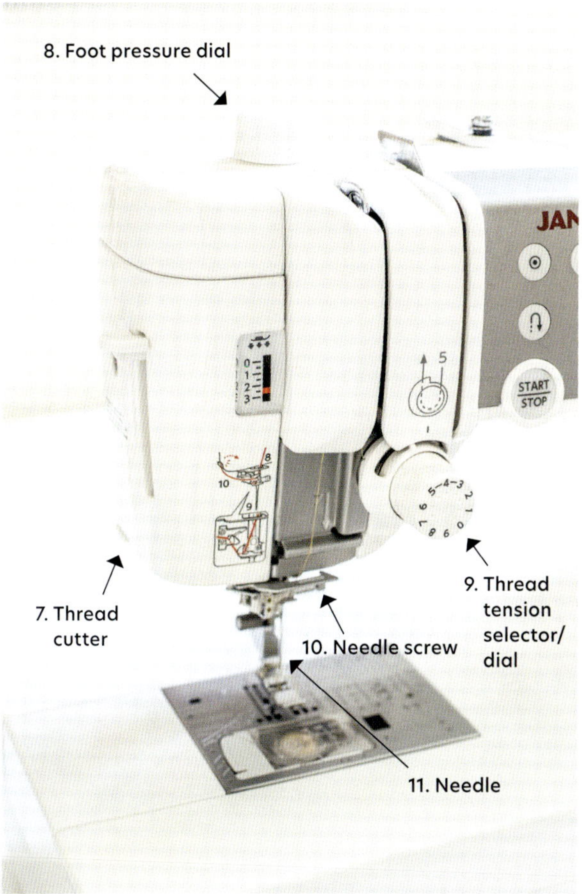

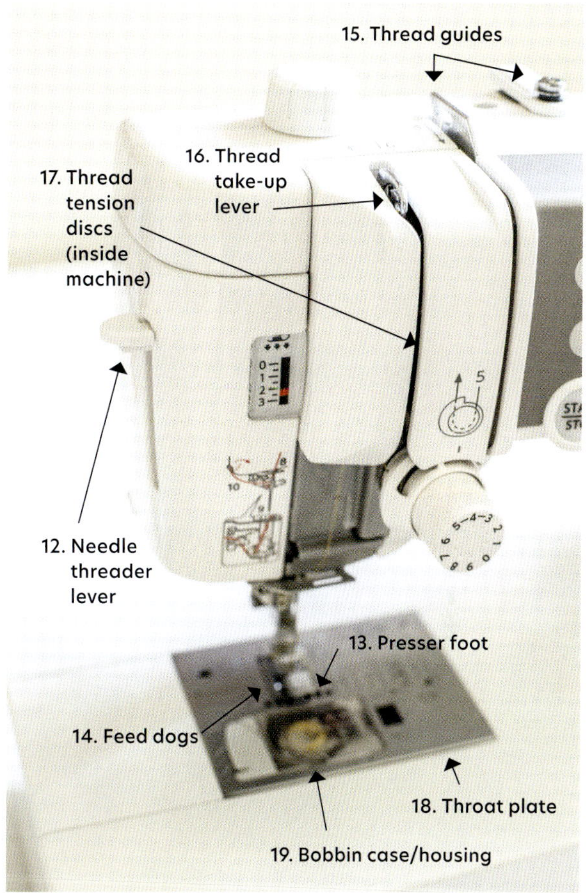

11. Needle—Pierces the fabric to bring the top thread down to meet the bobbin thread below the throat plate to create a stitch; thread is fed through the eye of the needle before sewing

12. Needle threader lever—Automatically feeds the thread through the eye of the needle

13. Presser foot—Keeps the fabric flat as it is moved under the needle

14. Feed dogs (under presser foot)—Mechanical teeth that move the fabric at an even pace

15. Thread guides—Position the thread so it goes through the machine smoothly

16. Thread take-up lever—Pulls the correct amount of thread off the spool for each stitch

17. Thread tension discs (may be inside machine)—Control thread as it passes through the machine to the needle

18. Throat plate—Covers the mechanics under the needle but leaves the feed dogs exposed; marked with a variety of seam allowance measurements

19. Bobbin case/housing—Secures the bobbin while its thread is pulled up through a hole in the throat plate to meet the top thread and create a stitch

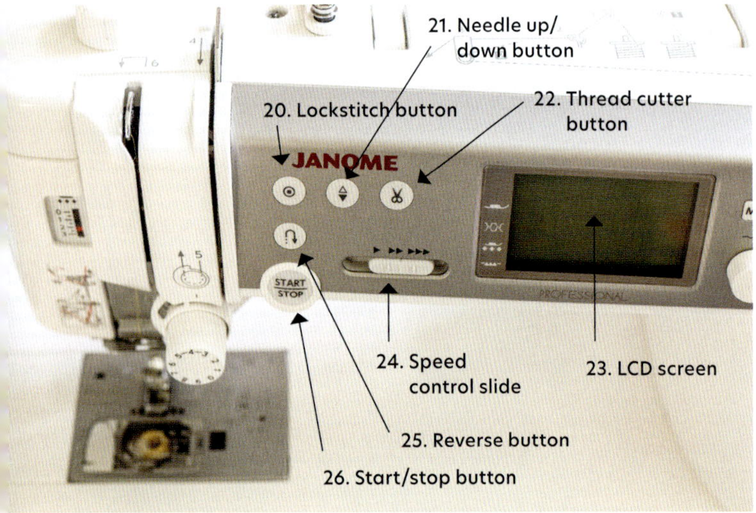

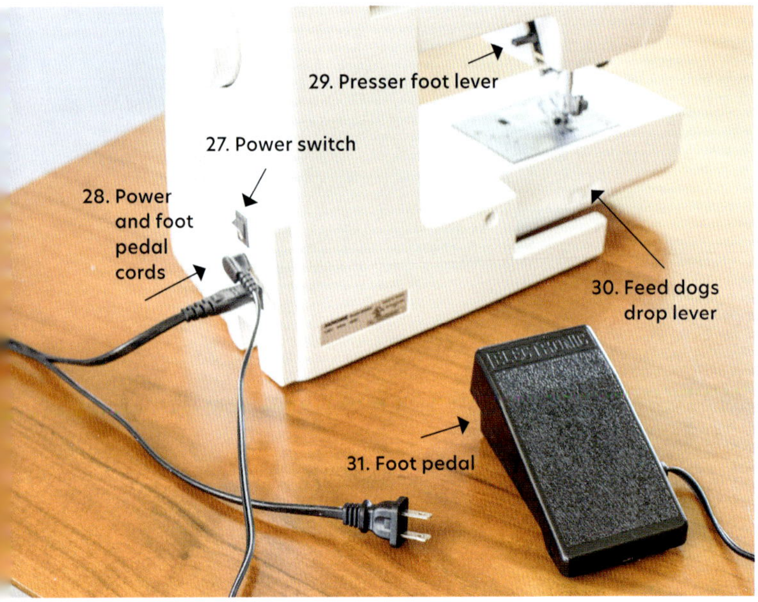

20. Lockstitch button—Sewing machine sews in place for a few stitches to secure the line of stitching

21. Needle up/down button—Brings the needle up or down; "needle down" setting is convenient for holding the needle in fabric to prevent shifting when changing direction

22. Thread cutter button—Automatically cuts both top and bobbin threads; use after stitching

23. LCD screen—Displays sewing machine settings

24. Speed control slide—Decreases or increases maximum stitching speed

25. Reverse button—Sewing machine sews in reverse while pressing this button

26. Start/stop button—Starts or stops stitching without using the foot pedal

27. Power switch—Turns the machine on or off

28. Power and foot pedal cords—Power cord supplies power to the sewing machine when plugged in; foot pedal cord brings power from the sewing machine to the foot pedal

29. Presser foot lever—Manually raises or lowers the presser foot

30. Feed dogs drop lever—Drops the feed dogs below the needle plate; use when free motion quilting to allow you to control how the fabric moves under the needle

31. Foot pedal—Controls how quickly your sewing machine stitches; just like a car's gas pedal, press lightly and the machine stitches slowly, add more pressure and the stitching speeds up

Mechanical Machines

Mechanical machines are often the first machines we learn to sew on. Why? Their simplicity makes for a good first sewing experience. Easy to use and easy to adjust, they are basic machines with manual controls using knobs or dials to adjust settings like stitch length and width. They are able to sew a straight stitch, a zigzag stitch, and a buttonhole, and usually won't have any decorative stitches. When starting out, a mechanical machine will let you focus on learning to quilt, rather than finding your way around a fancy sewing machine. While a mechanical machine might be a great introductory machine, its lack of stitch options might be limiting.

That said, some quilters swear by their mechanical machines. Many quilters take classes and learn to maintain and repair them. These workhorses are solid and reliable for piecing. They sew a consistent straight stitch with good tension and they rarely need repairs. Other steps in the quilting process may require more versatile machines, but even an advanced quilter appreciates the long-lasting reliability of these mechanical marvels.

Electronic Machines

Electronic machines are a mix of mechanical and computerized machines. Machine adjustments are more precise because they are pre-programmed. Some of these machines have small screens on the front of them, making adjustments quick and easy. Electronic machines offer more stitch options and other features than mechanical ones, giving you more flexibility for your projects. These machines often have alphabet stitches, too, which can be helpful when making custom quilt labels.

PROS	CONS
MECHANICAL MACHINES	
Inexpensive; simple to learn; uncomplicated to use, maintain and repair; many quilters take classes and learn to maintain and repair them themselves	Limited stitches; not as easy to make precise stitch width and length adjustments; won't memorize manually adjusted settings for you; no options for advanced or convenience features; you may quickly outgrow its capabilities
ELECTRONIC MACHINES	
Precision adjustments; more stitch options; availability of some advanced features such as a needle threader or thread cutter; you probably won't outgrow this machine as quickly as a mechanical one	More expensive than mechanical machines
COMPUTERIZED MACHINES	
Accuracy; large stitch assortment; smoother and faster stitching; virtually unlimited options for convenience, precision and customization; the ability to keep pace with your growing expertise and creativity; being the envy of your quilting friends	Price; expensive to fix; must be tech savvy (but buying at a local dealer makes this less of a hurdle); steeper learning curve

Computerized Machines

Computerized machines offer the most of everything and have the highest price tag. They are meant for the sewist who likes to learn and experiment. There are options for advanced features like variable speed control, automatic needle threaders, adjustable needle positioning, larger bobbins, more throat space, a variety of presser feet for specialty stitching, and large touchscreens. They can store your settings for future use, tell you when to change your presser foot or throat plate, have hands-free thread cutting, and warn you when your bobbin is almost empty. Some allow you to monogram or create stitches that look hand sewn. Others have a knee lift for the presser foot or allow the presser foot to hover when not stitching. Some have computer or tablet connectivity.

These are advanced machines and have a learning curve; they may be intimidating, especially for a newer quilter. This is a good reason to buy from a reputable, local sewing machine shop. They will review it all with you and help you pick the best machine for both your current sewing needs and your future sewing dreams. They usually include an introductory class with your purchase and are only a phone call away when you've got a question.

Longarm Machines

Longarm quilting machines are used exclusively for quilting, not piecing. A longarm has a large sewing-machine head mounted on a rolling carriage attached to a heavy frame. Metal poles are attached to the frame and hold the layers of the quilt sandwich in place while they are being quilted. Side clamps provide extra stabilization. Many longarm quilters use their machines for their personal quilts only, while others quilt for customers to earn income. I decided to buy a longarm when I wasn't able to create my desired quilting designs on a domestic sewing machine, (and I didn't want to wait for someone else to quilt my projects for me). You might consider buying a longarm if you are paying a longarm quilter to quilt for you, if you want specific quilting designs that you can't achieve with a domestic machine, if you'd like to quilt for others, or just for pure fun. Longarms come in a variety of sizes and price points and are either guided manually or by computer.

Hand-Guided Longarms

A hand-guided longarm is exclusively "driven" by hand. The majority of longarm owners have hand-guided machines. Many longarm quilters have incredible skill at free motion quilting, while others use rulers or pantographs (pre-printed patterns) to help them create beautiful designs that would be difficult and time consuming with free motion quilting on a domestic machine. Refer to Types of Quilting: *Hand-Guided Longarm Machines*, page 229, for more information.

Computer-Guided Longarm

Computer-guided longarm machines connect to a tablet mounted on the front of the machine head. This tablet contains software allowing the quilter to use digital files to design the quilting layout in full *before* quilting begins. After the design is finalized, the quilter sets up the machine to stitch, then presses a button to begin quilting. The computer drives the longarm, with no help from the quilter. Designs stitch out effortlessly and with precision. Computerized longarms are great for highly detailed, geometric, and intricate designs. They can be used with rulers and for hand-guided free motion quilting as well. Refer to Types of Quilting: *Computer-Guided Longarm Machines*, page 229, for more information.

NEEDLES

Fact: You cannot quilt without a needle. The needle is the smallest tool needed for quilting, and also the most important. Over 50,000 years ago, the first needles were made from bone shards or wood. Today, needles are made from materials like high carbon steel and iron, then plated with nickel, gold, titanium alloy or platinum. There are two main kinds of needles used in quilting: hand sewing needles and machine sewing needles. Each needle has defining characteristics: size, eye shape, length, and point type. There are many needle types out there, and let's be real...it can get confusing *fast*. Here is a guide to choosing the appropriate needle for your project.

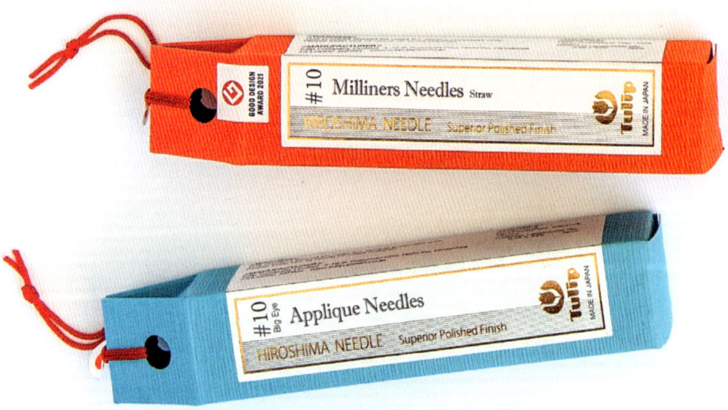

HAND SEWING NEEDLES

There are a range of sizes for each type of hand sewing needle. A higher number means a finer and shorter needle. For example, a #3 needle is longer and thicker than a #12 needle. There is no "correct" size needle to use; it truly is a personal preference. If you have larger hands, you may choose to use a longer needle because it is more comfortable and vice versa. As a beginning hand quilter, you might choose a larger needle to learn with, then move on to a smaller needle as your skills progress.

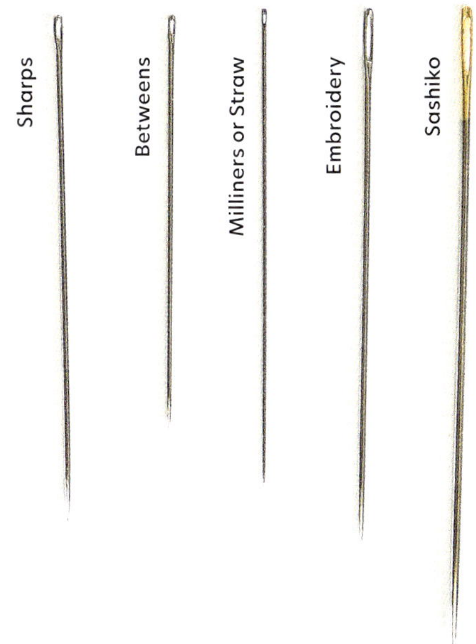

Types of Hand Sewing Needles

SHARPS	Medium length, strong, fine needles; round eye; sharp point	General purpose, including hand quilting, hand appliqué, quilt binding	A versatile needle that works for just about any purpose
BETWEENS	Short, fine needles with a round eye; sharp point	Designed for hand quilting, good for detailed stitch work	The short length allows for quick and easy stitches through the quilt sandwich without bending as much as a longer needle
MILLINERS/ STRAW	Long, fine needles with a small round eye; sharp point	Traditionally used in hat making; also good for basting, English Paper Piecing, needle-turn appliqué	Creates a very small hole in fabric; works well for needle-turn because the long, thin needle sweeps the seam allowance under with ease
EMBROIDERY	Similar to Sharps with a longer eye; sharp point	Embroidery, hand quilting with thicker thread such as embroidery floss, general sewing	The longer eye makes these easier to thread than a Sharp making them another good choice for general sewing
SASHIKO	Longer and stronger with a large eye, less flexible; sharp point	Sashiko and hand quilting with thicker threads, embroidery	Strong enough to pull a thicker thread through the layers of a quilt sandwich; inflexible so it can pick up more than one stitch at a time without warping

SEWING MACHINE NEEDLES

Once again, there are lots of differences between types of sewing machine needles. The labels can be intimidating if you don't know what they mean, but this section will help you understand all of the machine needles you will need to make a quilt. It's all pretty amazing. If you haven't already, check out some online videos on how a sewing machine works. Once I watched a few of those, I never took my sewing machine or its needles for granted again!

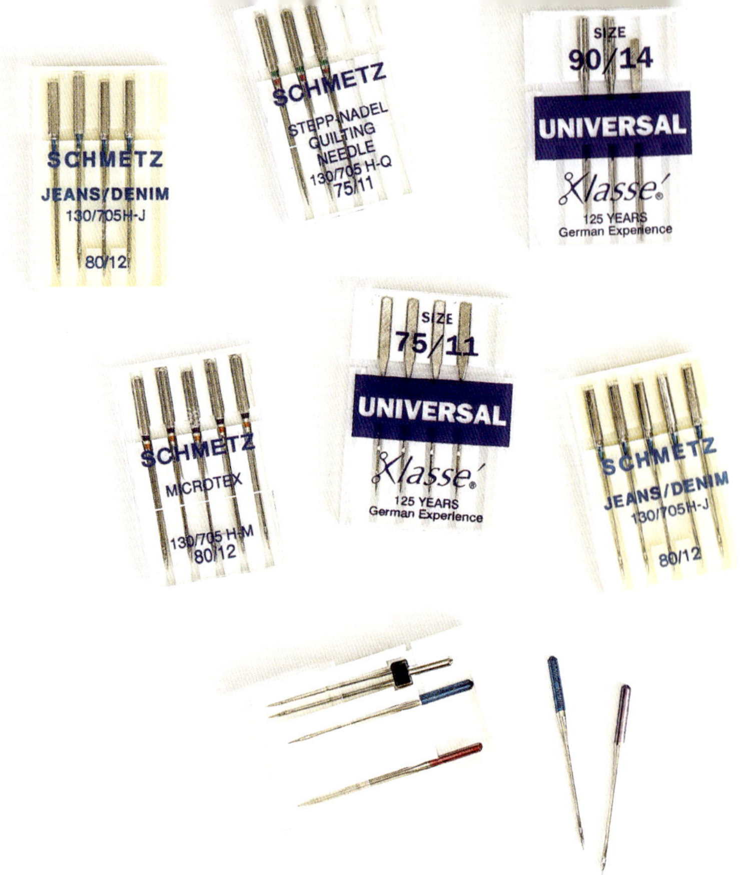

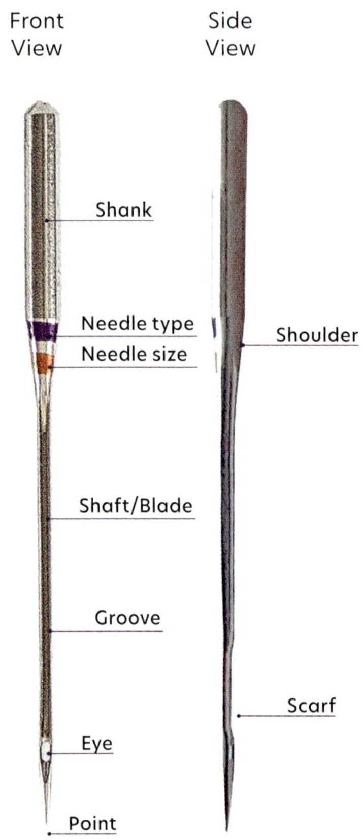

Anatomy of a Sewing Machine Needle

SHANK	Located at the top of the needle; inserted into the sewing machine's needle bar; rounded on the front and flat on the back so you can't put them into your sewing machine backwards. Nifty, right?
SHOULDER	Section where the shank tapers down to the shaft
SHAFT OR BLADE	Long, narrow section between the shoulder and the eye
GROOVE	Indentation at the front of the needle; allows the thread to track directly down into the needle eye
EYE	Open hole at the bottom of the needle; when threading the machine, guide the thread through the eye from front to back
POINT	Below the eye, this is the first part of the needle to penetrate the fabric
SCARF	Small indentation on the *back* of the needle above the eye, allows the bobbin hook to catch the top thread and make a stitch

Which Needle For Your Project?

When you look at the packaging on sewing machine needles, there is a lot of information. It can be very confusing. There are two numbers on every needle case and they look like this: 90/14. The first number (90) is the European size, and the second number (14) is the American size. Next you will see the *type* of needle it is. For example, needles will be labeled as Universal, Quilting, Denim, or Microtex. Picking the correct needle will depend on your project. Some manufacturers color code the individual needles. The colored band closest to the point represents the needle *size* and the one closest to the shank represents the needle *type*. Also, the needle size is etched into the shank of each needle.

CHANGE YOUR NEEDLE!
When I started sewing, I didn't change my needle often. Now, I try to change it with every new project. Why? Dull needles lead to thread breakage, skipped stitches, damage to your fabric, uneven sewing, and popping sounds while you sew. If you experience any of these, try changing to a new needle.

Types of Sewing Machine Needles

MICROTEX/ SHARP	Slim needle with a very sharp point	Topstitching and precision piecing; designed for precise, straight stitches	*Use sizes 70/10, 80/12, 90/14
TOPSTITCH	Extra sharp with longer groove	Topstitching and machine quilting; longer groove directs thread to eye of needle for smoother stitching with heavier weight threads	*Use sizes 80/12, 90/14
QUILTING	Tapered shape with slightly rounded point	Piecing, appliqué, and machine quilting; designed to avoid damage to layers of fabric	*Use sizes 75/11, 90/14
UNIVERSAL	Medium with a slightly rounded point	General purpose; piecing and appliqué; has rounded point needed for knit fabrics	*Use sizes 70/10, 75/11, 80/12, 90/14
DENIM	Medium and strong with a ball point	Machine quilting with thick fabrics or attaching thick binding such as denim, canvas, any extra-thick woven fabrics	*Use sizes 70/10, 80/12, 90/14, 100/16, 110/18

**Choose a needle size that matches your thread weight. If the thread is breaking frequently, try a larger needle.*

USED NEEDLES AND BLADES Used sharps should not just be thrown into the garbage. They will not only tear the bag, but can injure someone. Keep a small container (an empty Altoids™ box is perfect) to store your used needles and blades for disposal. That way, you won't inadvertently hurt yourself or others.

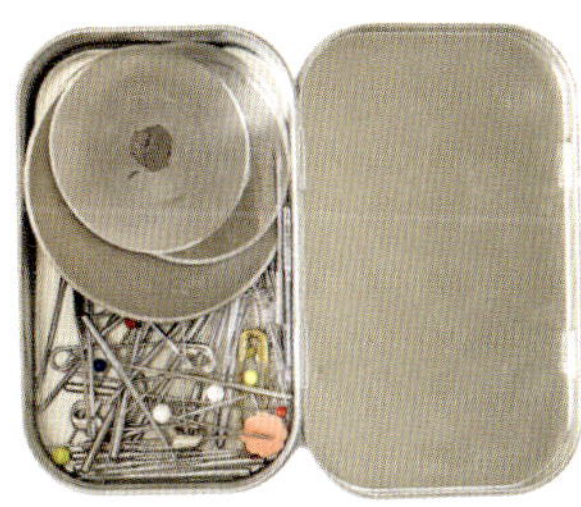

THREAD

Thread is so, so, so important! When I started quilting, I believed all threads were created equal. This is simply not true. Like any product, quality in thread will vary; it's always best to use a high-quality thread for your projects. Low-quality thread will break, snarl more and will not last over time. As quilters, we put a great deal of time and effort into our quilts and the thread we use literally ties it all together. Using a quality thread will ensure our quilts will stand up to years of use.

Ok, so we need thread. That's a given, but have you ever looked at the thread displays at the store and realized there are a LOT of thread types? Not only that, but there are different thread weights! As a beginning quilter, how am I supposed to know what any of this means?!

THREAD WEIGHT

Thread weight is a measurement of the length of the thread in kilometers, required to make one kilogram (2.2 lbs). For example, a 50wt thread is when 50 kilometers of thread weighs one kilogram. An 80wt thread is when 80 kilometers of thread weighs one kilogram, and a 12wt thread is when 12 kilometers of thread weighs one kilogram. It is a bit counterintuitive, but lower thread weights are actually thicker, heavier threads, and higher thread weights are thinner and lighter.

Thread Weights and Uses

Weight	Uses	Needle
12wt	Hand stitching and embroidery, Sashiko, hand quilting, visible mending, top stitching; will look thick and bold against fabric; thickest thread that can be used in a sewing machine	*Use a 90/14 needle with 40wt thread in the bobbin
28wt	Visible hand appliqué, hand stitching and embroidery, Sashiko, hand quilting, top stitching	*Use a 90/14 needle with 50wt thread in the bobbin
40wt	Ideal for hand or machine quilting, as well as machine appliqué	*Use a 80/12 needle with 40wt or 50wt thread in the bobbin
50wt	Best weight for machine piecing; fantastic for needle-turn appliqué, English paper piecing, machine appliqué, machine quilting	*Use a 80/12 needle with 50wt thread in the bobbin
80wt	Machine appliqué, English paper piecing, hand appliqué, hand piecing	*Use a 70/10 or 80/12 needle with 80wt thread in the bobbin
100wt	Hand appliqué, English paper piecing, hand piecing	*Use Sharps, Betweens, or Milliners/Straw hand needles

**Needle size and type will vary depending on fabric thickness and weight.*

THREAD TYPES

Cotton

The gold standard for quilt piecing, cotton is strong but soft, comes in a huge variety of colors, has a low to medium sheen, and can withstand high temperatures from an iron. High-quality cotton thread won't create much lint while sewing, won't easily break, and won't create extra bulk at the seams of your project (very important when trying to get those seams to lie flat on a quilt top). A 50wt cotton is the perfect thread for machine piecing.

SECURE THAT THREAD

The base of an Aurifil® thread spool is removable to make it easy to keep the thread from unwinding and to find the beginning of the spool.

Polyester

A fantastic thread for quilting. However, I don't recommend polyester for piecing because it can weaken, melt, or discolor when using high heat on an iron. Polyester thread is widely available and comes in a huge variety of colors, does not shrink, does not produce a lot of lint, and will hold the layers of your quilt sandwich together over time. It is much shinier than cotton thread. There are a few disproven myths about using polyester thread, the most common of which is that poly thread is *soooo* strong it will eventually cut through the weaker cotton fibers in your cotton fabric. This is untrue when using today's modern fabrics, so go ahead and use that poly thread! However, if you're working on an antique quilt or making a quilt using vintage clothing or fabric, best stick to cotton.

All-Purpose

Has a polyester single-core wrapped with either cotton or polyester. Usually found at big-box stores in a variety of colors. It will work if that is all you have access to, but most quilters do not use all-purpose thread, because 100% cotton thread sews more smoothly creating flatter stitches, making it much nicer to work with.

Silk

Flexible, thin, strong, colorfast, and lint free. It's perfect for needle-turn appliqué or English paper piecing.

Monofilament

Made from a single nylon strand. It is used when invisible stitches are the goal. Great for English paper piecing or appliqué. Avoid polyester monofilament; it's not as stable as nylon. When using it for hand sewing, be careful not to pull the stitches too tightly and stretch the thread. It will shrink back and cause puckering.

Variegated

Dyed in a repeating pattern of different colors over the length of the thread. It is used for topstitching, hand, or machine quilting.

Metallic

Made with a polyester core and wrapped with thin metal strips. Delicate and sometimes difficult to use, but adds sparkle to your project. Usually used for decorative stitches and embroidery. Not used for quilt piecing but can be used for hand or machine quilting.

Embroidery floss

Made from six strands of loosely twisted thread. Commonly made of cotton and used for cross stitch, crazy quilting, decorative stitching, or tying quilts. Threads may be separated to get a thinner strand.

Perle cotton

Another twisted cotton thread, but not divisible like embroidery floss. Used for embroidery, crazy quilting, crewel work, and Sashiko.

NEW VS. OLD THREAD

Thread degrades over time. Whether your thread has been exposed to sunlight, excessive heat, a very dry or humid climate, or even just time, it will fade and weaken. If you don't know how old your thread is, take a minute to do a couple of quick tests to see if it has kept its integrity.

- Pull a few yards off the spool. Is the thread underneath a different color? If so, discard it and use a spool that hasn't faded.
- Snip a 15" length of thread and hold one end in each hand. Pull the thread until it breaks. If the thread offers no resistance and snaps easily, don't use it.
- Don't use any threads purchased ultra-cheaply. There is a reason these threads are priced that way. Their quality mirrors the pricing.

MY GO-TO THREAD I like to use what I have on hand, which is Aurifil 50wt. This is a great multipurpose thread that works for piecing, appliqué, quilting, everything. I have a slew of colors I can use for all of my projects.

FABRIC

Quilting does not exist without fabric. It is the foundation of every quilt project, both aesthetically and structurally. That being said, if you're new to quilting, how do you know which fabrics are best? Can you simply go to the store, pick what you like and start sewing? The answer is yes and no. Here's the deal: There are certain fabrics that work for quilting and some that won't. The goal of this section is to show you which fabrics work best and why, so you are equipped with the knowledge you need before making those fabric purchases.

The best fabric for piecing and quilting is high-quality, 100% quilting cotton. Your local quilt shop will carry it. Big-box stores have both high- and low-quality fabrics, so it's best to actually feel each fabric and decide if you'd like to include it in your project. A quality quilting cotton will not only be easier to sew, it's less likely to run in the wash and will hold its color and texture over time. Some lower-quality fabrics are flimsy and thin, and others are stiff and rough. Using a fabric that feels good to the touch will result in a finished quilt that is soft, snuggly, and will stand up to years of use.

Fabrics Used In Quilting

QUILTING COTTON	100% cotton, medium weight (4+ oz. per square yard)	Average stiffness with a soft hand*; the most popular fabric used for quilting
COTTON LAWN	100% cotton, lightweight (2–3 oz. per square yard)	Silky, with a lighter hand than quilting cotton
COTTON FLANNEL	100% cotton, medium weight (5+ oz. per square yard)	Brushed with metal bristles during production to create a soft feel; often used for a backing on baby quilts
SHOT COTTON	100% cotton, medium weight (4–5 oz per square yard)	Has a bicolored effect achieved by weaving together different colors of thread on the warp and weft
CLOTHING	T-shirts, ties, denim, and other materials	Often used in memory quilts; stretchy or very delicate fabrics like knits and silk should be stabilized before being pieced into a project

"Hand" of a fabric refers to the feeling of it against your skin.

FABRIC KNOW-HOW

When fabric is woven, there are *warp* (also known as straight-of-grain) threads and *weft* (also known as cross-grain) threads. The warp threads are stationary and parallel the selvage. Think of the warp threads as the foundation for the weft threads to build on. Weft threads are woven back and forth over and under the warp threads, creating fabric. The density of these threads determines thread count.

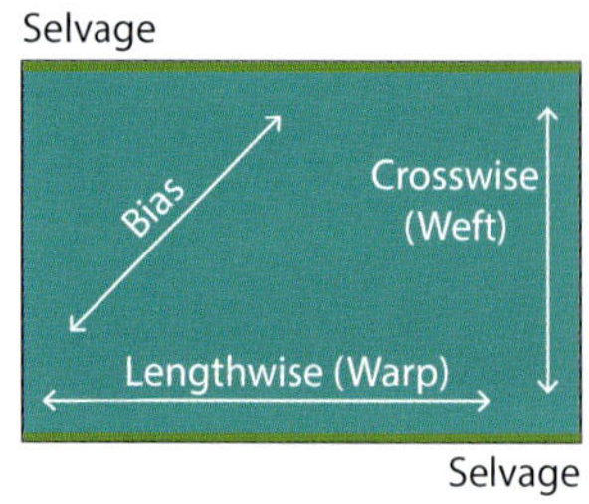

Fabric Selvage

- The selvages are the tightly woven edges of the fabric.
- Quilting cotton fabrics have selvages or are "self-edged" to keep the edges from fraying or raveling.
- The selvage has a different texture and is usually a different color than the main body of the fabric.
- Do not use the selvages in your quilting. It shrinks and stretches differently than the rest of the fabric.
- Avoid cutting the selvages off your fabric until you're ready to use it. Having the selvage is useful for a couple of reasons. First, if you need more of the same fabric later, the selvage often has the designer, manufacturer, and collection name which makes it easy to find. Second, the selvage is a quick reference to the grain of the fabric.

DON'T THROW IT AWAY Save your selvages for use in future projects. Selvages can be sewn together to make fabric, or even used as fun gift-wrap ribbon.

Fabric Grain

Fabric has 3 grains: crosswise, lengthwise, and bias. Each has its own features and uses.

Crosswise Grain

This is the grain used for all standard piecing. If an instruction in a quilt pattern does not specify a grain, it is using the crosswise grain.

- The crosswise grain runs from selvage to selvage.
- It has minimal stretch, a little more than the lengthwise grain and a lot less than the bias.
- The crosswise grain is very stable for piecing. Shapes will remain consistent.
- "Width of Fabric" or "WOF" in patterns refers to cutting on the crosswise grain. For example, "cut a strip, 3½" × WOF" means cut a 3½"-wide strip from selvage to selvage.

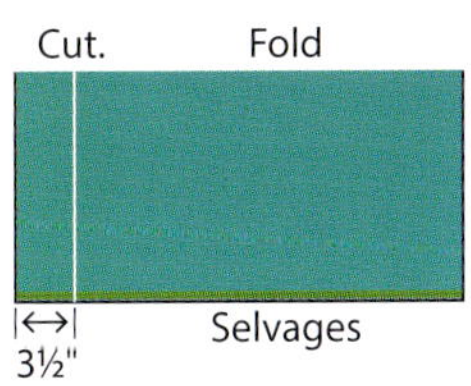

- Strips for quilt binding are usually cut on the crosswise grain. See Finishing: Binding, Facing, and More: *How to Make Binding*, page 236, for more on this.

Lengthwise Grain

- The lengthwise grain runs parallel to the selvages.
- This grain has almost no stretch, definitely the least of the 3 grains, and is used the most infrequently.
- The lack of stretch in this grain makes it extremely stable and it's sometimes used for long border strips to help prevent waviness in quilt edges.
- Using the lengthwise grain requires more fabric than the crosswise grain. For example, a 3½" × 36" border cut from the lengthwise grain, needs 36" or a yard of fabric. Cut on the crosswise grain, it needs only 14" or less than ½ yard.

Bias Grain

- Bias grain runs on the diagonal from one selvage to another.
- This is the stretchy grain! Use it for curves but be careful when it shows up in piecing straight edges.
- Fabric cut on a 45-degree angle to the selvage has the most give and is the standard for bias cuts.
- Bias wears longer than straight-of-grain. Quilt binding was traditionally made with bias-cut strips because the binding gets the most wear.
- The downside to bias strips is that cutting on the bias uses more fabric than cutting WOF (crosswise) strips. Quilters now almost always use WOF strips for binding.
- But . . . the exception to that is when you have a quilt with curved or scalloped edges. Bias strips stretch and conform smoothly to curves. Cut bias strips for binding curved edges.
- An angled cut has more stretch than a straight-of-grain cut. For only a little stretch, a 30-degree cut maximizes fabric usage.

- Double-fold bias strips are beautiful and versatile. See Machine Appliqué: *Bias Tape Appliqué*, page 112, for more on this.

- Bias edges stretch. Don't overwork them in your piecing. Be especially gentle when pressing. Otherwise, your finished shape may be a little wonky. Again—ask me how I know. [Sigh.]

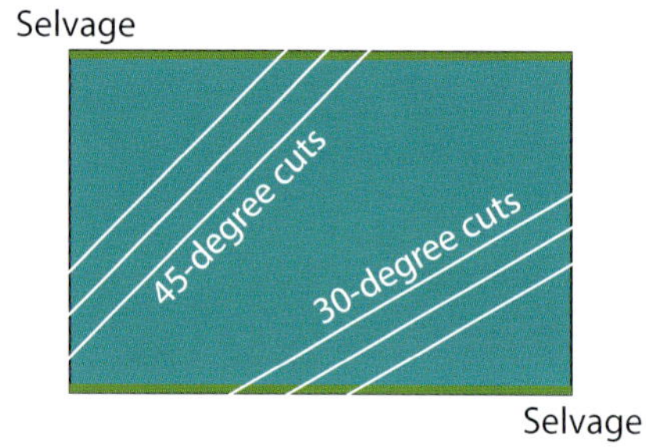

How Fabric is Sold

The most common quilting cotton purchases are by the yard, but it's not the only way!

By The Yard

- Fabric is cut from bolts that are 10 or 15 yards long. Priced by the yard, it's purchased in increments starting at ¼ yard.

- Standard quilting cotton is 42"-44" wide (Width of Fabric or WOF). Remove the selvages and there's 40" to 43" of usable width.

- Wide-back quilting cotton ranges from 106" to 120" wide. It's designed to be used for quilt backings which require no piecing.

Precuts and Bundles

- Precuts are quilting cottons sold in pre-cut sizes.

- Fat quarters (FQs) measure 18" × 21" and are the original pre-cut. If a ¼ yard (9" wide) isn't wide enough but you don't want a ½ yard, buy an FQ.

- Fat eighths measure 9" x 21". Buy these when you need a very small amount of fabric, potentially to fussy cut or use as an accent.

- Jelly rolls are coordinating strips, 2½" × WOF. They usually have 40 strips with 2 to 5 of each fabric.

- Layer cakes are 10" × 10" squares of coordinating fabrics sold in packs of 42 pieces.

- Charm packs are 5" × 5" squares of coordinating fabrics sold in packs of 42 pieces.

- Mini Charm packs are 2½" × 2½" squares of coordinating fabrics sold in packs of 42 pieces.

- Fabrics are also bundled by color, fabric line, or designer. Popular sizes are FQ, ¼ yard, ½ yard, and 1 yard bundles.

Fat quarter
(FQ)
Jelly
roll
strip
Fat eighth
Layer cake square
Charm
square
Mini
charm
square

Where to Buy Fabric

The local quilt shop (LQS)—This is the best place to shop! Your LQS will carry high-quality fabrics that you can see and touch. Employees are usually very knowledgeable about quilting and can help guide you with color selection and technical questions. Each quilt shop will carry different fabrics, so it's fun to explore and see which shop's selection speaks to you most. In addition to fabric, your LQS will likely have notions and batting available for purchase, and may offer longarm quilting services. Your LQS may offer online shopping in addition to in-person shopping.

Online—There are shops that are strictly online with no brick-and-mortar location. Shopping online can be great if you are looking for something specific, but it is more difficult to match fabrics and colors when viewing them over a computer screen. Buying online would be the easiest option for those living far from a quilt shop, or when looking for fabric that isn't available at your LQS. Sometimes it's the only way to find a very old fabric that you just need a little more of.

Custom fabric—If you have a design idea you'd love to incorporate into a quilt but can't find a fabric that works for you, custom-printed fabric is a fun and easy way to create a one-of-a-kind project. Upload a design or image to a website specializing in custom-printed fabric, and they'll print it and mail it to you.

Social media—Many quilters will sell their unused fabric on Instagram or Facebook. Search for destash accounts or hashtags like #thegreatfabricdestash on Instagram. This is a good way to find fabrics that might be out of print or no longer easy to find. I've found some real gems this way.

Big-box store—When shopping at a store that doesn't specialize in quilting fabric, quality can be hit or miss. Employees may or may not have knowledge of quilting and what it requires. These stores will offer competitive pricing with both in-person and online shopping, but select your fabric carefully.

Prewashing

Do you need to prewash your fabric? Let me start by saying this: there is no correct answer. Each quilter has their own personal preference when it comes to washing fabric before starting a project. Here are some reasons you might decide for or against prewashing:

Reason to Prewash

Colorfastness—Washing will remove any excess fabric dye. Use a "color catcher" sheet or two in the wash cycle to absorb excess fabric dye from the water so it's not transferred to other fabrics. Shout! Color Catchers are a common brand.

Fabric feel—This is personal preference. Prewashed fabric is softer. (But many people then starch their prewashed fabric so it's sturdy enough for piecing.)

Fabric age—If using a combination of fabrics of varying ages, prewashing is a bit of an equalizer.

Finishing agents—People who are sensitive to chemicals may find the finishing agents on fabric to be irritating.

Batiks—Many people prewash batiks because they may have "resist" left on them. Wax is a common resist that is used on batiks to control where the design dye is placed.

Shrinkage—There is little or no shrinkage of the finished quilt with prewashed fabric. Quilting cotton has a 3–5% shrinkage rate.

Reasons Not to Prewash

Colorfastness—Most quilting cottons are colorfast and won't bleed. The BIG exception here is red. If you plan on using red fabric with white, cream or any other light-colored fabric, I absolutely recommend prewashing.

Time—*Not* prewashing saves time. This is my #1 reason for not prewashing. In addition to the time spent washing and drying fabrics, prewashed fabric has to be ironed and often needs to be starched before being cut.

Ease—It is easier to cut and piece unwashed fabric. Fabric is slightly stiffer before being washed because of the finishing chemicals it is treated with during production.

That wonderful crinkle—I love crinkly quilts. Quilts made with fabric that hasn't been prewashed will shrink slightly when washed the first time. This shrinkage results in a quilt that has the crinkly, homemade look that is unique to quilts.

Fabric Storage

Some folks buy fabric, fold it up, and put it in a storage bin in their closet. While this is an easy *storage* solution, it does not make it easy to *find and use* the fabric when the time comes. My project inspiration usually comes from fabric first, and design second. Being able to see all of my fabric at once makes selecting colors and designs much easier. I'm able to pick and choose, try out different combinations, and switch fabrics out super easily.

With this in mind, I have a four-tiered storage system. I know this sounds a little intense, but bear with me.

FABRIC FADES It is important to know that fabric will fade over time if exposed to sunlight. It is best to keep fabric in cabinets away from light if possible.

- **Yardage over 2 yards**—Fold the fabric neatly and store it with other large pieces of fabric on a shelf. Alternately, store the fabric on bolts. (Bolts are the sturdy cardboard that fabric comes wrapped around). Ask your local quilt shop if they have any empty ones sitting around; they'll be happy to give them to you.
- **Yardage under 2 yards**—Store this on comic book boards. These boards are acid-free, lightweight cardboard and make fabric easily visible and neat on a shelf. The fabric does not wrinkle when stored on these. I find them at online retailers, like Amazon. To wrap fabric on a comic book board, first fold it in half lengthwise, then once again. Wrap it around the board and secure with a clip or a pin.
- **Fat quarters and smaller pieces**—Store these by color in clear shoe boxes. I buy snap-lid stackable shoe boxes for easy viewability. Fold the fabrics so they're all similarly sized. Store like-colors together to make them easy to find.
- **Scraps**—Store in clear drawers by color. I purchased a six drawer plastic storage tower for my scraps. Each drawer has a designated color. Store like-colors together.

  I keep scraps larger than 2" × 2". Some quilters toss anything they don't use when piecing, but I have been able to make some pretty awesome scrap quilts from leftover fabric, so keeping it works for me.

Standard Quilt Sizes

"Standard quilt sizes" is a bit of a misnomer. Mattress sizes vary, so a twin-sized quilt that will fit a mattress with an 8" depth will not work as well on a mattress that is 15" deep. Below you will find the "standards", but if you are going to make a quilt for a bed, measure the bed to be sure the quilt will be the correct size. A couple of things to think about when making a bed-sized quilt:

- **Drape**—How many inches would you like the quilt to hang over the edges of the mattress? Add that number to the mattress length; double it and add it to the mattress width.
- **Fold**—Would you like the quilt to be folded at the top of the mattress or do you prefer it to lie flat? If you want it folded, add the desired length of the fold to the mattress length.

Common Quilt Sizes

BABY	30" × 40"
CRIB	36" × 54"
LAP	45" × 45"
THROW	54" × 64"
TWIN	70" × 90"
FULL	80" × 90"
QUEEN	90" × 108"
KING	110" × 108"
CA KING	106" × 112"

BATTING

Have you ever snuggled up under a warm, cuddly quilt? It's a great feeling, right? Have you sat under a quilt that felt lumpy? Or a quilt that doesn't keep you warm? Have you had to throw a quilt off because you're roasting under it? If so, the reason for your comfort (or discomfort) was likely the quilt batting. Batting is the insulation in your quilt and determines the warmth, weight, drape, and look after quilting.

Batting (known as wadding in the UK) is a sheet of thick cotton, polyester, wool, silk, bamboo, or other material sewn between the quilt top and quilt backing to insulate the quilt. It comes in many lofts (thicknesses), weights, sizes, and even a few colors. Each batting material behaves differently, so choosing the appropriate material for your quilt is important.

BATTING CONSIDERATIONS

Batting Quality

There is a *huge* variation in batting quality. When I began quilting, I thought all batting was created equal. Wow, was I wrong! Quality batting is stronger, softer, more durable, easier to use, and the quality of your finished quilt will be far superior than with a cheaper batting. A low-quality batting is more likely to pull apart, feel scratchy or rough, and pull through your quilt top or backing (known as "bearding"). It won't retain warmth or breathe, and might be stiff and uncomfortable to use. While you may find acceptable batting at a big-box store, I encourage you to buy quality batting from your local quilt shop. You won't be sorry. I prefer Quilters Dream® batting because of the high quality and variety of products available.

Quilting Density

Each batting has a "quilting density" specified on the packaging. This refers to how close the lines of quilting stitches must be to keep that batting from pulling apart or shredding inside the quilt. Some batting requires close quilting (no more than 3"–4" apart), while others can accommodate less dense stitching (8"–12" of open space). A higher quality batting will allow for more space between stitching or tying.

Prewashing

Prewashing batting is not necessary or recommended. Batting is not made to be prewashed and can come apart in a washing machine. Most batting shrinkage is minimal, but if you'd like NO shrinkage with your project, choose a batting that does not shrink.

Loft and Drape

- Loft refers to the thickness or puffiness of the batting. Consider what you would like your quilting to look like and your machine's capabilities before choosing a loft.

The green batting from Quilters Dream is very light green and can be used in the same way as a natural batting.

- Drape refers to how the batting hangs. Some batting has a soft, easy drape, and some have a stiff one. Which drape you choose depends on how you would like your quilt to feel and look.
- Hand quilting is easier with low-loft batting because you can take small stitches and make them a consistent length; 10 to an inch is the standard. High-loft batting shows off the stitches more but stitch length is harder to keep consistent and you must take fewer stitches per inch. Personal preference!
- Use a low-loft batting if you want to show off the piecing more than the definition created by the quilting. If it's a project with a lot of open negative space, a low-loft batting shows off both.
- High-loft battings will give your quilt a puffy look; low loft will be flatter with a more traditional feel.
- The throat space on a domestic machine might not be able to handle a large, high-loft quilt batting, but would have no issue with a low-loft one.
- A longarm is able to handle any loft of batting.
- Very dense quilting will affect a quilt's drape, making it stiffer. Less dense quilting allows for a more flowing drape.

Batting Color

Batting typically comes in 3 colors: white (bleached), natural*, and black. Choose your batting according to the project you're working on. If you have a quilt top with a lot of white fabric, use white batting; even a natural-colored batting will dull the white fabric. Use natural-colored batting with cream-colored or colorful quilt tops, and use black for dark-colored quilts.

Standard Batting Sizes

CRAFT	46" × 36"
CRIB	46" × 60"
THROW	60" × 60"
TWIN	93" × 72"
DOUBLE	96" × 93"
QUEEN	108" × 93"
SUPER QUEEN	121" × 93"
KING	122" × 120"

What Else?

Scrim

Scrim is a thin layer of woven polyester fused to cotton batting to add stability. It enables the quilter to use less dense quilting. A batting with scrim feels scratchy and rough on one side, soft on the other. Do NOT iron the fabric on the scrim side of the batting as the fabric will fuse to the scrim and ripple. Scrim makes needling through the quilt sandwich a bit more difficult. Consider that when choosing; it's not ideal for hand quilting.

Bonded Batting

Bonded batting has a very thin layer of adhesive resin on both sides to stabilize fibers and keep batting from shifting or bearding. Thermally bonded batting is made by blending the batting fibers (cotton, wool, etc.) with low-melt polyester. Do not iron the fabric with the batting; the polyester or resin may melt and fuse to the fabric. As with scrim, resin and polyester are more resistant to needling and not a good choice for hand quilting.

Fusible Batting

Fusible batting has a thin layer of glue on each side, allowing the quilt back and top to be fused to the batting when ironed. This is most useful for small projects like wall hangings or placemats and should not be used on quilts. Hand quilting through the fusible can be especially difficult. Sometimes the fusible rubs onto the machine needle while quilting. Check the needle occasionally for residue and wipe it off with rubbing alcohol (*turn the machine off first*) or replace it with a new needle.

Needle-punched

Needle-punching is a process where thousands of needles punch small holes in a batting compressing the fibers together, securing them for stability. Polyester batting is needle punched to give it the feel of cotton batting. Although there is no officially correct placement, many quilters prefer to put their batting "dimples up, pimples down" in the quilt sandwich. This way, the sewing machine needle penetrates the batting in the same direction as the needle-punching machine.

Frankenbatting

As any quilter knows, there are always leftover pieces of batting from completed projects. Don't throw that batting away! Instead, keep those pieces, join them together, and make yourself some Frankenbatting. I have done this multiple times with batting scraps and I truly can't tell the difference between regular batting and Frankenbatting in a finished quilt.

- Straighten the edges of the leftover batting pieces.
- Place them next to each other so the edges are touching, but *not* overlapping. An overlap will cause an unwanted bump in the project.
- There are a few ways to connect the pieces:

Zigzag stitch—Stitch across both pieces of batting with a wide zigzag stitch. Use like-colored thread.

Seam tape—One-sided fusible seam tape is a lightweight, precut thin strip of interfacing which works perfectly for Frankenbatting. I use Pellon® Easy-Knit Fusible Batting and Seam Tape. Place the tape over the seam and press. This is my favorite method because it is easy and quick. (My neighbor introduced me to this technique. She makes stacks of charity quilts and uses every scrap of batting she can).

Lightweight fusible interfacing—If you happen to have lightweight fusible interfacing lying around, cut it into 1"-wide strips and use it to join pieces of batting together. Place the strip of interfacing over the seam between the two pieces of batting and press. Pellon SF101 Shape-Flex works well for this.

Loft of Various Quilters Dream Battings

1. Dream 80/20 (blend)
2. Dream Blend 70/30 (has a scrim)
3. Dream Cotton Request Loft
4. Dream Cotton Select Loft
5. Dream Cotton Deluxe Loft
6. Dream Cotton Supreme Loft
7. Dream Angel
8. Dream Bamboo
9. Dream Poly
10. Dream Green
11. Dream Wool
12. Dream Puff

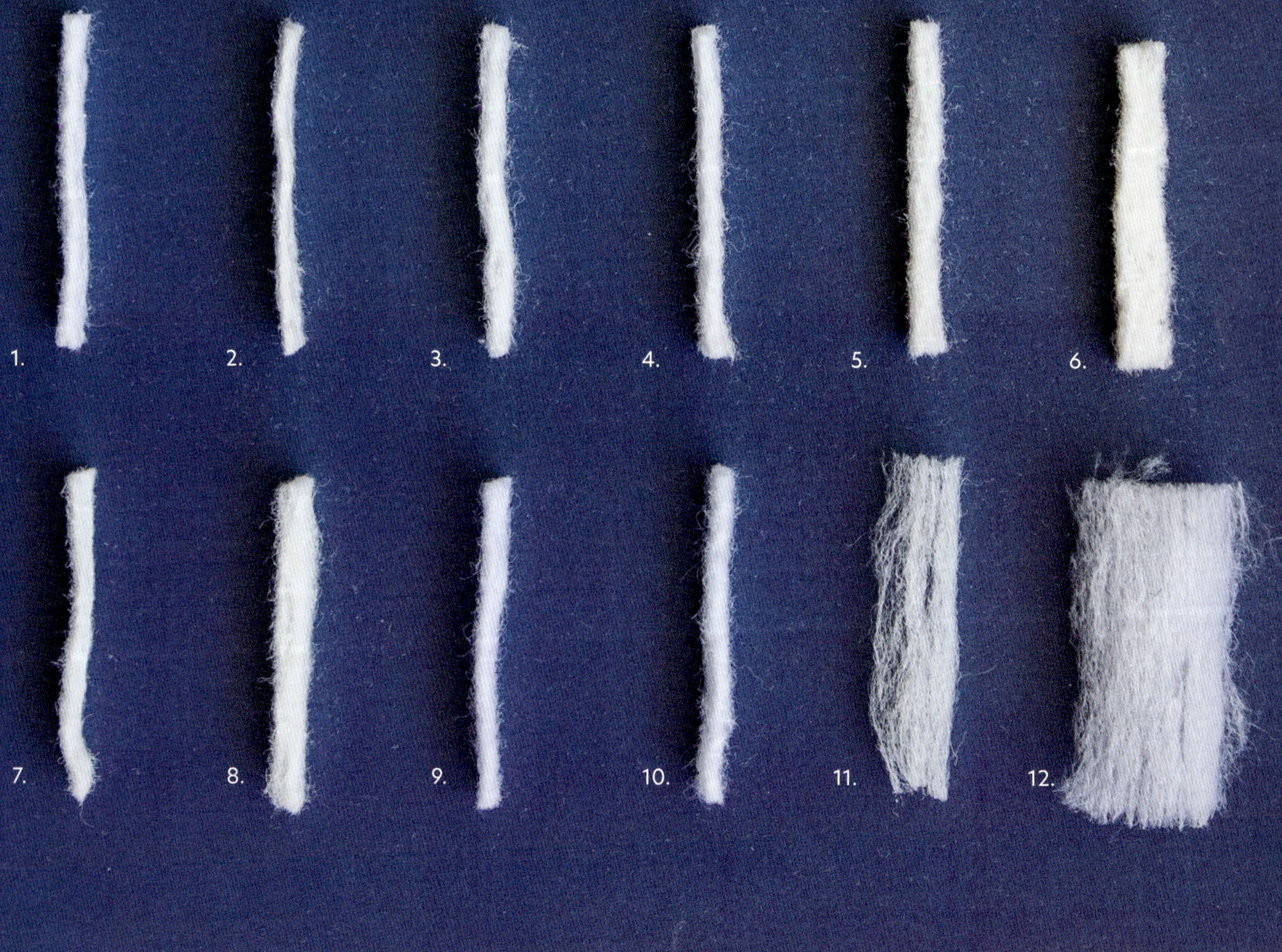

Batting Materials *Check the packaging for exact shrinkage, washing, and quilting density information.*

100% COTTON	Natural fiber available in various lofts	3–5% shrinkage; machine washable	Hand and machine quilting, up to 8" apart	Provides lightweight warmth; breathable with a soft drape
80/20 (80% COTTON/ 20% POLYESTER)	Partially synthetic fibers; low loft, ⅛" thick	3–5% shrinkage; machine washable	Hand and machine quilting, up to 8" apart	Cotton provides stability and poly reduces wrinkling; breathable with a soft drape
BAMBOO	Natural fiber; low loft; often comes in a blend with cotton, silk, and Tencel™	2–3% shrinkage; machine washable	Hand and machine quilting, up to 8" apart	Lightweight with a silky drape; bamboo is popular because it's renewable, sustainable, grows quickly, and requires less water than cotton; good for people with allergies; almost indistinguishable from cotton inside a quilt
WOOL	Natural fiber; medium to high loft	Little or no shrinkage; machine washable; do *not* iron or put in the dryer	Hand and machine quilting, up to 8" apart	Lightweight and warm; quilting will stand out; non-quilted areas will puff up; wool is renewable and sustainable
POLYESTER	Synthetic material; available in various lofts up to ½" thick	No shrinkage and resists wrinkling; machine washable	Hand and machine quilting, up to 12" apart	Use a thicker loft for more quilting definition
GREEN	Synthetic material, made from recycled plastic bottles	No shrinkage; machine washable	Hand and machine quilting, up to 12" apart	Eco-friendly; lightweight and warm
SILK	Natural fiber	3–5% shrinkage; hand wash or delicate machine wash with no agitation or spin; lay flat to dry	Hand and machine quilting, up to 4" apart	Luxurious, lightweight but strong with flowing drape

Batting alternatives There are all kinds of materials that can be used as batting in quilts. Mattress pads, flannel sheets, blankets, and fleece are batting alternatives that can be upcycled to use in your quilts. Re-using keeps materials out of the landfill, and can result in a super warm, snuggly quilt! *Before choosing, consider how an alternative will wash, shrink, and wear compared to the fabrics in your quilt.*

Layered Batting

Yup, this is a thing! Quilters often use two layers of batting to achieve the look or feel they want. Maybe you want a heavy quilt for the cold winter, or maybe you'd like the quilt to look "poofy" when it is quilted. Using two layers of batting will allow you to get the result you want. There is no right or wrong way to layer. You can even layer different types of batting but keep track of the washability of both. Have fun!

Batting Solutions

Wrinkly Batting

Wrinkly batting doesn't lie flat in a quilt sandwich making it very difficult to effectively baste. There have been a few times where I've pulled batting out of its snug plastic packaging and found myself looking at a wrinkled mess. There are a couple of ways to fix this.

▷ The Solutions

- Hang the batting over an ironing board, couch, or table and use a fine mist sprayer to moisten it. As the batting fibers relax and slowly dry, the wrinkles will fall out.
- Put the batting into the dryer with a wet washcloth. The heat of the dryer combined with the moisture from the washcloth will help smooth the batting. I usually put the batting in the dryer for 20 minutes on low, longer if needed.
- Drape the batting over an ironing board and use a steamer or steam iron to steam the wrinkles out.

Ripped Batting

I once caught my batting under the leg of my chair and ripped the heck out of it. I momentarily freaked out, then realized it could easily be fixed.

▷ The Solutions

- If the tear isn't bad, nudge the ripped section back together.
- If you've got a good hole going, replace the ripped section using the Frankenbatting method, page 39. (This is why we keep our batting scraps!)

Low-Quality Batting

I've had clients bring me low-quality batting that I consider unusable. It is thin, rips, and even falls apart. Batting should be a quality addition to your quilt, not something that makes you want to tear your hair out. If you've purchased a batting that is not working for any reason, move on and consider it a lesson learned.

▷ The Solution

- Going forward, work with tried-and-true, good-quality batting that won't give you problems.

Bearding

When fibers from the batting are pulled through the quilt top or backing, it looks terrible. I've never had this happen, but I wanted to include it because I've heard how horrible it can be. There are a few theories as to why bearding occurs. If you notice it when you begin quilting, here are a few suggestions on how to avoid it.

▷ The Solutions

Static electricity theory

More static electricity than usual is created with the sulfur-based chemicals used to dye vivid or darker-colored fabrics. This static electricity, paired with the movement of the sewing machine needle, attracts the batting fibers, especially in low humidity environments.

- Use an anti-static spray on both finished and unfinished quilts.
- Put a couple of dryer sheets and water into a fine mist spray bottle, and spray the quilt both during quilting and when the quilt is finished.
- Use anti-static dryer sheets when drying the quilt after washing.

Low quality theory

Stiff batting fibers from lower-quality batting can migrate through fabrics, especially low-quality ones. It's most common with polyester or wool batting.

- Use high-quality quilting cotton and high-quality batting.

Dull needle theory

A dull needle will push batting fibers through the quilt backing.

- Change the needle on your sewing machine before starting each project and check frequently for a problem.
- Finishing agents on some battings, especially lower quality brands, can dull needles more quickly.

Spray basting theory

Using spray baste to make the quilt sandwich can gum up the sewing machine needle and result in batting fibers sticking to it and pulling through the quilt backing and top.

- Use a minimal amount of spray baste.
- Turn off the sewing machine and clean the needle with rubbing alcohol to remove any gunk.
- Change the needle more frequently.
- If this problem continues, pin baste your next quilt.

PIECING BASICS

Quilts are made from all different sizes and shapes of fabric. Many quilters start with squares and some stick with them. They don't think they have the skills to try anything else, or are scared to try a new technique. This chapter is about building your basic piecing skills to branch out *beyond* squares. Don't get me wrong, quilts made with only squares are versatile and can be beautiful. I still make them! My quilt, *Such a Square*, page 72, is an "all-squares" quilt.

Adding rectangles and triangles to your quilting repertoire will boost your confidence and then you'll be ready to jump into the rest of this book. There are basics and tips for every level of quilter in this chapter. Read on—there are lots of skills and fun techniques to learn!

SUPPLIES

Scissors Galore

There are many different types of scissors out there and, honestly, I find I need very few of them. I recommend having three pairs of good quality scissors: a large pair for cutting yardage or larger pieces of fabric, a medium-sized pair that work well for small hand projects, and small needlecraft scissors with super sharp tips for snipping threads. I keep multiple pairs of needlecraft scissors around my workspace and my ironing board because I use them so frequently.

To keep your scissors at their sharpest, avoid cutting anything but fabric with them. Even paper (a wood product) dulls them faster than fabric.

- Here are some other useful scissors:

Small curved-blade scissors—helpful when cutting threads close to the surface of the fabric, in order to avoid accidentally cutting into it.

Snips—different from standard scissors in that they have a spring action. I keep curved-blade snips at my ironing board to snip off errant threads when pressing.

Embroidery scissors—small with thin blades. These are good for accurate cutting on hand projects.

Medium- and large-sized scissors with micro-serrated blades—keep the fabric from slipping and are useful when cutting lengths of yardage.

Scissors with blunt tips—avoid snagging adjacent fabric when cutting. Use these to reduce bulk in multiple layers of appliqué.

Pinking shears—give a zigzag edge that's decorative and prevents fraying. If you prewash your fabric, pink the edges first to prevent raveling. Pre-cut fabrics often come with pinked edges. In general, don't pink fabric pieces for patchwork. The zigzag makes it hard to align the edges for consistent seam allowances.

Rotary Cutters

Rotary cutters cut quickly and accurately and are the stars of quilting. They are extremely sharp so the first thing I'll say here is "Be careful!".

Make it a practice to always (always!) retract the blade and engage the safety lock when you put your cutter down. It will quickly become a habit and prevent injuries.

- There are a few sizes of rotary cutters with different uses.

60 millimeter (mm)—Multiple layers of fabric, straight cuts, and heavy materials.

45mm—Straight cuts or gentle curves. This size is the most common used in quilting.

28mm—Templates and curves.

18mm—Best cutter for tight curves and small templates.

- Change the blade on your rotary cutter when it misses threads when you cut. The blade should glide over your fabric like an ice skate on fresh ice, smooth and easy.
- As with scissors, only use your rotary cutter on fabric. Paper and other substrates dull the blades more quickly.

DISPOSING OF USED BLADES Properly dispose of rotary cutter blades. It's not safe to simply throw a blade into the trash. I keep a small metal box for "sharps" like old rotary cutter blades and used sewing needles. An Altoids™ box is perfect for this.

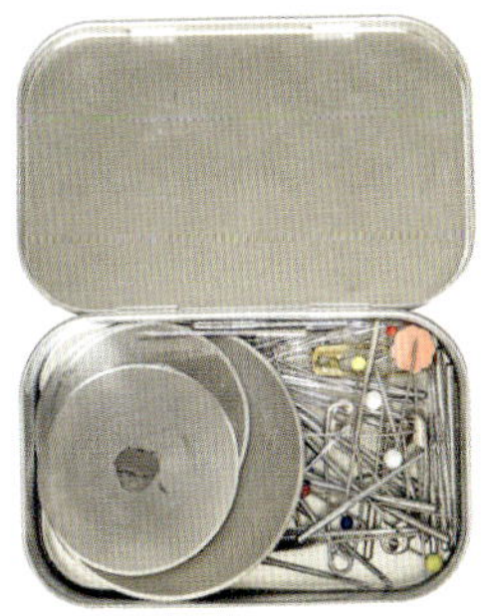

Rulers

Specialty rulers are made for rotary cutting. These are heavy-duty, transparent, acrylic rulers with a grid on them for accurate measuring. Most will have angle markings for 15-, 30-, 45-, and 60-degree cuts.

There are many different brands out there. My favorite rulers are Quilter's Select® because they have a non-slip treatment on the underside that prevents the ruler from shifting while cutting. These rulers are also marked with numbers that can be read right-to-left or left-to-right, so my brain doesn't go into overdrive figuring out measurements. Olfa® Frosted Advantage, Omnigrid®, and Creative Grids® are three other popular brands.

These are my favorite rulers and their uses:

6" × 24"—My workhorse! It makes cutting strips and blocks a breeze. It's comfortable to handle for both long or short pieces of fabric.

2½" × 12½"—For smaller pieces of fabric. It's perfect when the larger ruler is too unwieldy.

18" × 18"—For squaring the corners of a quilt after quilting.

- When sewing blocks, an exactly sized ruler makes squaring them up easier. Common block sizes are 6½" and 12½" square. Many quilters buy these sizes, too.
- There are triangles, diamonds, circles, rulers with slits for cutting strips; you name it, they make it. Talk to your local quilt shop and your fellow quilters about what works for them.
- As a general rule, use the smallest ruler you can for the size pieces you're cutting. This helps keep the ruler from sliding around on the fabric.

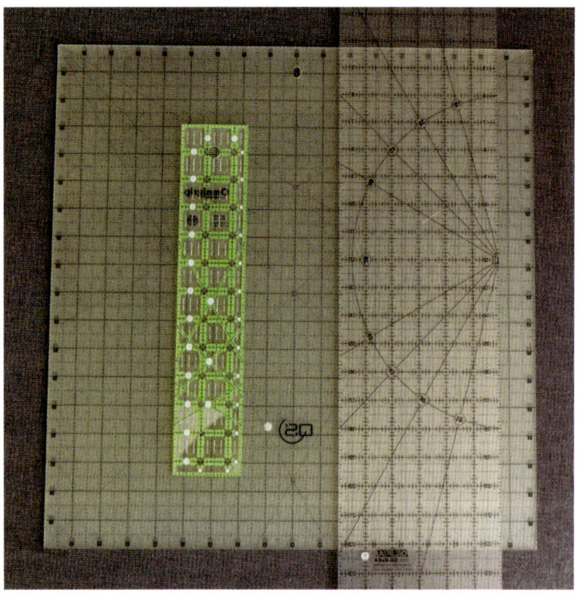

USE 2 RULERS

When you need to cut pieces of fabric larger than the rulers you have, use 2 rulers side by side or end to end.

Cutting Mats

Quilters cut fabric with a rotary cutter on a self-healing cutting mat. These mats protect your table and extend the life of the rotary blade. Self-healing means that you can cut on the mat many times without ruining it. My mats have lasted years!

- Mats come in an almost endless variety of sizes, colors, and types. Start by buying a cutting mat as large as your primary cutting table. Mine is 24" × 36". If you're lucky enough to have a bigger cutting area, splurge on the bigger mat! It's worth it. Then add in other sizes as needed for specific quilting projects.
- Consider buying a small mat for next to your sewing machine. I have a 6" × 8" one there. This is convenient, especially when you're working on a foundation-paper piecing project like *Triangle Sunburst* (page 90).
- Mats come in the standard flat style and also in foldable and rotary styles. Foldable mats are compact to travel with and to store. A rotary mat spins fabric around to cut other edges without shifting the fabric. This is handy for tasks like cutting around hexie templates (see *Hex Key*, page 168).
- Mats have measuring grids printed on them that are great for estimating fabric cuts and for designs that don't require precision. However, when doing precision cutting, always use a ruler to measure.
- Various mat colors are available, too. Green and grey are the most common but I love that a bright, fun color can add personality to my sewing station.
- Store your mats flat and away from heat. They are temperature sensitive and will warp if exposed to heat, as in a hot car or from an iron.
- You need a new mat when your cutter has a fresh blade but still misses here and there or the mat feels "fuzzy" from lint left behind after cutting fabric. This means your mat has slight grooves cut into it and it's time for a new one.

Cutting Tables

Rotary cutting is best done while standing. This provides stability and accuracy, and is safest for the quilter. If you're lucky enough to have a dedicated cutting table, fantastic! If not, a kitchen counter with a cutting mat works perfectly well.

- The ideal cutting table is counter height, around 36". This saves your back because you don't bend or hunch while cutting fabric. You can buy tables made especially for quilters and sewists from the big-box sewing stores.
- Most cutting tables have shelves or drawers for storage. If you're new to quilting and don't know it yet—this extra storage will come in handy!
- Some people buy bed risers and put these under a table's legs to get the same result. Go for whatever works for you and suits your budget.
- If you have the room, place your cutting table where you can walk around it and cut from both sides. This avoids swiveling your fabric to cut after straightening an edge or removing selvages.

Presser Feet

My favorite presser foot is a walking foot (also known as a "dual-feed" foot). I use one 95% of the time on my domestic machine. This foot moves all layers of fabric under the needle at the same rate. It eliminates fabric pulling, sliding, or bunching. Many machines come standard with one.

These are my recommendations:

- For accurate straight-line piecing, a ¼" walking foot is fantastic. If your machine doesn't have one or dual-feed capability, a ¼" foot is an ok substitute.
- When piecing, I use a ¼" foot with an edge guide. Why? My fabric slides along the guide and makes sewing a perfect ¼" effortless and consistent.
- For curved piecing, a standard ¼" foot works best.
- For straight-line or gently-curved quilting, use a standard walking foot to ensure the quilt sandwich moves under the needle evenly. I don't recommend quilting with anything else.
- A free motion foot, or darning foot, is used for free motion quilting on a domestic sewing machine. Choose open or closed-toe, plastic or metal, depending on the visibility you need. Talk to your local sewing machine shop about these when you start free motion quilting.

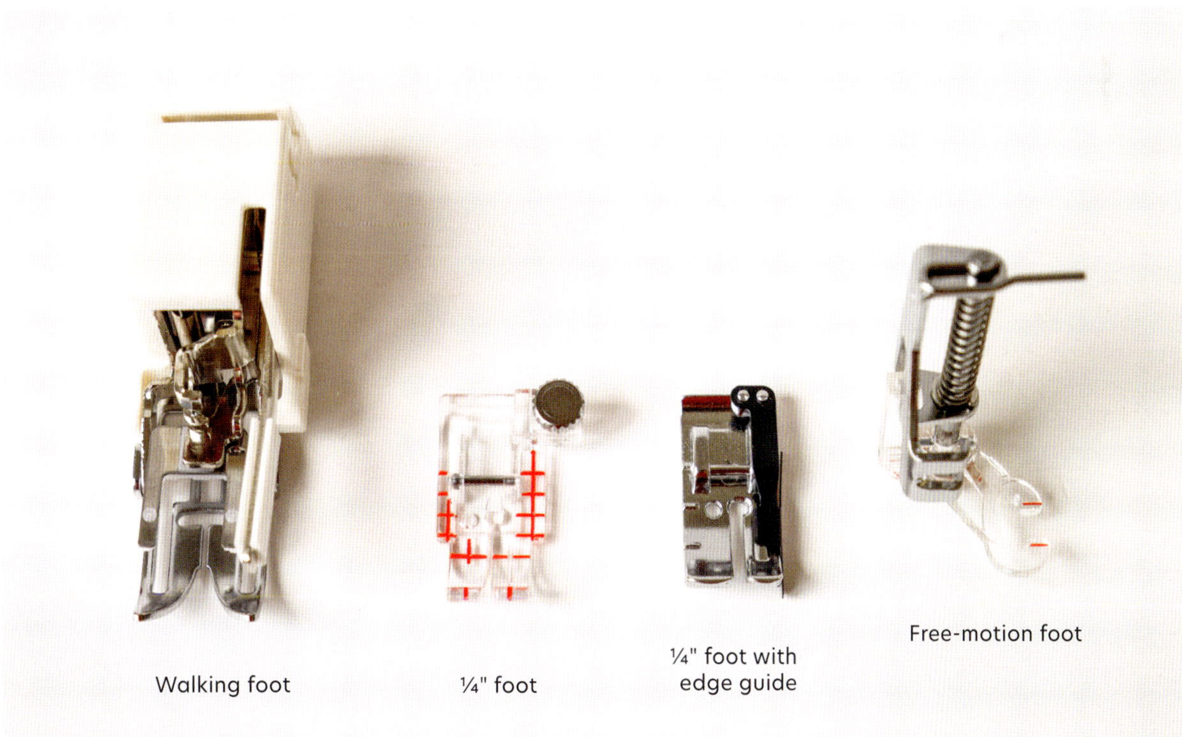

Fabric Markers

Not all markers are "created equal", always test a marker on your fabric and check that it's easy to remove.

Temporary Markers

Pilot FriXion® pens—have a ton of uses in quilting. They leave a crisp dark line that disappears with heat from an iron. FriXion pens are widely used for tracing templates, drawing cutting lines, and for temporarily marking fabrics. *Lines from a FriXion pen may re-appear in extreme cold—not a problem for most, but good to know. Also, they can leave marks on batik fabrics. Test to be sure.*

Disappearing pens—are used in much the same way as FriXion pens, but disappear when exposed to moisture or air, not heat. Keep in mind you need to wet your fabric to get rid of the water-soluble marks. If you plan to wash your quilt immediately, this is a non-issue.

Hera™ markers—are made of hard plastic with a thin, rounded edge. Running that edge over fabric creates a gentle crease that's visible under the sewing machine needle. Use these to mark quilting lines that disappear under quilting or by scratching the fabric with a fingernail. Lines from a Hera marker will last for days.

Chalk markers—are used in the same way as the other markers. Chalk can be shaken off, washed off, or brushed off with a soft cloth or old toothbrush.

Heat may set some disappearing ink or the dye in chalk markers. Don't iron over a mark until you've tested.

Permanent Markers

Pigma® Micron pens—are used for permanent marks on projects or quilt labels. They come in a variety of point sizes and colors. They don't bleed and last for years and through many washings.

Pentel® Gel Roller for Fabric pens—are also used for projects and labels. They come in black with a 1.0mm point size. They don't bleed and leave a dark line that lasts through washings.

Ultra-fine point Sharpie®—works for a quilt label in a pinch. I don't recommend using them as they can bleed and do not have crisp lines.

Iron with high heat to set ink before washing.

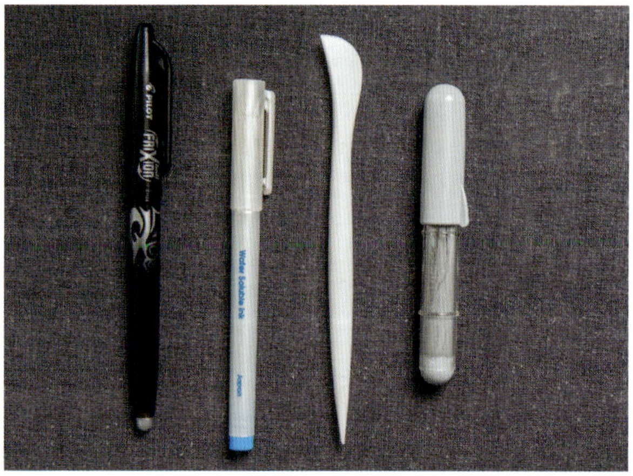

FABRIC AND DESIGN

How do you choose the right fabric for your project? This is a tricky question, and there is no right or wrong answer. Of course, we all want a beautifully finished quilt and our fabric choices are the first step toward it. Choosing fabric is my absolute favorite part of the quilt-making process. Think about which colors you'd like to work with. Ask yourself these questions: Is there a color palette that appeals to you? A combination that you've thought about using but haven't? Does the person you'd like to make a quilt for have a favorite color? When choosing, I audition different fabrics, placing them next to each other. Most times, a combination that works for me emerges quickly. When it doesn't, I try different combinations, switching fabrics in and out until I like what I see. This should be a fun process, not a stressful one!

If you're unsure about picking colors, never fear, there is inspiration all around. If I can't come up with something on my own, I look to the world around.

- Many quilters choose a "focus fabric" to begin their selections. Find a fabric you love that has the colors you want, then select other fabrics that look good with it.
- I once took color inspiration from the packaging of an oil diffuser because I loved the colors on the box.
- Your closet likely has colors you love sprinkled throughout. See what color combinations on your clothes speak to you.
- Use an online random color palette generator to get yourself started. Browsing through beautiful color palettes is a great way to kick-start creativity.
- Nature, in every changing season, has color combinations that are awesome. What's your favorite season and what are the colors in it?
- Pick someone or something to design for. For my quilt *Winging It*, page 146, I chose my wonderful friend, Margaret, for inspiration. She loves Day of the Dead, sugar skulls, Frida Kahlo, bright and colorful fabrics, and jewel tones. I pulled fabrics based on what I thought *she* might like. I started with yellow, green and orange; then auditioned different pinks and blues to arrive at a combination that made me happy.

What Kind of Shopper Are You?

There are a couple of different fabric shopping styles that I've seen among quilters, and each has its own advantages and drawbacks.

THE IMPULSE SHOPPER

This is me! When I look for fabric, I'm not usually searching for anything in particular. I just love perusing the fabrics at my local quilt shop, looking for something that speaks to me. It always feels like a bit of a treasure hunt. Sometimes I find a gem, and other times I leave without buying a thing.

Once I find a fabric I love, I'll either design a quilt around it, or find a pattern that showcases it. This is a fun way to shop. It is a spur-of-the-moment, fly-by-the-seat-of-your-pants fabric hunt. It works for me.

ADVANTAGES

- You have a collection of fabrics you love and an abundance on hand to begin new projects.
- You can design spur-of-the moment and start sewing right away.

DRAWBACKS

- You've purchased fabric you may never use.
- Your fabric stash is always growing.
- You almost always need to buy additional coordinating fabrics when starting a project which makes it difficult to stay on a budget.

(It's still worth it!)

THE MEASURED SHOPPER

Some quilters are more methodical about their fabric needs. First, a pattern is selected. Next, they shop *only* for the fabric needed for the project. It's very efficient!

ADVANTAGES

- You only buy what you need and don't have a big fabric stash to store at home.
- It saves money.

DRAWBACKS

- You can't design from your own stash.
- You have to go to the fabric store every time you start a project.
- No flexibility to swap out a fabric mid-project without going shopping.

Whether you're an Impulse or Measured Shopper, the question surrounding fabric selection is the same. What will look best? Here are some things to consider when choosing fabrics for your next project.

- **Color selection—**Warm vs cool, contrasting colors, complementary colors?
- **Solids vs. prints—**What's the best way to use these, separately or together?
- **Tone-on-tone prints—**Add in fabrics that read as solid from a distance?
- **Print scale—**Are large-scale prints, small-scale prints, or both appropriate for your project?
- **Directional fabric—**How will a directional fabric look in the project?
- **Color tone and saturation—**Where do you want your project to be among the variations in every color of the rainbow?

If you're anything like me, sometimes you know exactly what palette and fabrics to use, and other times you might not know where to start. You may have a color you'd like to use, but no direction beyond that. Read *Fabric and Design*, in this chapter starting on page 53, for more details and tips.

The Fabric Trifecta

The most successful fabric combinations have a mix of these 3 criteria: color, value, and scale.

Color

- Color preferences are different for everybody but we know what we like when we see it. It's the planning before we see it that can trip us up.
- A color wheel is an excellent tool for beginner and experienced quilters alike. This defines and shows color combinations like complementary, split complementary, triadic, and analogous. Some color wheel tools also have lots of design information and other suggestions for successful combinations.
- The internet is a great resource. Search for a "color palette generator" and you'll find all sorts of sites with gorgeous color combinations.

Value

- Value refers to the lightness or darkness of a color. Using a variety of values from light to dark adds visual appeal.
- A fabric's value is determined in relation to the fabrics around it. For example, a medium-value fabric looks light next to a dark color and looks dark next to a lighter color. It's all about contrast.
- A design with fabrics of only one value will be static. The pieces may all fade together making it hard to distinguish one from another and difficult to see the design.

Scale

- Scale refers to the size of the print in the fabrics.
- Use a variety of scale (small, medium, and large patterns) from fabric to fabric to amp up the visual appeal.
- A combination of small and large pieces of fabric in the design will vary the scale, too, particularly when using solids and tone-on-tone fabrics.

FUSSY CUTTING Fussy cutting highlights a specific motif from a printed fabric. A motif is cut out with a seam allowance added around it, then placed strategically in the piecing. Fussy cutting is often used with hexagons. If you plan to fussy cut, buy more fabric than the project calls for.

Solids, Prints, and the In-Betweens

Small-scale prints— Small-scale prints feature a motif the size of your fingernail or smaller. The motif is repeated all across the fabric. These often feature only one or two motifs.

Large-scale prints— Patterned fabrics that feature larger repeated design elements are large-scale prints. They often feature many colors and motifs.

Low-volume—A fabric that's increasing in popularity, low-volume prints feature a small-scale print on a white or near-white background.

Tone-on-tone—A patterned fabric using a variety of shades, tints, and tones of one color is a tone-on-tone. These are also called blenders.

Solids—Solids are a single color. They have a right and wrong side, but in some the difference can barely be seen so they're a good choice for beginners. Mix solids with prints for visual interest.

Neutrals—Neutrals are generally in the white, cream, gray, and black color families. They blend with any color and allow the others to stand out. Often neutrals are background fabrics but sometimes entire quilts are made from them.

Directional prints— Fabrics with a clear orientation are called directional. They can be tricky to work with as pieces placed in different directions are easily noticed. That can be accidental or an intentional design element. Buy extra fabric to accommodate directional cutting.

Finalizing the Design

Whether you're designing your own quilt or working from a pattern, visualizing the fabric placement and color combinations ahead of time is important. Here are some planning tips.

- Use a coloring sheet to design your quilt. How you think a quilt will look is often very different from how it will actually look. A coloring sheet gives you an idea of what to expect, especially if you plan to use more than two fabrics. Color multiple versions until you home in on your favorite layout.
- Before starting to sew the pieces together, arrange them on a design wall, floor, bed or table. This gives you a chance to see how your finished quilt top will look.
- When you're happy with your design, snap a photo. This provides another frame of reference to evaluate it. Change the photo to black and white to better show value and contrast.
- Things to consider as you plan: Do you like the layout? Does it feel heavy or light in areas? Are the colors distributed nicely? Do they work together the way you intended? Is there enough value or color change between pieces to distinguish one from another? If the answer to any of these questions is no, don't be afraid to go back and *change it*! Sometimes we get stuck in a rut of what we "should" be doing, but quilting is art, and art is subjective, so do what makes you happy. You aren't spending this much time on a project just to feel "ok" about it. Give yourself permission to make changes!
- Finally, a photo of the final design is a great reference as you sew. Believe me when I say that it is not difficult to mix up pieces (or even rows!), or sew a block in the wrong spot, or lose track of where you are. Having a picture will save you from extra work and prevent you from getting off track—ask me how I know!

TECHNIQUES AND TIPS

Straightening the Edge

Before you start cutting strips and pieces, you have to straighten or "square up" the edge.

- Fabric comes off the bolt folded with the selvages together. Leave the fabric folded to cut width-of-fabric (WOF) strips.
- Press the fabric so the cuts will be accurate. Avoid ironing too crisp a crease at the fold because it can be hard to "un-iron" later.
- Align a ruler with the fold and close to the edge you are squaring up. Cut the edge of the fabric at a 90-degree angle to the fold. (Fig. 1)
- *Always cut away from yourself.* Cutting towards your body is not only awkward and inaccurate, it can be dangerous.
- Cut standing up to get the most stability for the ruler and accuracy of the cuts.
- Press the ruler securely in place with one hand; use a rotary cutter to cut with the other hand.
- Be sure the hand holding the ruler is away from the ruler's edge. Quilters have had severe cuts from rotary cutters. (Fig. 2)
- Pause cutting as you go to move your hand further up the ruler. Press the ruler down next to where you are cutting. This keeps it from sliding or shifting. (Fig. 3)
- When moving your hand up the ruler, don't lift the hand completely, "crawl" it up. It's easy to accidentally shift the ruler out of alignment when you place your hand back down.
- When you need a lot of strips of the same width, cutting through more than two layers of fabric is tempting. But too many layers may cause the bottom layers to be less accurate. Inaccurate cutting leads to more squaring up later. I cut my WOF strips through two layers, but I subcut through more layers.
- Close and lock the rotary cutter blade with the safety—EVERY time you put it down.

Fig. 1

Fig. 2

Fig. 3

Cut Strips and Subcut Pieces

Most piecing starts with cutting strips, then smaller pieces are subcut from the strips.

- Now that the edge is squared up, move around to the other side of the fabric (or rotate the fabric) to start cutting strips.
- Align the ruler with both the squared edge and the fold. Place the mark for the strip width at the edge. In this example, I am cutting a 4½" strip. (Fig. 4)
- Remove the selvages before you subcut smaller pieces. Align the ruler with the top and bottom edges of the strip and cut off the selvage with your rotary cutter. (Fig. 5)
- To progress from strips to squares and rectangles, align the measurements on the ruler with three edges of the strip: the top, bottom and cut edge. (Figs. 6 and 7)

Fig. 4

Fig. 5

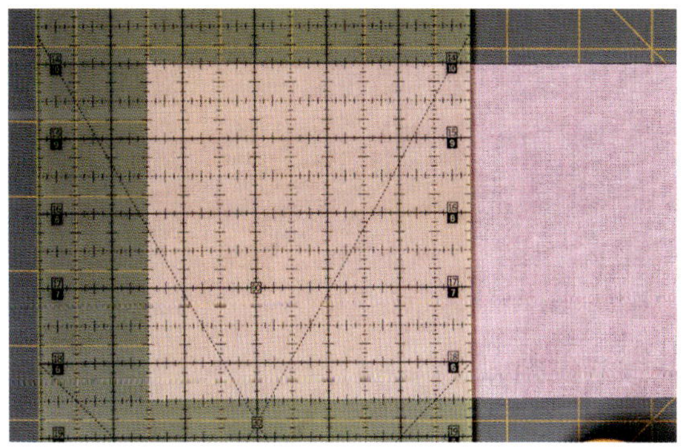

Ruler aligned to cut a 4½" x 4½" square. Fig. 6

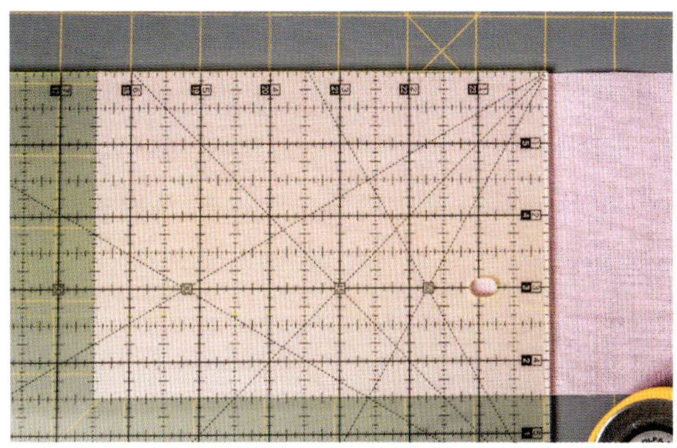

Ruler aligned to cut a 4½" × 6½" rectangle Fig. 7

SQUARE IT AGAIN?

After cutting multiple strips, recheck that the edge is still at a 90-degree angle to the fold. If it's not, re-square it. Otherwise, your strips will come out skewed. This happens, believe me, especially when cutting a series of narrow strips, like for binding.

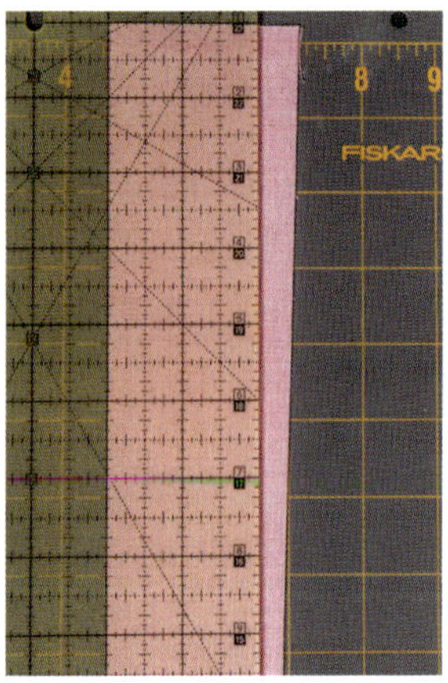

Re-square by cutting the edge to 90 degrees with the fold to avoid skewed strips, like this one.

The Infamous Scant ¼"

Have you ever heard of a scant ¼"? I'll be honest and tell you that when I first heard about it, I was intimidated and I actually avoided learning about it because I thought it was too advanced. Turns out it's not intimidating at all and it greatly improves piecing accuracy.

A scant ¼" seam allowance is simply this: it's about one thread width narrower than the standard ¼" seam allowance. That's it! Why does this matter? When our fabrics are sewn together and the seam is pressed, we lose a tiny bit of the fabric to the fold of the seam allowance. A scant ¼" seam allowance accounts for that tiny loss so our blocks are exactly the intended size.

So, how do we go about getting that scant ¼" seam allowance? On my machine, I use a button to nudge the needle to the right, one position. If your presser foot or sewing machine won't allow the needle to move from center, align the fabric just inside the edge of the ¼" foot.

- Keep your seam allowance accurate and all your blocks and sections should end up the same size.
- This accuracy only matters for quilts with a traditional look, such as with matched corners and points. Improv or free-form designs don't need to be as accurate. My quilts *Winging It* (page 146) and *Riding the Waves* (page 152) are examples of this.
- The easiest way to get a consistent ¼" seam allowance is to use a ¼" presser foot. Some machines come with these. If yours didn't, I recommend buying one. Another option is to move your needle to sew ¼" from the edge of whatever foot you have.

Tension

Tension refers to the balance in a line of stitching between the bobbin thread and the top thread.

Even tension is when the bobbin thread doesn't show on the top and the needle thread doesn't show on the bottom. It's pretty straightforward.

Uneven tension causes problems. Seams may be weaker and/or they may pucker.

- To start, always raise your presser foot before threading the machine. This assures the tension mechanism is ready for the top thread.
- For most piecing with quilting fabrics, the pre-set tension works perfectly. But check now and then, especially when starting something new.
- To check your tension, join two scraps of fabric with a sample line of stitching. Evaluate the seam to see if the thread is pulling harder from one side or the other.
- Adjust the tension on your machine until it sews a smooth seam.

Even tension

Top tension is too loose

Top tension is too tight

Stitch Length

- Sew with a moderate stitch length. Aim for about 12 stitches per inch. That's a setting of 12 on some machines and 2.2 on others. You can always sew a sample seam and measure to double check.
- Use a shorter stitch length for foundation paper piecing. (Refer to Foundation Paper Piecing: *Techniques and Tips*, page 83, for more on this.)
- A longer stitch length isn't strong enough to last a lifetime for a quilt. It might also cause the seams to press unevenly and look crooked.

A SAMPLE SEAM If you're new to this, sew a sample seam. Cut 2 squares, each 2½" × 2½". Sew them together using a ¼" seam allowance. After pressing, the resulting rectangle should be 2½" × 4½". If it's not, adjust your seam allowance accordingly. It probably means just a slight change in how you align the edge of the fabric with the edge of the presser foot.

BACKSTITCHING Some folks say that backstitching is unnecessary when piecing a quilt. I disagree! Sewing backward over 2 or 3 stitches is a simple way to ensure your seams are strong and secure as you progress through piecing the quilt top. I backstitch at the start and end of every block, even when chain piecing. Is this overkill? Maybe. But I like knowing that my blocks won't come apart if accidentally stretched or pulled.

To Pin or Not to Pin?

Pinning is individual to each quilter. I don't use pins unless it's necessary. First—I don't like to take time to pin if I can easily hold the fabric with my fingers. Second—I can't seem to avoid sticking myself with pins, so when needed, I use binding clips instead. And third—a dab of washable glue set with a hot iron holds tricky spots together long enough to sew them. Play around with different techniques to find what works best for you. There are a few times when pinning is absolutely worthwhile.

- When there are seams to match, pinning makes it easier to keep everything lined up and in place.
- Pin long seams at the beginning and end, and then throughout the middle. This prevents the fabric from shifting as you sew.
- Use glass-head or other heat-resistant pins because it's awful when a plastic pin melts onto your fabric and iron's soleplate.
- Flat-head pins, as you might think, lie flatter on the fabric. This helps when aligning bulky seams.
- Appliqué pins are shorter with slightly blunter tips. Use them for hand-appliqué because they stay out of the way and don't hurt as much if you stick yourself.

Pressing

- *Pressing* is different from *ironing*. Pressing is a gentle up and down motion. Ironing is more aggressive—sliding the iron and pushing the wrinkles out. Pressing avoids stretching the fabric which can distort the grainline and skew the seams.
- Pressing "to one side" means both seam allowances are pressed in the same direction. (Fig. 1) When possible, press towards the darker fabric so it will not show through to the front of the lighter one.
- When you press "open", the seam allowances are pressed away from each other, away from the seam. (Fig. 2)

Fig. 1

Fig. 2

- One of the major quilting debates is whether to press seams open or to the side. Want to know what I think? Do what works for you. I prefer to press my seams open for two reasons: 1) I never have to figure out which way I need to press my seams for them to nest. I can't be bothered. If I press open, the seams always match. 2) When seams are pressed open, bulk is reduced. Both sides of the seam allowance share the bulk, and the block lies flatter.
- If you are planning to quilt in the ditch, *always* press your seams to the side. In-the-ditch quilting can weaken or break the thread in the seams if they are pressed open.
- For effective pressing, use the cotton setting on your iron (with steam). Some wrinkles need an extra spritz of water, too.
- A wool pressing mat is a great option to press smaller blocks at your sewing station. The wool heats up and you're effectively pressing from both the bottom and the top. It's like magic.

SUPER FLAT Press seams with a hot steam iron, then use a tailor's clapper to get them super flat. A tailor's clapper absorbs the steam from the fabric while pressing the seam and cooling it. These have become very popular in the last couple of years, with quilters acheiving great results.

Chain Piecing

Chain piece together repetitive piecing or blocks to save thread and time. Chaining is similar to an assembly line; all the pieces are ready to sew and there's hardly any thinking from one set to the next.

- Place your pieces within reach of your machine at your sewing station. Sew the first set.
- Sew 2 or 3 stitches past the end of the set, then sew onto the next set.
- The stitches are easy to clip between sets when you're done.

Seam Ripping

- Seam ripping is sometimes jokingly called "un-sewing" and is never welcome, but everyone has to do it sooner or later.
- Seam rip from the *wrong* side of the fabric so you don't accidentally rip or snag the right side.
- Cut the thread every few stitches on one side. The thread on the other side can then be pulled off in one long string.
- Seam rippers come in different sizes for travel and for ergonomics. There's also one with a rubber cap to easily brush away the cut thread.

Nesting Seams

One way to ensure seams match is to "nest" them for sewing. It's a simple technique.

- Press one seam or a whole row of seams to the side in one direction and press the corresponding seam(s) in the opposite direction. That's pretty much it!
- When seams are pressed in opposite directions, they butt up to each other (nest); you can feel the alignment with your fingers. Pin on both sides of the seam in the seam allowances.
- Sew slowly and remove the first pin just before stitching over it. Remove the second pin after the needle has secured the intersection.

Nested seams

AN INTRODUCTION TO BASIC BLOCKS

Half-Square Triangle Blocks

A slew of quilt patterns have half-square triangle (HST) blocks in the design. There are two easy methods for constructing HST blocks. Both start with 2 squares cut from different fabrics and a diagonal line drawn from corner to corner on the *wrong* side of one of the squares.

DOG EARS The little bits of fabric that extend past the blocks on half-square triangles are called "dog ears". Trim these square with the block.

HST Blocks—Method 1

This method yields two half-square triangle blocks for each set of squares.

- Add ⅞" to the desired *finished* size of the half-square blocks to get the *cut* size for the squares. For example, if you want the blocks to be 3" × 3" in the finished quilt, cut the squares 3⅞" × 3⅞".
- Draw a diagonal line from corner to corner on the *wrong* side of one of the squares.
- Align the squares, *right* sides together.
- Sew using a ¼" seam allowance on *both* sides of the drawn line. Cut on the drawn line and press. You have two half-square triangle blocks!

HST Blocks—Method 2

This method yields one half-square triangle block for each set of squares.

- Add ½" to the desired *finished* size of the half-square blocks to get the *cut* size for the squares. For example, if you want the blocks to be 3" × 3" in the finished quilt, cut the squares 3½" × 3½".
- Draw a diagonal line from corner to corner on the *wrong* side of one of the squares, the same as in Method 1, above.
- Align the squares, *right* sides together.
- Sew *on* the drawn line.
- Trim to a ¼" seam allowance and press.

Flying Geese

Flying Geese blocks are another commonly used element in quilt designs. They make the arrows in my quilt, *Going Out*, page 74.

- Start with a rectangle from one fabric and 2 squares from another.
- For the rectangle, add ½" to the *finished* measurements of the block. For example, if you want your block to measure 3" × 6" in the finished quilt, cut the rectangle 3½" × 6½".
- The squares are the same as the short side of the rectangle. In this example, that's 3½". So cut 2 squares, each 3½" × 3½".
- Draw a diagonal line from corner to corner on the *wrong* side of both squares.
- Align a square *right* sides together with one end of the rectangle and sew on the drawn line. Trim the seam allowance to ¼". Press. (Figs. 1 and 2)
- Repeat the process with the other square at the other end of the rectangle. (Figs. 3 and 4)
- Check the orientation of the second square before sewing. The drawn diagonal lines should meet at one side of the rectangle.

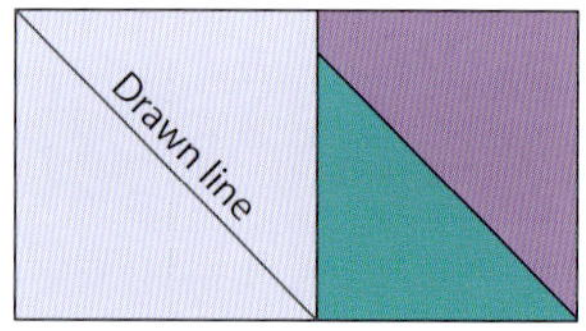

Incorrect orientation of the second square

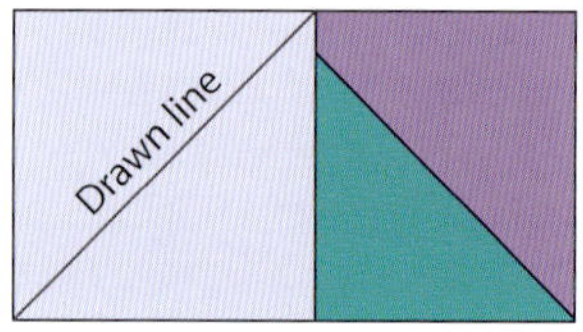

Correct orientation

Fig. 1

Fig. 2

Fig. 3

Fig. 4

AN INTRODUCTION TO SEWING CURVES

Most quilt patterns are made by sewing straight lines. This is all well and good, but what happens when you want to sew shapes with curves? Curves can be intimidating at first. They were for me. After learning the technique, I realized I wasted time worrying because it's actually pretty darn simple. Once you learn the basics, you'll tackle curved piecing with no issue at all.

Make the project *Riding the Waves*, page 152, to try your hand at improvisational curves.

- Draw a line ¼" away from one straight edge of your template paper for the seam allowance.
- Use a compass to draw a half-circle centered on the drawn line. If you don't have a compass, cut a string to the length you need and use that to guide your drawing.

TEMPLATES There are many premade acrylic templates that make cutting the fabric pieces uncomplicated, but I love to use what I already have on hand. Make your own template from a piece of thick paper, cardstock, or thin cardboard.

- Make 2 templates: one for the background fabric with a ½" *smaller* diameter than the finished circle and another for the half-circle fabric with a ½" *larger* diameter. For example, for a finished diameter of 9", the background template's diameter will be 8½" and the half-circle's will be 9½".
- Trace around the templates onto fabrics and cut out the fabric pieces.
- Fold each piece of fabric in half across the straight edge and finger press to mark the middle of the arcs. (Fig. 1)
- Pin or glue-baste the 2 pieces *right* sides together at the middle and ends. Ease the fabrics together between those locations and pin/glue to match the curved edges. (Fig. 2)

Fig. 1

Fig. 2

- Sew together with a ¼" seam allowance. Use a standard presser foot, not a walking foot. Sew slowly being careful not to sew any tucks into the seam. When needed, stop (with the needle down) and reposition the fabrics under the presser foot. (Fig. 3)
- Press toward the background fabric. Voilà! You've sewn a curve.
- To make a full circle, join two half-circles. (Fig. 4)

Fig. 3

Fig. 4

SUCH A SQUARE

Question: What's a simple quilt you can make as a complete beginner? Answer: One made from fabric squares! Its simplicity is its strength. Use two fabrics for simple contrast; make a vibrant statement with a range of colors; or choose fabrics with novelty prints for babies and children. This is the perfect project to launch you into the world of quilting!

Seam allowances are ¼"

WOF=Width of Fabric

Fabrics by Alison Glass for Andover Fabrics: Foxglove, Cosmos, Thistle, Lavender, Periwinkle, Hydrangea, and Blue Jay from the Kaleidoscope collection

CUTTING FABRIC This quilt uses 70 squares and any size can be used. I chose 6" squares because a 6"-wide acrylic ruler makes cutting them a breeze. Another simple way to go is to use the 5" precut squares in a charm pack.

FINISHED SIZE 39" × 55½"

MATERIALS

If you use fat quarters, you can get 9 squares from each one.

Six fabrics (A–F): ⅜ yard each

One fabric (G): ⅝ yard

Backing: 2½ yards

Batting: 45" × 62"

Binding: ½ yard
(for 2¼"-wide, double-fold, diagonally pieced binding)

CUTTING

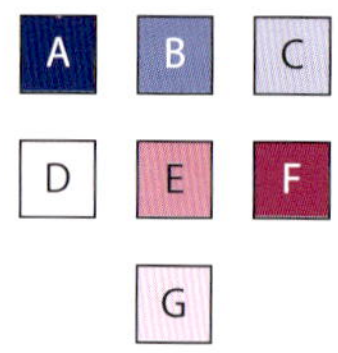

Fabrics A–F: From each fabric, cut 2 strips, 6" × WOF.

- **Fabrics A and F:** Subcut 7 squares, 6" × 6".
- **Fabrics B and D:** Subcut 10 squares, 6" × 6".
- **Fabrics C and E:** Subcut 11 squares, 6" × 6".

Fabric G: Cut 3 strips, 6" × WOF. Subcut 14 squares, 6" × 6".

Backing: Cut 2 pieces, each 45" × WOF. Join along the 45" edges using a ½" seam allowance. Trim to 45" × 62".

Binding: Cut 5 strips, 2¼" × WOF.

PROJECT INSTRUCTIONS

For each row, stack the 7 squares on top of each other in the correct left-to-right order. Label the top square in each stack with the row number, 1–10. This keeps things organized as you bring the stacks to your sewing table to sew the rows together.

1. Sew the squares in each row *right* sides together.

2. Press the seams to one side, alternating the pressing direction from row to row. (Refer to Piecing Basics: *Nesting Seams*, page 66.)

3. Sew rows 1 and 2 together, creating a wider strip. Do the same for rows 3 and 4, 5 and 6, 7 and 8, and 9 and 10.

4. Sew the wide strips together. Nest the seams from one row to the next to easily match the corners. Press.

5. Quilt and bind any way you like.

6. Add a label to the back and you're done!

Row 1	A	B	A	B	A	B	A
2	B	A	B	A	B	A	B
3	C	B	C	B	C	B	C
4	G	C	G	C	G	C	G
5	C	G	C	G	C	G	C
6	G	D	G	D	G	D	G
7	D	G	D	G	D	G	D
8	E	D	E	D	E	D	E
9	F	E	F	E	F	E	F
10	E	F	E	F	E	F	E

GOING OUT

My quilt is a scrappy mix of colors with the warm hues at the top left moving to the cool ones at the bottom right. I used 14 different fabrics. Use as many fabrics or as few as you like. Arrange them on a design wall to find the look that's right for you. In all, you need 36 arrows.

Seam allowances are ¼"

WOF=Width of Fabric

Fabrics are by Alison Glass for Andover Fabrics: Pomegranate, Cosmos, Cherry, Poppy, Persimmon, Carrot, Sunflower, Citrus, Fern, Grass, Dragonfly, Beetle, Bluebonnet, Hydrangea, Blue Jay, and Charcoal from the Kaleidoscope collection

MATERIALS

Arrow fabrics: 1 fat eighth or fat quarter each of 15 fabrics

Background fabric: 2¾ yards

Backing: 3½ yards

Batting: 61" × 61"

Binding: ½ yard (for 2¼"-wide, double-fold, diagonally pieced binding)

CUTTING

For each arrow:

Cut 1 rectangle, 3½" × 6½"
Cut 1 rectangle, 3½" × 2½"

From the background fabric:

Cut 7 strips, 3½" × WOF
Subcut: 72 squares, 3½" × 3½"

Cut 4 strips, 6½" × WOF
Subcut: 13 squares, 6½" × 6½" and 4 rectangles, 6½" × 12½"

Cut 2 strips, 12½" × WOF
Subcut: 4 squares, 12½" × 12½" and 4 rectangles, 12½" × 6½"

Cut 5 strips, 3½" × WOF
Subcut: 72 rectangles, 3½" × 2½"

Backing: Cut 2 pieces, 61" × WOF. Join along the long edges using a ½" seam allowance. Trim to 61" × 61".

Binding: Cut 6 strips, 2¼" × WOF

FINISHED SIZE 54½" × 54½"

PROJECT INSTRUCTIONS

Use the techniques and tips on pages 60–66 to guide you through the process for this project.

The Arrows

1. Make a Flying Geese block using 1 arrow rectangle, 3½" × 6½", and 2 background squares, 3½" × 3½". Follow the instructions for Flying Geese on page 68.

2. Press. Make 36 Flying Geese.

3. Make an arrow stem by joining 2 background rectangles, 3½" × 2½", with 1 arrow rectangle, 3½" × 2½".

4. Press. Make 36 arrow stems.

5. Sew an arrow stem to a Flying Geese block to make an arrow.

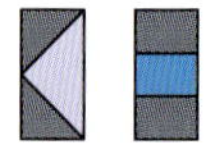

6. Press. Make 36 arrows.

7. Join 2 arrows to make a double-arrow block.

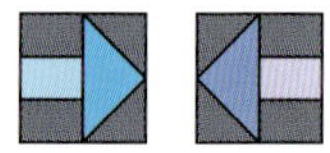

8. Press. Make 12 double-arrow blocks.

Quilt Assembly

1. Join the arrows, double-arrows, and background pieces into rows, as shown.

2. Sew the rows together.

Finishing

1. Quilt and bind your quilt any way you like. I decided to quilt mine with an all over geometric pattern which echoes the style of the arrows. Then I used the background fabric as the binding to keep the emphasis on the arrows.

2. Remember to add a label to the back!

PIECING BASICS

WHAT COULD GO WRONG?

ISSUE The seam folded over as I was sewing and it is no longer open, but sewed to the side.

SOLUTION This actually happens to me a lot. No biggie if the block still finishes to the right size. But if not or if you're a perfectionist, you may want to go back and unpick the stitches over the folded seam and re-sew. Otherwise, just let it stay but make sure it's pressed super flat from the front.

ISSUE I sewed my blocks together in the wrong order.

SOLUTION This is why seam rippers were invented. Realizing you've sewn blocks in the wrong order can be frustrating, but it is totally fixable. Use your trusty seam ripper to take the blocks apart, then rearrange them until they're in the right order and re-sew. Can't seem to figure out where those squares were supposed to be? I recommend taking a photo of the quilt layout once you finalize the design (page 59). Refer to it and you'll be back in business in no time.

ISSUE My squares and rectangles aren't the same size when I put them together to sew.

SOLUTION Been there! Sometimes we make mistakes when cutting fabric. Maybe the ruler slipped, maybe we just weren't paying attention.

If a single piece is ⅛" smaller or larger than the others, it can probably be dealt with by easing or stretching to fit. If an entire row has pieces that are ⅛" smaller, that is going to be a problem that needs to be fixed.

If the project has points like the arrows in my quilt, *Going Out*, page 74, the solution is to cut new pieces. You may have to buy more fabric for this, so it pays to be extra careful when cutting.

For a project with all 90-degree angles, you can sometimes trim the larger pieces or blocks to match the smaller ones.

ISSUE I messed up on my ¼" seam allowance. Not all of my seams are the same.

SOLUTION It's usually not a big deal if the seam allowance is off by a tiny bit, but if there are big variances from one seam to another, take out that seam ripper and pull those stitches out.

A small problem will stay small if it occurs only once, but if you repeat that problem throughout the quilt, it will be exacerbated and show in the finished product.

ISSUE I sewed all of the finished blocks together the wrong way.

SOLUTION Fun little story for you...

When I designed and pieced the arrows quilt, *Going Out,* page 74, I knew exactly how I wanted it to look. I drew it out, chose fabrics with intention, and arranged the cut fabrics on my design wall just to double check it was going to look the way I wanted. Even with all of this deliberate preparation, I made a mistake. Life can be stressful, right? Even with the best intentions (and perceived focus on what I was doing), I put the finished blocks together the wrong way. My carefully planned blocks with 4 arrows facing away from each other? Well—I pieced them facing toward each other. I didn't realize my error until I had literally sewn the very last seam on the quilt top. I spread the top out and realized that the color transitions were no longer smooth. I had really mucked it up. Honestly, if the quilt hadn't been for a book, I would've marveled at my own lack of focus, laughed a little, then moved on to the next project.

But, being as this *was* for a book, I had a choice to make: pull the individual blocks apart using a seam ripper and reassemble, or remake the whole thing. I decided to give myself a break and not get more stressed out by pulling the quilt all apart. So...I remade everything! That option felt better to me.

The moral of the story? Give yourself a break. Mistakes like this happen all of the time, to all of us. Life has all sorts of ways of pulling your focus away from the project you're working on. If it does happen, know you are not alone and give yourself some grace.

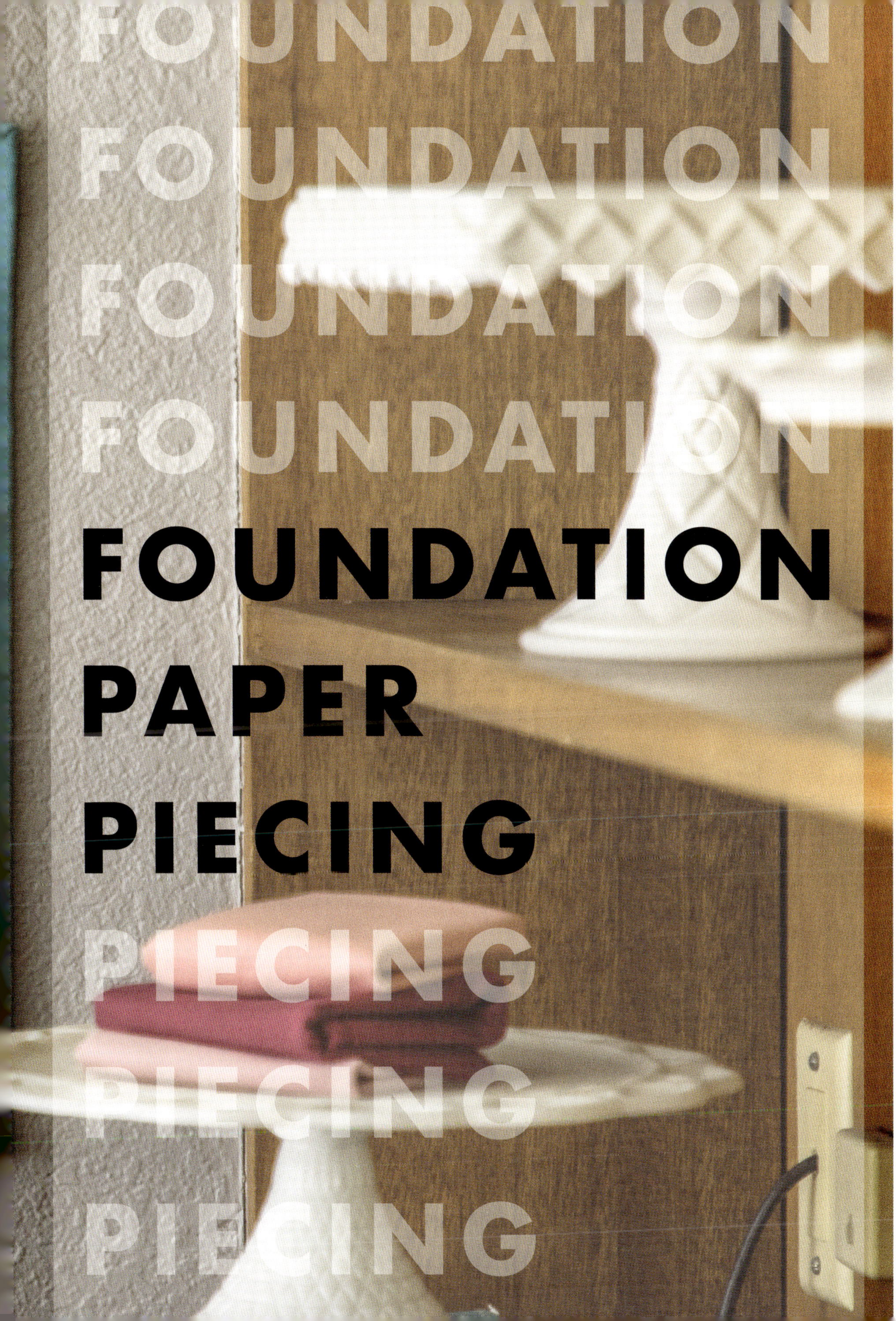

FOUNDATION PAPER PIECING

FOUNDATION PAPER PIECING

When I began quilting, I was content to stick to simple quilts made with squares, rectangles and triangles. Over time, I realized that I wanted to create more intricate designs with non-traditional shapes. This is accomplished with foundation paper piecing.

What is foundation paper piecing (FPP)? FPP is sewing pieces of fabric directly onto a "foundation", usually a piece of paper preprinted with a pattern. Hands down, FPP is the most accurate way to piece a detailed quilt. You can be assured that each piece of fabric will be sewn accurately because you're sewing directly onto a template. I personally love FPP because it is easy to achieve accurate designs with minimal brainpower (my favorite way to sew). FPP is a very popular technique and many patterns are available, both for free and for purchase online with instant downloads. All you need is a printer, and your pattern pieces can be printed out at home.

FPP can be intimidating to new quilters or quilters who haven't tried it. Although it is a new and different way of piecing, it is simply another valuable tool in your quilting toolbox. Once you get used to FPP, worlds of quilting possibilities open up.

TECHNIQUES AND TIPS

Your Sewing Station

- There is lots of pressing with FPP. To avoid constantly getting up and going to your ironing board, set up a pressing station right next to your sewing machine.
- Use a small seam roller to flatten seams quickly and easily.
- Alternately, a small wool pressing mat and mini iron are comfortable to use at your sewing station.
- Avoid the printer ink on the foundation paper when ironing because it may get the iron plate dirty.
- Save pressing with a large iron for the finished sections.

Notes on the Foundation Paper

There are plenty of options for FPP templates, but I prefer to use what I already have at home:

Printer Paper

I use good old printer paper for all FPP projects. It's always around and inexpensive. Remember to shorten your stitch length to 1.6 or less, otherwise the paper's tough to tear out and your stitches may loosen or pull out with the paper. Use tweezers, if needed, to pull pieces out in small corners.

Blank Newsprint

This is usually sold in quilt shops and is packaged as "Foundation Paper." It's lightweight and tears away the easiest of all the options, so it's more forgiving if you forget to shorten your stitch length. It runs through your printer and comes in both letter and legal size, which helps for larger patterns. It's inexpensive, too.

Vellum

Vellum is translucent and very easy to see through and line up the fabrics with the seam lines. Vellum is expensive and not readily available at quilt shops, but can be found at art supply stores or online.

Freezer paper

This is great because the shiny waxy side temporarily sticks to fabric when ironed. Print or trace the pattern on the paper side. Iron shiny side down and the fabric will stick to the freezer paper making it very stable. No floppy fabric pieces when you turn the paper over! You can find 8½" × 11" freezer paper that runs through your printer at quilt stores and online. (Take extra care not to let your hot iron touch the shiny side of the freezer paper; it's a total mess if the plastic melts onto the iron plate).

DON'T FORGET THE MIRROR IMAGE! If you're designing your own FPP pattern, remember that the block will be the mirror image of what's printed on the foundation paper. That's because you're sewing on the wrong side of the pattern. This happens with letters and other non-symmetrical designs.

Most printers have an option to print the mirror image. If yours doesn't, tape the design with its *right* side to a bright window, then trace it. A light box is another option.

TO CUT OR NOT TO CUT?
Cutting fabric pieces to size before sewing them to the foundation paper wastes less fabric. Most FPP patterns don't specify fabric piece sizes, so we have to figure it out ourselves. This is a personal pet peeve of mine. When I was new to FPP, I found it confusing to try and figure out which shapes I needed, especially triangles and odd shapes. To solve this, I use a large square of fabric cut at least an inch larger than the widest part of the piece.

Sewing Sections

- Cut pieces ahead of time, if desired, and label them with stickers.
- Shorten your stitch length to 1.6 or less. A shorter stitch length makes it easier to remove the papers after sewing. A longer stitch length creates fewer perforations in the paper. This makes the paper very difficult to remove after sewing without loosening or pulling out stitches.
- Chain piece your blocks assembly-line style, to save time. (Make one complete section first to work out any kinks before chain piecing everything.)
- Sew the pieces to the foundation paper in numerical order.
- Start with Section A, piece 1 (A1). Center the A fabric under the A1 piece on the *unprinted* side of the foundation paper with *wrong* side of the fabric to the paper. Make sure the fabric extends at least ¼" over all the piece's edges for the seam allowances.
- Hold the paper and the fabric up to the light or place on a lightbox to double check the fabric is placed correctly. (Fig. 1)
- Using a dab of glue stick, adhere A1 in place. (Fig. 2)
- Next up is piece A2. Look at the printed side of the pattern and cut a piece that's larger than A2 by about 1" on all sides. Cut a straight edge on this piece for the A1/A2 sewing line.

Fig. 1

Fig. 2

- To check that the A2 piece is correct, place it over its location on the pattern next to the glued A1 piece, *right* side up. Overlap the straight edge of A2 at least ¼" with A1 for their seam allowances. Hold it up to the light, and make sure the A2 fabric is large enough to cover its space. Check that you have enough extra fabric around all edges to account for seam allowances.
- Flip A2 over onto A1, fabrics *right* sides together and ready to sew. Check the alignment by holding it up to the light again.
- Hold A2 in place, turn the pattern printed side up, and sew on the A1/A2 seam line.
- Start and end the stitching about ¼" outside the seam line. The stitching will be crossed by other stitching later which will anchor it in place so keep it outside the seam line for this to work. (Fig. 3)
- Trim the seam allowance to ¼". For very small pieces, like the ones in *Triangle Sunburst*, page 90, trim to about ⅛". To be precise, use a ruler to trim. As you become more proficient, you may choose to trim by eye, with either a small rotary cutter or scissors.
- Turn the pattern fabric side up, open A2, and press the seam with a dry iron or a seam roller. (Fig. 4)

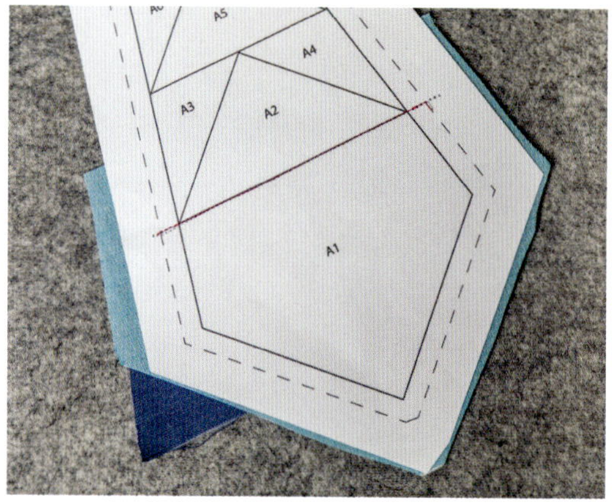

Fig. 3

Fig. 4

GO EASY ON THE GLUE Don't use a lot of glue; use just enough to keep the fabric from shifting as you sew. Using too much glue makes it difficult to remove the paper from the fabric.

I use standard washable glue sticks, because I like how easy they are to find and the price can't be beat. Choose the small size glue stick, it's easier to use than the chubby kind. Another option is white school glue, like Elmer's, in a bottle with the pointy orange tip to control how much glue comes out. There are specialty quilter's glues, too, with needle-nose applicators to apply the small dabs you'll need.

- Move on to A3. As you did for A2, cut a piece for A3, place it over its space on the pattern overlapping A2 enough for the seam allowance. Hold it up to a light, and double check it will fit its space.
- Flip A3 over onto A2, fabrics *right* sides together and ready to sew. Check the alignment by holding it up to the light one more time.
- Hold the fabrics in place, turn the pattern printed side up, and sew on the A2/A3 seam line. (Fig. 5)
- Trim the seam allowance and press. (Fig. 6)
- Continue adding pieces until the section is completed.
- Give the entire section one more press with a dry iron.
- Trim the seam allowance to an exact ¼" on all edges of the section. Remember to trim on the *dashed* line. *If there is no dashed line, add ¼" outside of the solid one.* (*Fig. 7*)
- Follow the same process for all the sections in your pattern.

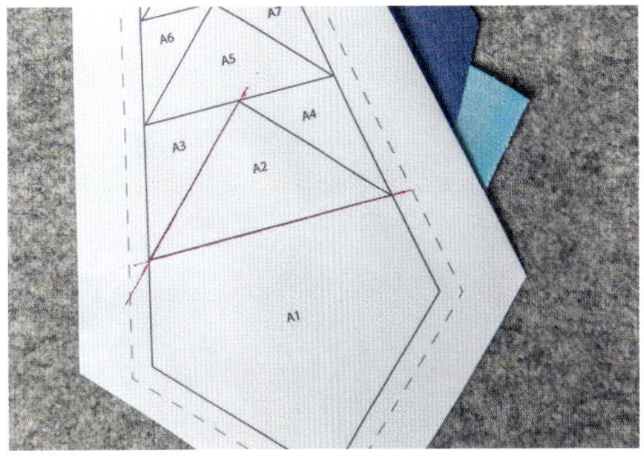

Fig. 5

Fig. 6

Fig. 7

Joining Sections

- Align the edges of Sections A and B along their join line.
- For sections that are bulky, use binding clips to keep the sections from shifting. (Fig. 8)
- Match corners and align or nest seams from one section to the other. For more information on this, refer to Piecing Basics: *Nesting Seams*, page 66. To get the points matched and seams aligned with the least struggle, glue baste or machine baste at each of these spots before stitching.
- Take caution matching points, they should meet where the stitching will go, not at the outer edge of the seam allowance. (Fig. 9)
- Another option is to sew the bulkiest sections first to hold them in place. Then go back and sew the whole seam. Those sections will not shift and will be super strong.
- Stitch the entire seam with the 1.6 stitch length.

Fig. 8

Fig. 9

SUCCESS FROM THE START There can be a lot of bulk in some of the seams when joining sections. Glue or machine baste the bulkiest bits first to check the alignment of your seamlines.

- Remove the seam allowance paper from the sections. Leave all of the other paper intact. Press open. (Figs. 10, 11, and 12)
- Removing the paper from the seam allowances reduces bulk. Pressing the seams open reduces bulk even more. Less bulk means the block will lie flatter and allow for smoother quilting. But if you're planning to stitch in the ditch while quilting, do *not* press open; press to one side.
- Follow these steps to join all the sections until your block or design is complete.

Fig. 10

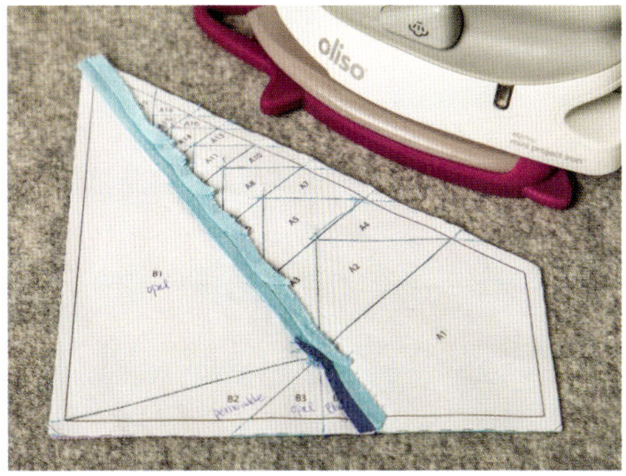

Fig. 11

Fig. 12

BE CAREFUL TRIMMING

FPP patterns usually have two outer lines: a solid line which is the outer line of the design, and a dashed line which is the seam allowance line. Always trim at the dashed line. (Fig.7) If you trim at the solid line, you won't have a seam allowance and your finished design will not be the correct size and the sections will not fit together. Some patterns (inexplicably!) don't come with a built-in seam allowance. If you come across one of these, add ¼" to all of your pattern pieces. Thankfully, patterns without seam allowances are few and far between.

TRIANGLE SUNBURST

This mini quilt project will teach you the ins and outs of Foundation Paper Piecing, and results in a stunning small project. This pattern can also be made into a large quilt by making multiple blocks and joining them with or without sashing.

Seam allowances are ¼"

WOF=Width of Fabric

LOFQ = Length of Fat Quarter (the longest edge of the FQ)

Fabrics by Alison Glass for Andover Fabrics: Opal, Cosmos, Foxglove, Thistle, Periwinkle, Hydrangea, and Blue Jay from the Kaleidoscope collection

MATERIALS

Bright pink: 1 fat quarter

Light pink: 1 fat quarter

Purples: 1 fat quarter each of 3 fabrics; a light, a medium, and a dark

Dark blue: 1 fat quarter

Blue for the background and the binding: 1¼ yards (for 2¼"-wide, double-fold, diagonally pieced binding)

Backing: ¾ yard

Batting: 22" × 22"

CUTTING

To simplify the cutting, there's one strip size for the fabrics. You use a little more fabric this way but it's much easier than cutting lots of different sizes for so many small pieces.

Bright pink:
Cut 2 strips, 2" × LOFQ

Light pink:
Cut 3 strips, 2" × LOFQ

Purple 1 (light):
Cut 2 strips, 2" × LOFQ

Purple 2 (medium):
Cut 4 strips, 2" × LOFQ

Purple 3 (dark):
Cut 3 strips, 2¾" × LOFQ

Dark blue:
Cut 3 strips, 2½" × LOFQ

Blue:
Cut 9 strips, 1½" × WOF
Cut 1 strip, 4¾" × WOF
Cut 2 strips, 6" x WOF

Backing: Cut 1 square, 22" × 22"

Binding: Cut 3 strips, 2¼" × WOF

FINISHED SIZE 18½" × 18½"

Cut the Section Pieces *Subcut these pieces from the strips.*

FABRIC	SIZE TO CUT	HOW MANY TO CUT	WHERE TO PLACE THEM
Bright Pink	2" × 1½"	4	A17
	2" × 3¼"	4	D1
	2" × 2½"	8	E18 and F18
Light Pink	2" × 1½"	4	A14
	2" × 3"	8	D2 and D3
	2" × 2½"	8	E15 and F15
Purple 1 (Light)	2" × 2½"	12	A11, E12, and F12
Purple 2 (Medium)	2" × 3"	4	A8
	2" × 5"	8	B2 and C2
	2" × 2½"	8	E9 and F9
Purple 3 (Dark)	2¾" × 3½"	4	A5
	2¾" × 1½"	8	E1 and F1
	2¾" × 2"	8	E6 and F6
Dark Blue	2½" × 4¼"	4	A2
	2½" × 1½"	8	B4 and C4
	2½" × 2"	8	E3 and F3
Blue	4¾" × 4¾"	4	A1
	1½" × 2¼"	120	A9, A10, A12, and A13 E2, E4, E5, E7, E8, E10, E11, E13, E14, E16, E17, E19, and E20 F2, F4, F5, F7, F8, F10, F11, F13, F14, F16, F17, F19, and F20
	1½" × 3"	20	A3, A4, A6, A7, and A19
	1½" × 1¼"	12	A15, A16, and A18
	2½" x 1½"	8	B3 and C3
	6" × 9"	8	B1 and C1

PROJECT INSTRUCTIONS

Seam allowances are ¼″.

Use the techniques and tips on pages 83–89 to guide you through the process for this project.

The Sections

- Photocopy the pattern for each section onto your choice of foundation paper. The patterns are in the envelope at the back of the book.
- Set your stitch length to 1.6. Add the pieces to the foundation in numerical order.

AVOID CONFUSION

It's easy to get fabrics mixed up, especially the pinks and purples in this project.

Make a key by gluing a piece of each fabric to a piece of paper and labeling it. Keep this at your sewing station and double check you are sewing the correct fabric in the correct spot.

▶ Make 4 of each section.

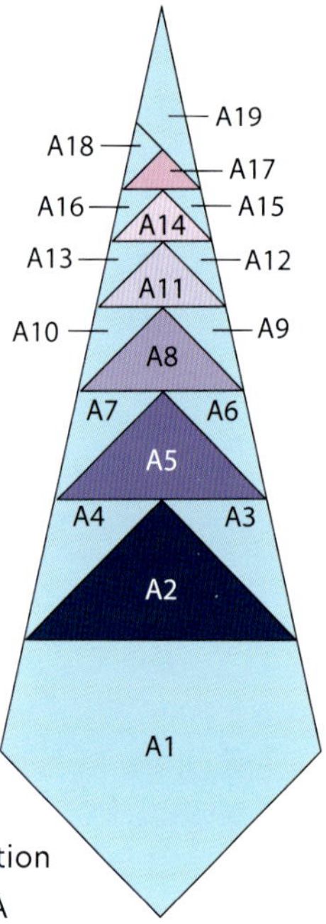

Section A

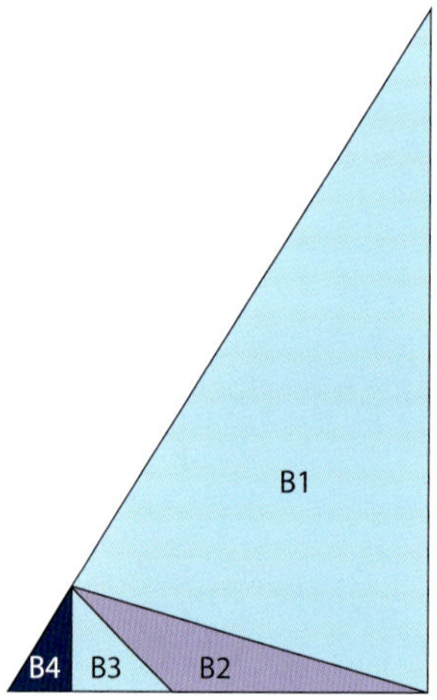

Section B

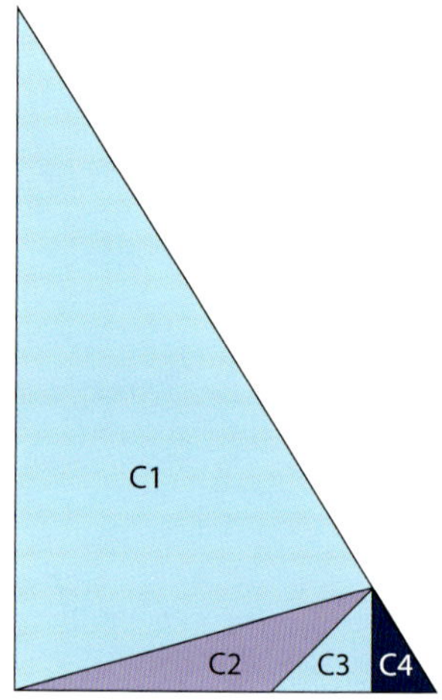

Section C

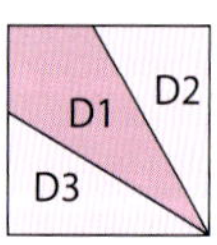

Section D

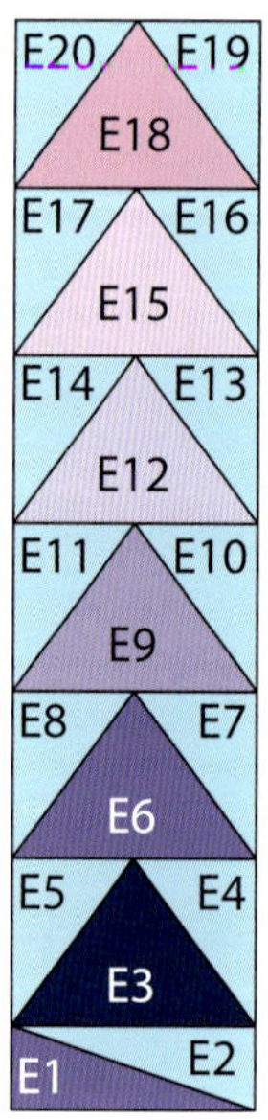

Section E

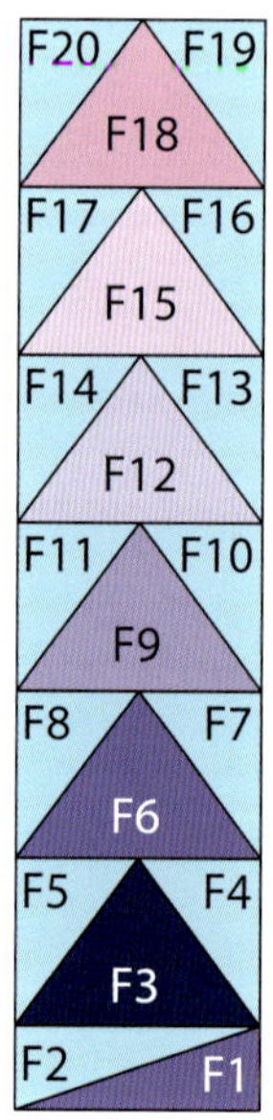

Section F

The Quarters

1. Join Section B to Section A, matching the corner of A2 with B2. Press open.

2. Join Section C to the other side of Section A, matching the other corner of A2 with C2. Press open.

Note the placement of pieces B4 and C4 in relationship to Section A. The B and C sections are mirror images.

3. Join Section E to the B/A/C unit. Press open.

4. Join Section D to the F unit. Press open.

Note the placement of pieces E1 and F1 in relationship to Unit B/A/C. The E and F sections are mirror images.

5. Join the D/F unit to the E/B/A/C unit, aligning the seams so that the corners of E1 and F1 match. Press open.

6. Trim some of the seam allowances a little to get the seams to lie flatter after pressing.

7. This completes a quarter of the wall hanging. Make 4.

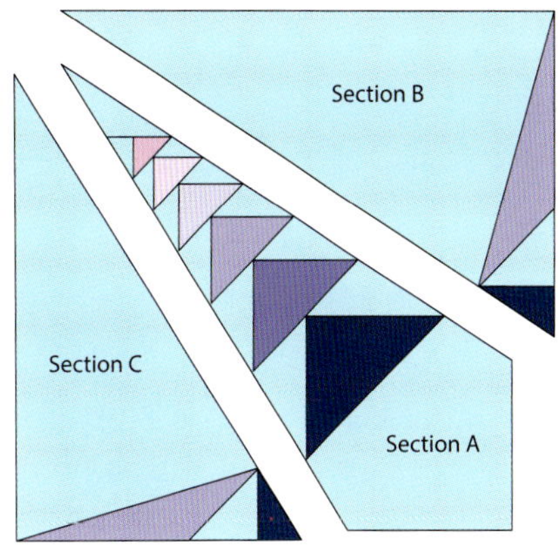

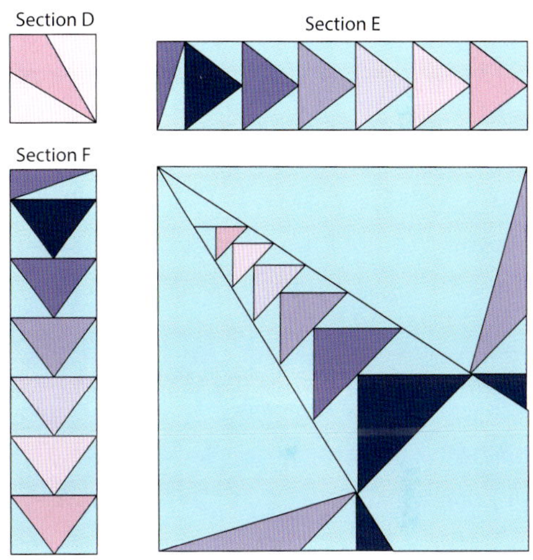

Final Assembly

1. Join 2 quarters to make half of the wall hanging. Press open.

2. Join the other 2 quarters to make the other half of the wall hanging. Press open.

3. Join the 2 halves, aligning the main seams and matching the points on all the others. Press open.

Final assembly

Finishing

Quilt and bind your quilt any way you like. Here's what I did.

Quilting— I wanted the quilting to pack a punch. Using a walking foot on my domestic sewing machine, I quilted around the pink and purple triangles to make them pop. Then I used a Hera marker (page 226) to mark the quilting for the negative space and stitched over those lines.

Binding—I bound the wall hanging with the background fabric for a finish that doesn't distract from the design.

Hanging sleeve—On small wall hangings, I like to put easy corner pockets on the back instead of a hanging sleeve. See Finishing: Binding, Facing, and More: *Facing with Corner Triangles*, page 249.

Label—Remember to add one. A quilt's not finished without it!

FOUNDATION PAPER PIECING

WHAT COULD GO WRONG?

ISSUE I sewed a piece of fabric on backward/upside down and it doesn't cover its space.

SOLUTION Grab that seam ripper! Even if you are a seasoned foundation piecer, sewing a piece on incorrectly happens. It is a total pain, but that is why a seam ripper is one of the most important tools to have.

ISSUE I trimmed my block at the solid line, not the dashed line; now I don't have a seam allowance.

SOLUTION I'm sorry to say, there is no great solution here. Cutting your seam allowance off means you'll sew your design into the seam. The only way to guarantee your block will be perfect and align with the other blocks is to go back and remake it. (I know, such a bummer!)

darling,
you
are
magic

MACHINE APPLIQUÉ

MACHINE APPLIQUÉ

Welcome to the wonderful world of machine appliqué! It's a quick way to add intricate design without complicated piecing or hand stitching. It's a perfect technique for layering elements over a pieced design. The possibilities are endless: add fussy-cut pieces, page 56, letters, complex motifs, or fun organic shapes to your quilts.

TECHNIQUES AND TIPS

Once you've picked your design, follow these few steps, then get sewing!

Make the Templates

Freezer Paper Templates

Many appliqué-ers use freezer paper as a template for their designs. It's a tool quilters use that isn't actually made for them, but it's cheap, easy to find, and easy to use. Most quilters purchase it from the grocery store.

Specialty freezer-paper sizes are also available to buy. An advantage of 8½" × 11" sheets is they can be run through your printer to make templates.

Freezer paper has two sides: a paper side and a shiny, plastic-coated side. The plastic side sticks when ironed to fabric, and later pulls away leaving no residue. This makes it great for appliqué.

Trace, draw, or print the appliqué designs on the paper side, dry-iron the shiny side to the fabric, and cut them out. Freezer-paper templates can be used more than once.

Rigid Templates

If you have shapes that are repeated multiple times, rigid templates are the way to go and heavyweight cardstock works well for this. Another inexpensive method is ironing two or three layers of freezer paper together to create a thicker template.

Some appliqué patterns come with premade templates which are convenient and easy to use.

Prep the Appliqué Fabric

Double-sided fusible interfacing creates clean lines for your appliqué, is easy to sew through, and is readily available at craft stores. My preference is HeatnBond® Lite Sewable Iron-on Adhesive.

Fuse one side of the iron-on adhesive to the wrong side of your appliqué fabric. Leave the paper on the other side.

Place a non-stick pressing sheet on the ironing board under the appliqué fabric. If any adhesive sticks over the fabric's edge, it will peel off the pressing sheet instead of sticking to your ironing board!

Trace the Templates

- Flip the appliqué fabric over so the fabric is *right* side up. Place the templates on the *right* side of the fabric. This is raw-edge appliqué so there's no need to leave space for a seam allowance between the templates.
- If the templates are freezer paper, iron them on with a dry iron. For rigid templates, use a light swipe from a glue stick or hold them in place by hand.
- Trace around the templates with a disappearing pen. I like to use FriXion pens. They draw a fine line that disappears when ironed. Test the pens first; FriXion pens can leave a line on batiks after ironing.
- If you don't have a disappearing pen handy, use whatever you have in your house. Any pencil or fine-lined pen that's dark enough to see but doesn't bleed to the other side will work. Test any marker on a bit of fabric. Double check it truly disappears and doesn't bleed so you can cleanly trim it off later.

Cut Out the Appliqué Pieces

- No seam allowance is needed for raw-edge appliqué!
- Use a combo of large and small scissors to cut out the appliqué pieces. Large scissors are useful for general cutting along straight lines or gentle curves, while small scissors give easy access to tight spaces.
- To cut out the center of a design, use a rotary cutter to make a small slit in the fabric. Then use your small scissors to cut out the rest.
- Cut *just inside* the traced line.

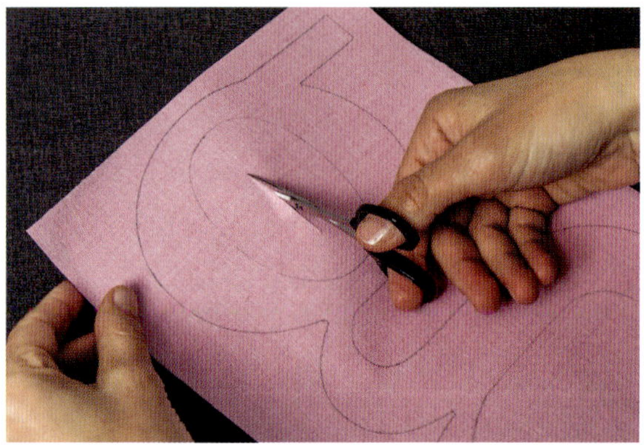

Fuse the Appliqué to the Background

- With the background *right* side up, place the appliqué on it, adhesive side down.
- Once it's all arranged and you're happy with the placement, peel off the paper backing from each piece, and place them back where they were.
- Check the placement again and begin ironing the pieces to the background, following the fusible instructions.
- Take care not to push or pull your iron, *press* the letters to the background fabric.
- Once ironed, the letters should be adhered to the fabric quite well. If you see any lifting, especially at the edges, press again.

Machine Stitch the Appliqué

Once the appliqué pieces are fused or basted to the background, you're ready to sew them down!

Stitch Options

After washing raw-edge appliqué, the edges may fray a little, giving them a rustic feel. Denser stitches cover more or all of the raw edge so it frays less. Choose a stitch for the results you desire.

Straight stitch—is uncomplicated; simply sew a straight stitch around the inside edge of your design. Use this with a turned seam allowance or when you want to see the frayed edges of raw-edge pieces.

Satin stitch—is a tight zigzag that keeps raw-edged pieces from fraying. It's perfect for stitching around precise designs giving them a smooth finish. Set the length to about 0.8. The width depends on how far you want the stitch to extend into the design.

Blanket stitch—is another popular option. It anchors the appliqué while adding a minimal design element.

Decorative stitches—bring a fun and unexpected element to your design. Most sewing machines come with a variety of these stitch options. Check your machine, it may have designated appliqué stitches. My machine has 16 stitches intended for appliqué.

Thread choice is as important as stitch choice. A contrasting thread color can add depth to a design. A color that blends can add cohesion or harmony. It depends on you and your eye. Go with your gut!

Aurifil 50wt cotton thread is perfect for machine appliqué. It's smooth, produces minimal or no lint, and comes in tons of colors. I keep a variety on hand so I have just what I need when I need it.

Stitching Around Curves and Corners

- Machine appliquéing around curves is precise work, so go slowly.
- Keep all of the stitching *at or inside* the edges of the design for a clean, neat look.
- The needle should be down in the fabric *before* you lift the presser foot, unless you're done stitching.
- To change direction in corners or around tight curves, don't stretch or pull the fabric. Stop with the needle down, lift the presser foot, then turn the fabric.
- On tight curves it can help to lift the presser foot with every stitch for small adjustments.

REDUCE BULK If appliquéing more than two layers of fabric, cut out underlying fabrics to reduce bulk. To do this, make a small slit in the backing fabric and, when you add a new layer, cut away the previous layer leaving a ¼" seam allowance.

PRACTICE FIRST Practice with the same weight fabrics and thread as in your project. Check the tension and how the stitch length and width look with your design. Adjust these until you're happy.

If the background puckers, use a lightweight one-sided fusible interfacing on the wrong side. I like Pellon SF101; it's flexible and doesn't noticeably shrink or change the drape of a quilt. It's easy to machine quilt through, too.

If you don't want a layer of stabilizer in your project, try a wash-away stabilizer or an iron-on, tear-away one, like Sulky Totally Stable.

MACHINE APPLIQUÉ

YOU ARE MAGIC

When designing this quilt, I chose big, bold lettering to create a modern, impactful design. I wanted a short phrase as the focus but I didn't have a concrete idea so . . . I did an internet search. I typed in "short quotes" and scrolled until two criteria were met: One, the quote was short enough to fit without feeling crowded and two, it was uplifting and meaningful to me. (Double check the quote is in the "public domain". If it's not, it's ok for personal use but credit the author if you put your project in a show.)

Seam allowances are ¼"

WOF=Width of Fabric

Fabrics are by Alison Glass for Andover Fabrics: Daisy, Fern, Salmon, Periwinkle, Thistle, Opal, and Hydrangea from the Kaleidoscope collection

SCRAPS It's possible to cut the letters in "*magic*" from large scraps. If you like this idea, make the templates before buying the yardage for Appliqué fabrics 2-6 to see what size pieces you'll need.

FINISHED SIZE 60½" × 72½"

MATERIALS

Appliqué fabric 1: (for "darling, you are"): ¾ yard

Appliqué fabrics 2-6: (for "magic"): 1 fat eighth or fat quarter each of 5 different fabrics

Heat N Bond Lite Sewable Iron-on Adhesive: 17" wide x 2 yards

Background fabric: 3½ yards

Backing: 3¾ yards

Batting: 66" × 78"

Facing: ⅝ yard

CUTTING

Appliqué fabrics: Cut these later, after you've made the templates.

Background fabric: Cut 10 strips, 12½" × WOF. Join strips at short ends.
Subcut 6 strips, 12½" × 60½".

Facing: Cut 7 strips, 2½" × WOF.

Backing: Cut 2 pieces, 66" × WOF. Join along the long edges using a ½" seam allowance. Trim to 66" × 78".

darling,
you
are
magic

PROJECT INSTRUCTIONS

Use the techniques and tips on pages 100–105 to guide you through the process for this project.

Prepare the Appliqué Letters

- Print or draw the letters for your phrase and make templates for them. I used a digital cutter to cut the letters out of cardstock for my templates. I picked the Georgia font, size 1000. Either print that on your home computer or use the patterns in the envelope at the back of the book.
- Use appliqué fabric 1 for the letters in "darling, you are".
- Use appliqué fabrics 2–6 for the letters in "magic", a different fabric for each letter.
- Iron double-sided fusible interfacing to the wrong side of the appliqué fabrics.
- Flip the appliqué fabrics over so the fabric is *right* side up. Arrange the letter templates on top of the fabric and trace them.
- Remove the templates and cut out your letters. To cut the centers out of the **d**, **a**, **g**, **o**, and **e**, make a small slit in the center with a rotary cutter. Then cut out the rest with your small scissors.

"PUZZLE" ARRANGEMENT The letters in "darling, you are" are cut from one fabric. In the interest of fabric conservation, both for the environment and your wallet, arrange them on the fabric like a jigsaw puzzle.

ANOTHER OPTION FOR THE EDGES I used raw-edge appliqué for this project because it's simple and gives fast results. If you prefer a turned-under seam allowance (turned-edge), learn about that technique in Hand Applique: *Other Turned-Edge Techniques*, page 120.

Position and Sew the Appliqué

- Place a background fabric strip on your ironing board. Smooth it flat and line it up with a ruler so that it's straight.
- Place the letters ¾" above the bottom edge of the strip. Constructing the background using strips makes it very easy to place the letters so they look straight when the strips are sewn together.
- Place the first letter in the line 3" away from the left edge of the strip. This provides enough spacing between the edge of the quilt and the first letter of each line. Continue placing the letters in the line. There is no "perfect" spacing. Approximate the distance and adjust until you're happy with the way it looks.
- Peel the paper backing off each letter and place it back on the strip. Double check the alignment. Then, starting with the leftmost letter, fuse them all to the fabric.
- The lower section of letters **g** and **y** will extend below the cut edge of the background fabric strip. Only fuse the top third of those letters to the strip.

- When fusing, do not push or pull your iron, simply press the letter to the background fabric. Once ironed, if you see any lifting of the letter, especially at the edges, go over it with an iron again. Repeat this process until each letter is adhered to the background fabric.
- Using a zigzag stitch, sew around the edges of each letter, except the partially fused ones. They will be zigzagged later. I use a 2.8 stitch width and 1.0 stitch length, which provides plenty of stability.
- Sew the rows together, including the top and bottom strips of background fabric. Flip up and pin the un-fused portions of letters **g** and **y** so they don't get caught in the seam allowances.
- From the *wrong* side, press the seam allowances open after each strip is added. *Do not apply heat to the partially fused letters or they will be fused to the wrong place!*
- Turn the quilt over, *right* side up, and give the seams one more press.
- Iron and fuse down the partially fused letters. Sew around them using the same stitching you used for the other letters.
- Quilt and finish the edges of your quilt any way you like. I used a facing instead of a binding to keep the look clean with a modern aesthetic. Refer to Finishing: Binding, Facing, and More: *Facing*, page 248, to finish your quilt this way.
- Remember to add a label to the back!

DON'T LET THE BULK GET YOU DOWN Roll up the excess fabric on the sides of the letter you're sewing. This makes it easier to handle the bulk of the material as you sew around the letter.

MACHINE APPLIQUÉ

WHAT COULD GO WRONG?

?

ISSUE When stitching around an appliqué piece, my fabric bunches up in front of my presser foot.

SOLUTION This is pretty common. With the needle down, raise the presser foot. Shift the fabric bulk from the front to the back of the needle. This is a simple and easy way to prevent puckering when sewing.

ISSUE I zigzagged right off the edge of my piece, and now it looks weird.

SOLUTION Seam ripper time! Simply rip out all of the threads that aren't where you want them, and start again. Backstitch where you started "un-sewing" to keep that thread from raveling later.

ISSUE I ironed a piece down and realized I don't like the placement.

SOLUTION A cool thing about Heat N Bond Lite is that it isn't immediately permanent. You may be able to pull the piece up. Then press the backing to remove any distortion and reposition the piece. If the piece becomes distorted when you pull it off, cut out a new one, press the backing, and try again.

BIAS TAPE APPLIQUÉ

Bias-tape appliqué is a lesser-known quilt-making technique, but one that deserves attention. Double-fold bias tape sewn to a fabric background creates striking shapes that are only limited by your imagination. One of my very favorite things about bias-tape appliqué is the ease with which delicate, thin curves can be added to your quilt.

CUT BIAS STRIPS OF FABRIC

You can purchase double-fold bias tape but making your own gives you unlimited design options!

- Decide on the width for the bias tape in your project and multiply that by 2. That is the width to cut your bias strips. For example, for ½"-wide bias tape, cut your strips 1" wide.
- If the design needs long continuous lengths of tape, use the tube method to make the bias strips. Instructions for this are in Finishing: Binding, Facing, and More: *Bias Binding*, page 238.
- If the design only needs a few short lengths, align the 45-degree line on your ruler with the straight grain to cut strips.
- Use a diagonal seam to join strips. See the Tip, *Why Diagonal Seams?*, page 237.

TWO WAYS TO MAKE DOUBLE-FOLD BIAS TAPE

Double-fold bias tape starts with a strip of fabric cut on the bias. The two long edges of the strip are folded in to meet at a center crease and the strip is ironed flat.

Bias-Tape Maker

This is my preferred method. It's quick, easy, and produces consistently sized strips. You don't absolutely need a bias-tape maker but, especially if you're making a lot of tape, they're worth buying.

- Cut the leading edge of a bias strip at an angle to make it easier to thread into the maker.
- Thread the fabric strip *wrong* side up into the maker and pin the leading edge of the strip to the ironing board.
- Feed the strip through the maker and iron it flat as it comes out. This keeps it crisp and easy to handle as it is appliquéd onto the quilt top.

Freehand

- This takes a little longer but the results are just as good.
- Fold the bias strip in half lengthwise *wrong* sides together and press to create a crease. Unfold.
- Fold each edge of the strip in to meet the center crease and press the strip as you fold. You can either fold and press both edges at the same time or fold and press them one at a time.

STARCH HELPS

Spray starch or a starch alternative help keep the strips' edges crisp and folded longer. It's especially helpful for the freehand technique.

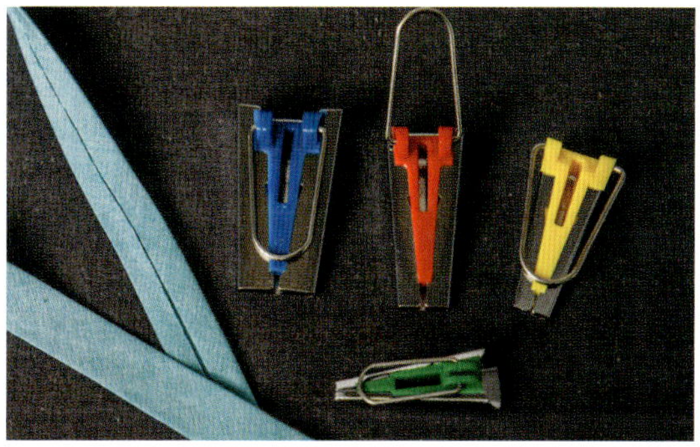

BIAS-TAPE APPLIQUÉ: TECHNIQUES AND TIPS

For an intricate design, like a Celtic knot, adhere a stabilizer to the wrong side of the background fabric before starting. This prevents your fabric from puckering or stretching when the appliqué is added.

- Draw the design your bias tape will follow on the background fabric. The tape will cover this line. Do not use a marker that will disappear when the fabric is ironed.
- Cut a length of bias tape about 3" longer than the starting section of the design.
- Center the tape over the beginning of the design line. If the end of your tape will not be sewn into a seam, fold the end under about ½" before sewing it down. (Fig. 1)
- Backstitch at the beginning and end of each line of stitching.
- Stitch down one edge of the bias tape, staying very close to its edge. Use a standard foot or a zipper foot.
- When possible, stitch along the concave edge of the tape first.
- Sew slowly, enough to keep the tape smooth on the background and your stitches just inside the edge.
- Place the tape as you go, keeping it centered over the line.
- When you need to adjust the direction of your presser foot, stop with the needle down, move the fabric, and continue stitching. If your design has sharp curves or angles, stop and adjust frequently.
- Continue placing and stitching the tape to the end of your traced design.
- The unsewn edge of the bias tape may stand up off the background fabric a bit. Press with a hot iron with steam so it lies flat (Fig. 2). Then sew down that edge of the tape. (Fig. 3)
- Repeat this process until the design is complete.

THE THREAD ELEMENT The thread color you choose will add another element to your design. A thread that matches the fabric will blend in, and hide any imperfections in your sewing. A contrasting color will give a bolder look. Do what makes your design look best.

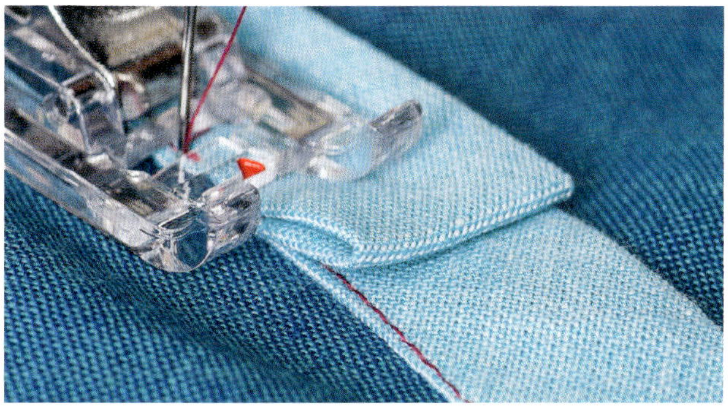

Fig. 1

Fig. 2

Fig. 3

WHY BIAS? Can't I just cut strips on the straight-of-grain strips and use those? Fabric cut on a 45-degree angle to the selvage (on the bias) stretches so it can be manipulated to make curves and round organic shapes. Straight-of-grain strips will not let you do this. Refer to Equipment and Materials, *Fabric Know-How,* page 28, for more details.

HAND APPLIQUÉ

HAND APPLIQUÉ

Hand appliqué is a beautiful technique to add designs to your quilt. Instead of being pieced in, the design is hand sewn on top. For the project in this chapter, I chose the traditional method of hand appliqué, needle-turn. This technique uses the *needle* to *turn* under the seam allowance on the appliqué pieces as you're hand sewing them to the background.

The very first quilt I ever made was entirely needle-turn appliqué. Living on the west side of Maui after graduating from college, I decided to take a Hawaiian quilting class. Back then, I didn't know anything about appliqué or hand vs. machine work, and that was probably a good thing. Had I known about the time commitment needle-turn appliqué and hand quilting require, I might have moved on to a sewing machine right then. Thankfully, I took the time to learn the art of Hawaiian quilting from the two ladies working at the local quilt shop and completed a twin-sized quilt.

A wonderful thing about hand appliqué is its meditative quality. There's a quiet simplicity to working repetitively with your hands and a needle and thread. Also, no sewing machine is required, so it's easy to do anywhere (couch, car, airplane) which makes it a great choice for vacation or road-trip sewing.

TECHNIQUES AND TIPS

There are 4 basic steps to hand appliqué: making (or buying) templates for the appliqué design, tracing and cutting out the design, basting it to the background, and sewing it to the background.

If you prefer to turn your seam allowances ahead of time instead of with your needle while stitching, refer to *Other Turned-Edge Techniques* (pages 120 and 121). Then use the same technique described here; just leave out the needle-turning and you're good to go!

Make the Templates

Use a purchased template or make a template for each piece of the design. Techniques and tips for this are detailed in Machine Applique: *Make the Templates*, page 100.

Trace and Cut Out the Design

Once you've got your templates, it's time to trace them and cut the fabrics for the appliqué pieces. Select fabrics with a standard or tighter weave, such as quilting cotton or batiks. The edges of a fabric with a loose weave will fray more easily.

- Place the template *right* side up on the *right* side of the appliqué fabric. Take care with placing the template. If your design isn't symmetrical and the template and fabric are not both placed right side up, the design will be reversed when sewn to the background. If the design *is* symmetrical, right and wrong sides of the template aren't important.
- Trace a thin line on the fabric around each template. Make the line dark enough to see but light enough that it doesn't show through to the other side.
- I use a mechanical lead pencil or a specialty fabric marker. The Sewline® Trio Mechanical Pencil is a good one because it has multiple lead colors and makes a thin crisp line. Use whichever is handy!
- Cut out your pieces with a ⅛" to ¼" seam allowance.
- Use a larger seam allowance for a project that will be washed; it's more durable. Use a smaller seam allowance for wall hangings and intricate designs.

HAND APPLIQUÉ

OTHER TURNED-EDGE TECHNIQUES

In this chapter, I'm focused on traditional needle-turn appliqué. What if you don't want to needle-turn the seam allowances or you're going to appliqué by machine rather than by hand? In the interest of giving you choices, here are two other techniques. These turn the seam allowance *before* basting the appliqué design to the background fabric. The *right* side of the template is placed on the *wrong* side of the appliqué fabric and the seam allowance is ironed over it.

If your design isn't symmetrical, be careful with the right *and* wrong *side placements. If the template and fabric are placed incorrectly, the design will be reversed when sewn to the background.*

GLUE STICK

- Use a very small swipe of glue to temporarily hold the template in place on the *wrong* side of the design fabric. (*Right* side of the template against the *wrong* side of the fabric.)
- Trim the seam allowance around the template to your desired width, usually between ⅛" and ¼". Use a wider seam allowance for a project that will be washed; it's more durable. Use a smaller seam allowance for wall hangings and intricate designs.
- Put a *thin layer* of glue on the seam allowance surrounding the template. Using too much glue makes things difficult later. Less is more here! (Fig. 1)
- Use your fingers to fold the fabric over the template one edge at a time. Neatly fold under the corners and pleat the curves. The glue will adhere the fabric to the template creating a temporary bond. Continue all the way around the template.
- Dry iron the entire design. Don't slide the iron, only press down, so you don't distort the shape. The glue will dry with the heat of the iron.

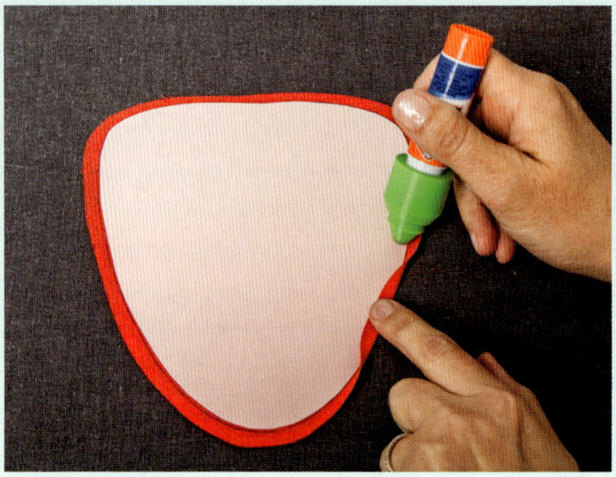

Fig. 1

- Choose a section of the template that's not near a point or a valley, and gently pull the seam allowance fabric away from the template. It should release easily.
- Use your fingernail or a stiletto to carefully slide between the fabric and the template (Fig. 2). Once you are able to pull the template out without altering the shape, do so.
- Dry iron (press, don't slide) the entire piece again without the template, securing all of the seam allowance in place.
- Your appliqué piece is now ready to baste to the background.

STARCH

This process is similar to the glue-stick method (at left) except, in place of glue, you'll use starch or a starch alternative.

- ▶ Use liquid starch or spray some starch into the cap of the spray-starch bottle.
- ▶ With the *right* side of the template adhered to the *wrong* side of the fabric, paint the starch directly onto the seam allowance. (Fig. 3)
- ▶ Fold the fabric over the template, one edge at a time. Iron the seam allowance down as you go. Neatly fold under corners and pleat curves.
- ▶ The starch will create a firm crease around the template.
- ▶ Carefully remove the template from the fabric (Fig. 2) and your appliqué piece is ready to baste to the background.

COMBINE THE TWO METHODS

When working on an intricate design or if the appliqué will sit awhile before being sewn to the background, combine the glue and starch methods. Follow the steps for the glue method. Before removing the template, spray starch the seam allowance and press again. Remove the template and give the piece a final press.

Fig. 2

Fig. 3

USING STARCH If you're not going to wash the finished appliqué (like a wall hanging), avoid starch. It attracts silverfish and other little critters that may eat away at your fabrics. Use a starch alternative, like Mary Ellen's® Best Press, that doesn't contain a food product.

Baste the Design to the Background

For needle-turn appliqué, keep your basting away from the appliqué pieces' edges. Leave free *both* the width of the seam allowance *and* the space to turn it under.

Thread Basting

- Traditionally, appliqué pieces are sewn to the background using thread, a basting needle, and a long stitch. This stabilizes the design and prevents it from shifting while it is being appliquéd.
- Use a contrasting thread color so it's easy to see and remove later.
- This is a very secure technique, but it takes longer than other methods.

Glue Basting

- As I've said many times, I like to use what I have; if there is a shortcut, I'll take it. The quickest way to adhere appliqué to the background is by using a washable glue stick. It's easy and disappears when the quilt is washed. Even if you won't be washing, the glue isn't stiff, so it's a total win.
- Rifle through your kid's backpack for a glue stick—any brand will do! Elmer's® glue comes in a bottle with a pointy orange tip that makes it really easy to control the amount of glue you're using.
- Use minimal glue where you'll quilt later. The glue can gum up the needle and make it harder to get through the fabrics by hand or machine.

Pin Basting

- Basting with pins is almost as quick and easy as basting with glue. Pins made specifically for hand appliqué are slightly blunted and are short so they stay out of the way when hand stitching.
- Place a pin or two at the center of your appliqué piece.
- Smooth the piece out from the center and add pins where needed.
- Remove pins as you get close to stitching an area so your fabric lies completely flat where you're sewing.

NEW AND FANCY

Getting just a small smudge of glue from a standard glue stick onto your template or fabric may be tricky. Too much may come off in a swipe. Since standard glue sticks are so economical and widely available, I went looking for a solution to this problem. The Glue Stick Precision Tip from Krebsbachhuber Crafts™ fits snugly on the end of a regular glue stick! Roll the glue up and it's squeezed out in tiny amounts at the point. Perfect for glue basting.

THREAD THOSE NEEDLES!

You'll go through many threaded needles, so load up. I usually thread 8 at a time. I prefer Tulip Hiroshima needles: #10 Appliqué Big Eye.

Cut the thread the length of the distance from your thumb to your elbow or about 14". If the thread is too long, it'll fray and knot as the needle is pulled through the layers of fabric.

Use a quilter's knot (page 223) and cut the tail shorter than ½".

Stitch the Appliqué to the Background

Needle-turn isn't as hard as you might think. This section gives uncomplicated steps to make it manageable and relaxing. Once you've got it, you may never appliqué another way!

- If you've already turned your seam allowances, as described on pages 120 and 121, use the same stitching process described here, but leave out the needle-turning.

  Note: The dark, contrasting thread in these photos is for demonstration purposes only.

- Use a lightweight thread that matches the appliqué fabric, not the background fabric. I use matching Aurifil 50wt thread. I like its strength and versatility. A heavier weight will make it more difficult to hide your stitches. For wall hangings, some quilters use lighter weight threads, like silk 100wt which is also strong and nearly invisible.
- Starting at a straight section of the design piece, finger-press the fold. Be sure the drawn line is turned under so it does not show on the finished piece. (Fig. 1)
- Thread a needle and make a quilter's knot (page 223) at the end of the thread.

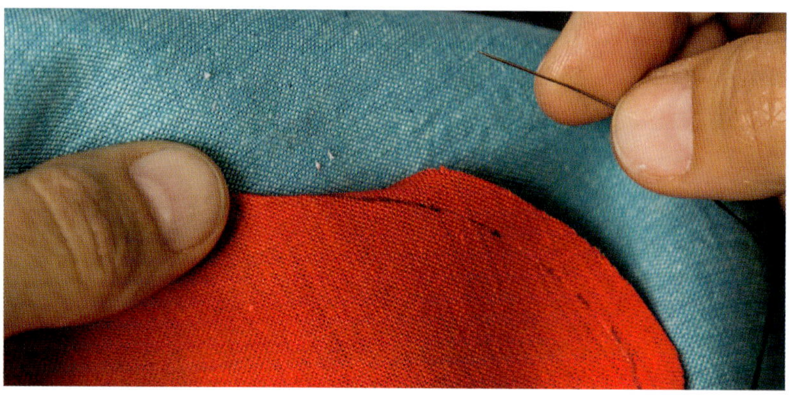

Fig. 1

- Bring the needle up from the back of the fabric directly below the edge of the appliqué piece.
- Pick up a thread or two of the fold. Try to bring the needle out through the crease in the fold. (Fig. 2)
- Stitch back down into the background right next to the stitch in the fold. Catch a few threads from the background and stitch up into the fold again about ⅛" beyond the last stitch. (Fig. 3)
- Continue stitching down into the background fabric and up into the fold moving along the design's edge.
- As you come to the end of a section of turned seam allowance, use your needle to turn under the next bit. To do this, hold the needle flat next to the fabric, catch a bit of the edge of the appliqué fabric and slide the needle between the piece and the background. Gently pull the seam allowance under with the needle. (Fig. 4)
- Turn under and finger press about an inch of seam allowance at a time.
- When you reach the end of a length of thread (or the design!), bring the thread to the back and make a small knot to anchor it behind the seam allowance where it won't show on the front. (Fig. 5)

CURVES For gentle curves that aren't sharp enough to be considered points or valleys, clip the seam allowances as needed to needle-turn them smoothly without any puckering. For sharp curves, points, and valleys, refer to pages 126 and 127.

Fig. 2

Fig. 3

Fig. 4

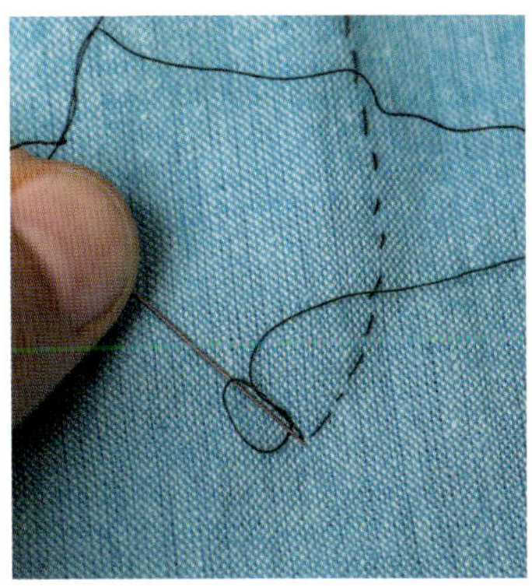
Fig. 5

Stitching Points

This technique will make your points sharp and they'll last for the life of your quilt.

- When the stitching gets close to a point, needle-turn the fabric under on the drawn line. Finger press to the tip of the point. This creates a little flag. Stitch to the point. (Fig. 1)
- Turn over the point fabric so you're looking at its wrong side and can see the seam allowance of the section you just stitched.
- With a small, very sharp pair of scissors snip off most of the seam allowance leading up to the point. This reduces bulk and guarantees a sharp point. (Fig. 2)
- Trim a small amount of the fabric "flag". (Fig. 3)
- To start sewing down the other side of the point, "sweep" your needle and seam allowance under until the needle hits the last stitch at the top of the point. Finger press. (Fig. 4)
- Reinforce the point with one or two extra stitches. Points receive more stress when the quilt is used, so stitch them down well. Using thread that matches the appliqué piece pays off here. (Fig. 5)

Fig. 1

Fig. 2

Fig. 3

Fig. 4

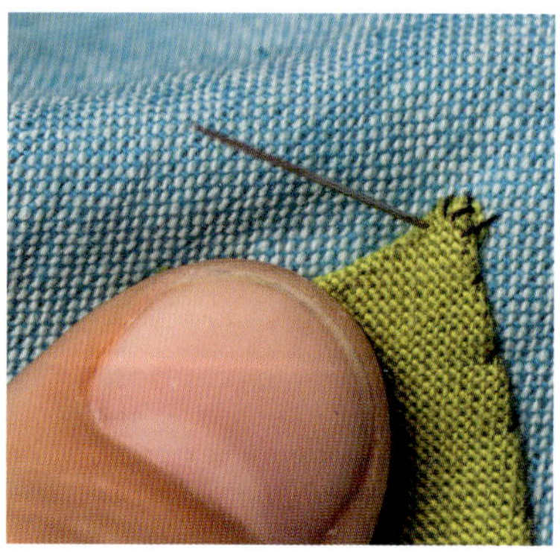

Fig. 5

Stitching Valleys

Valleys have a technique that makes them durable and a cinch to sew.

- Stitch until you're about 1" from the valley or "V".
- Use a small pair of scissors to snip the seam allowance of the design, cutting on an angle toward the inner point of the "V". Snip to a few threads short of the drawn line of the design. (Fig. 6)
- Needle-turn and finger press the seam allowance all the way to the inner point of the "V".
- Continue stitching toward the valley.
- At the snipped inner point, there will be no seam allowance at all, so take 3 or 4 extra stitches to tack down the fabric and keep its edges from fraying or looking messy. Just like at a point, this is a place where using thread that matches the design fabric is important.
- Sweep under the other side of the "V" with your needle and finger press the fold. (Fig. 7)
- Continue stitching around the remainder of the design.

KEEP IT SHARP! To snip or trim the seam allowance of a design, use scissors that are very sharp at the tips. This gives you the precision you need. It also helps keep your fabric from fraying before you turn it under and stitch it down.

Fig. 6

Fig. 7

MOXIE

For this design, I wanted something simple, modern, and approachable. Not everyone has time to finish an entire needle-turn appliqué quilt so this project is a mini quilt that can be used as a wall hanging. While it's not a traditional Hawaiian quilt, I hope it pays homage to Hawaiian quilting and the two traditional quilters who taught me the technique.

Fabrics are by Alison Glass for Andover Fabrics: Charcoal and Fern from the Kaleidoscope collection

SNOWFLAKES Do you remember cutting out paper snowflakes as a kid? Folding the square of appliqué fabric is basically the same technique. Refer to the diagrams and fold precisely as directed; it's easy as can be.

FINISHED SIZE 21" × 21"

MATERIALS

Appliqué design fabric: ½ yard or a square, 18" × 18"

Background fabric: ⅝ yard or a square, 21" × 21"

Backing: ¾ yard or a square, 25" × 25"

Batting: 25" × 25"

Binding: ¼ yard
(for 2¼"-wide, double-fold, diagonally pieced binding)

PROJECT INSTRUCTIONS

Use the techniques and tips on pages 118–127 to guide you through the process for this project.

Prepping the Design

1. Make a template from the pattern on page 131. (Refer to Machine Appliqué: *Make the Templates*, page 100.)

2. Fold the square of appliqué fabric following the technique in *Fold Before Cutting*, page 130.

3. Place the template on the folded fabric with their *longest* sides aligned. Align the stem end of the template with the triangle's short folds, *not* raw edges. (Fig. 1, page 130) This matters! If you align the stem with the raw edges, you'll end up with 4 separate pieces.

4. Pin or glue the template in place. Trace around the template with a thin line. Remove the template.

FOLD BEFORE CUTTING

- Fold the square of appliqué fabric in half, wrong sides together. Press and crease well. (Fig. 2)
- Fold it in half again, left to right. Press. You'll have a 9" × 9" square. (Fig. 3)
- Fold the top left corner of the square down to the bottom right corner. Press. (Fig. 4)
- Place the template on the folded fabric. Align the long edge of the template with the long fold of fabric. Align the stem end with the short folds. (Fig. 5)

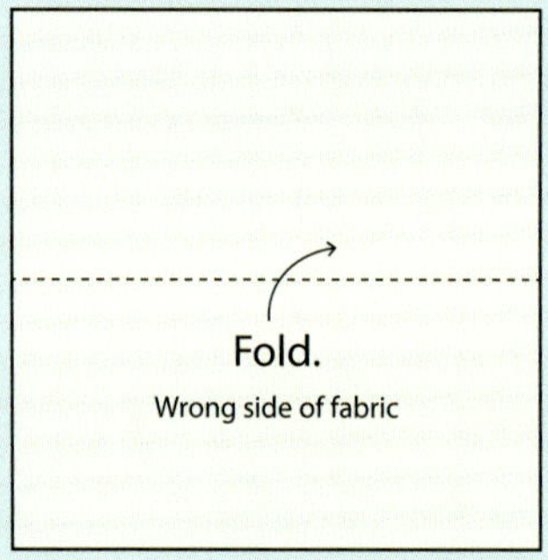

Fig. 2

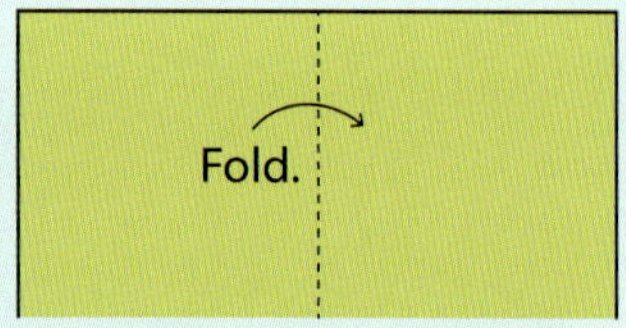

Fig. 3

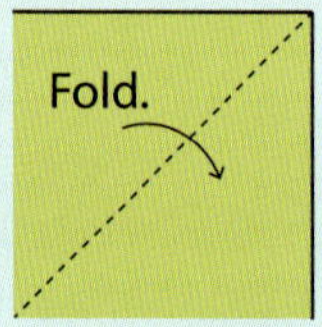

Fig. 4

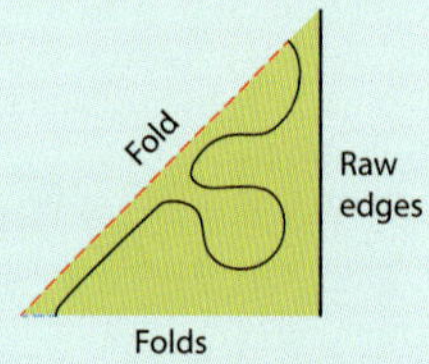

Fig. 5

5. Cut ⅛" outside the traced line using sharp scissors. The extra ⅛" is for the seam allowance. Do not cut on any of the dashed lines of the pattern. When cutting, hold the open edges of the folded fabric so they don't shift. The most reliable way to prevent shifting while cutting is to hand baste the layers of the triangle together.

Fig. 1

Stitching the Design to the Background

1. Find the center of the background by folding it in quarters and finger-pressing the folds.

2. Center the design on top of the background fabric, both *right* sides up. Press.

3. Baste the design to the background fabric. Leave at least ¼" free at the edges of the design for turning the seam allowance.

4. Hand appliqué using the needle-turn technique to fold under and hide the traced line. Press.

5. If needed, square up the background.

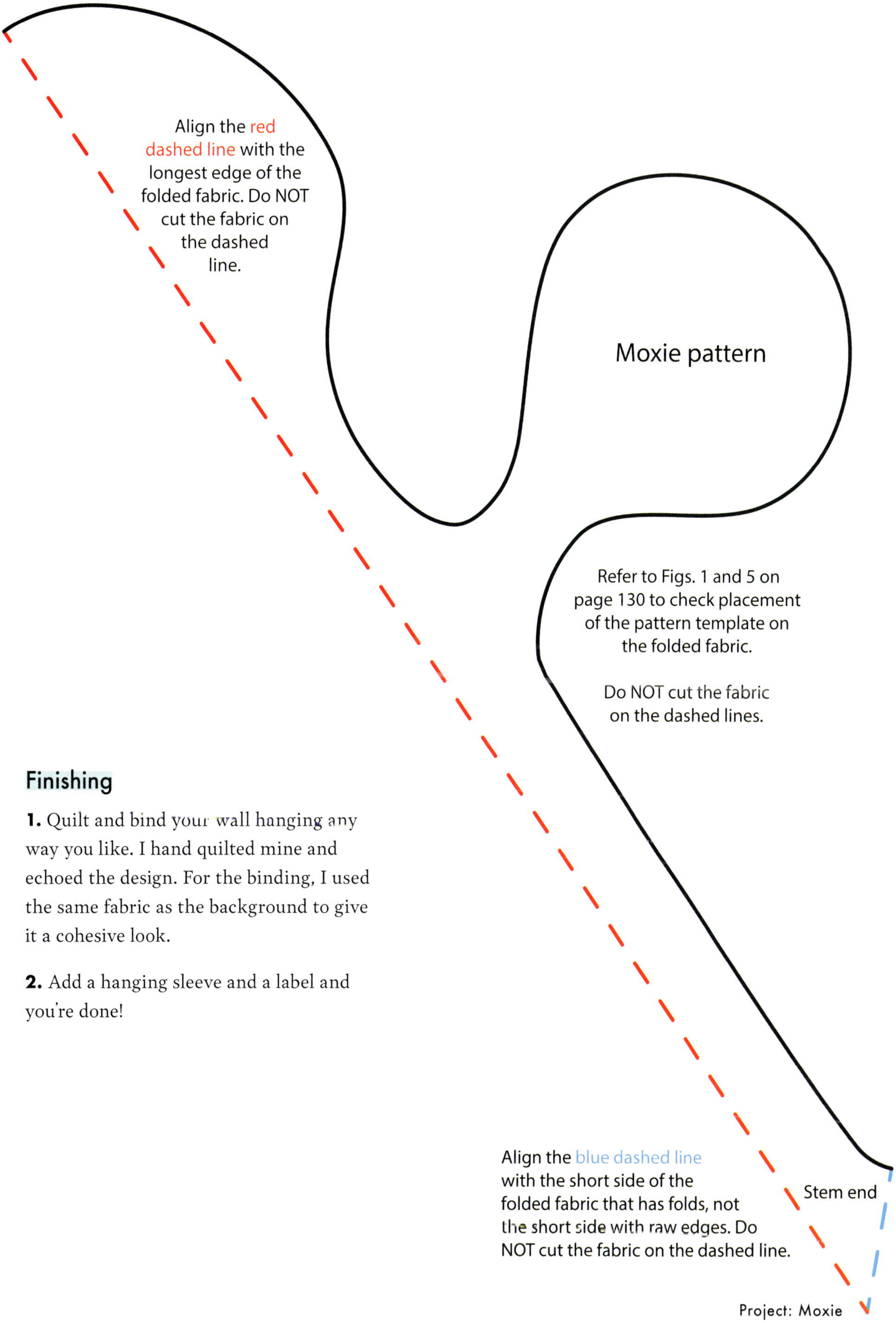

Finishing

1. Quilt and bind your wall hanging any way you like. I hand quilted mine and echoed the design. For the binding, I used the same fabric as the background to give it a cohesive look.

2. Add a hanging sleeve and a label and you're done!

REVERSE APPLIQUÉ

Reverse appliqué is a fun technique that allows the quilter to create little "windows" through a top fabric to see a background fabric behind it. It's great for simple shapes but can work well for more intricate ones. I made this reverse appliqué quilt back in 2012.

You can finish the edges of the reverse-appliqué windows with a raw edge or with a turned-under seam allowance. The quilt pictured above, designed by John Serrao and titled *Warrior Pride*, has turned-under seam allowances appliquéd by hand. Here I'm describing the raw-edge technique for speed and simplicity and so you can get to what you want to do . . . create!

- Make templates for your design pieces. Refer to Machine Appliqué: *Make the Templates* on page 100.
- Cut a piece of lightweight double-sided fusible about an inch larger than your template. I use Heat N Bond fusible.
- Center the fusible on the *wrong* side of the top fabric in the location you want the cut-out window to be. Fuse one side in place. Leave the paper on the un-fused side.
- Place the *right* side of the template down on the paper. Trace the template. (Fig. 1)
- Cut on the traced line to make the windows, using sharp scissors. (Fig. 2)
- Remove the remaining paper from the fabric.
- Cut a piece of window fabric about an inch larger on all sides than the windows in the top fabric. Note: the "window" fabric is orange in the quilt (above) and my example photo on page 133.

- Place the window fabric *right side up* on your ironing board. Center the top fabric *right side up* over the window fabric. Iron and fuse the top fabric to the window fabric. (Fig. 3)
  Place a teflon sheet under the whole piece so that excess fusible doesn't stick to your ironing surface.

- Check that all the edges are fused down. If not, press again.

- Machine or hand stitch the window's edges to finish. Use a straight stitch or any decorative stitch you like. (For stitching techniques and tips, refer to Machine Appliqué, pages 104–105, and Hand Appliqué, pages 124–127.)

- Repeat this process for all the windows in your design. Beautiful!

INTRICATE DESIGNS If you're making an intricate design with many windows close to one another, iron fusible to a large area of the top, instead of to a small area for each window. Cut a large piece of background fabric, too, and fuse that to the top after the windows are cut out. You won't have to deal with a stack of little pieces.

ANOTHER POSSIBILITY If you use single-sided fusible, fuse it to the back of the top fabric. Cut out the design and remove the remaining paper. Pin, glue, or thread baste (page 122) the background fabric to the top before stitching it in place. It's not as effortless as double-sided but it works! Remember, I'm all about using what you have.

Fig. 1

Fig. 2

Fig. 3

HAND APPLIQUÉ

WHAT COULD GO WRONG?

ISSUE Fabric is fraying as it is turned under.

SOLUTION This can be super annoying! It can be because the fabric has a loose weave which allows the edges to fray more easily. Use a high-quality quilting cotton or a batik. The fabric may have been cut with dull scissors. Use sharp scissors for a crisp, straight edge that is less likely to fray.

ISSUE Your stitch length and/or space between stitches is too long or uneven.

SOLUTION To prevent unintended wonky spots, go slowly and take small, even stitches. If you're anything like me and want everything to move quickly, going slowly isn't always easy, but taking the time to be precise makes a world of difference in the finished product.

ISSUE You're aiming for an invisible stitch but can't achieve it. Stitching is visible around the outside of the appliquéd design.

SOLUTION There may be too much contrast between the appliqué fabric and the thread color. We can't always color match thread perfectly, especially with fabrics that have multiple colors. For a multicolored fabric, choose a thread that coordinates with the most prevalent color in it. When using solid fabrics, if you don't have a perfectly matched thread (and don't plan on buying one), choose a lighter shade of thread vs. a darker shade. The lighter shade will be less visible.

The thread weight may be too heavy. Don't use anything heavier than 50wt. If you're finding even 50wt thread is showing, try a lighter weight thread.

Check your stitching technique. Sew a sample and see if you can hide the stitches. Practice small stitches and having the needle come out through the fold of the appliqué fabric.

ISSUE The appliquéd design looks lumpy or misshapen.

SOLUTION There is nothing worse than spending tons of time on a project, only to have it look...um, not great. Check often that the piece still lies flat. The basting may have been uneven, or what's more likely, as you've sewn, the piece has shifted slightly and the basting needs readjusting. It's worth it to take the time to smooth the piece before stitching further.

ISSUE The appliquéd curves aren't lying flat.

SOLUTION If you're using an appliqué design that has sharp curves, plan for it before you sew it to the backing fabric.

Concave (inner) curves need small notches cut in the seam allowance so it doesn't bunch up when being turned under.

Convex (outer) curves need small cuts in the seam allowance so it can stretch slightly when turned under.

These notches and cuts should be small and not close to the traced line that will be the piece's edge.

IMPROV PIECING & FREEFORM CURVES

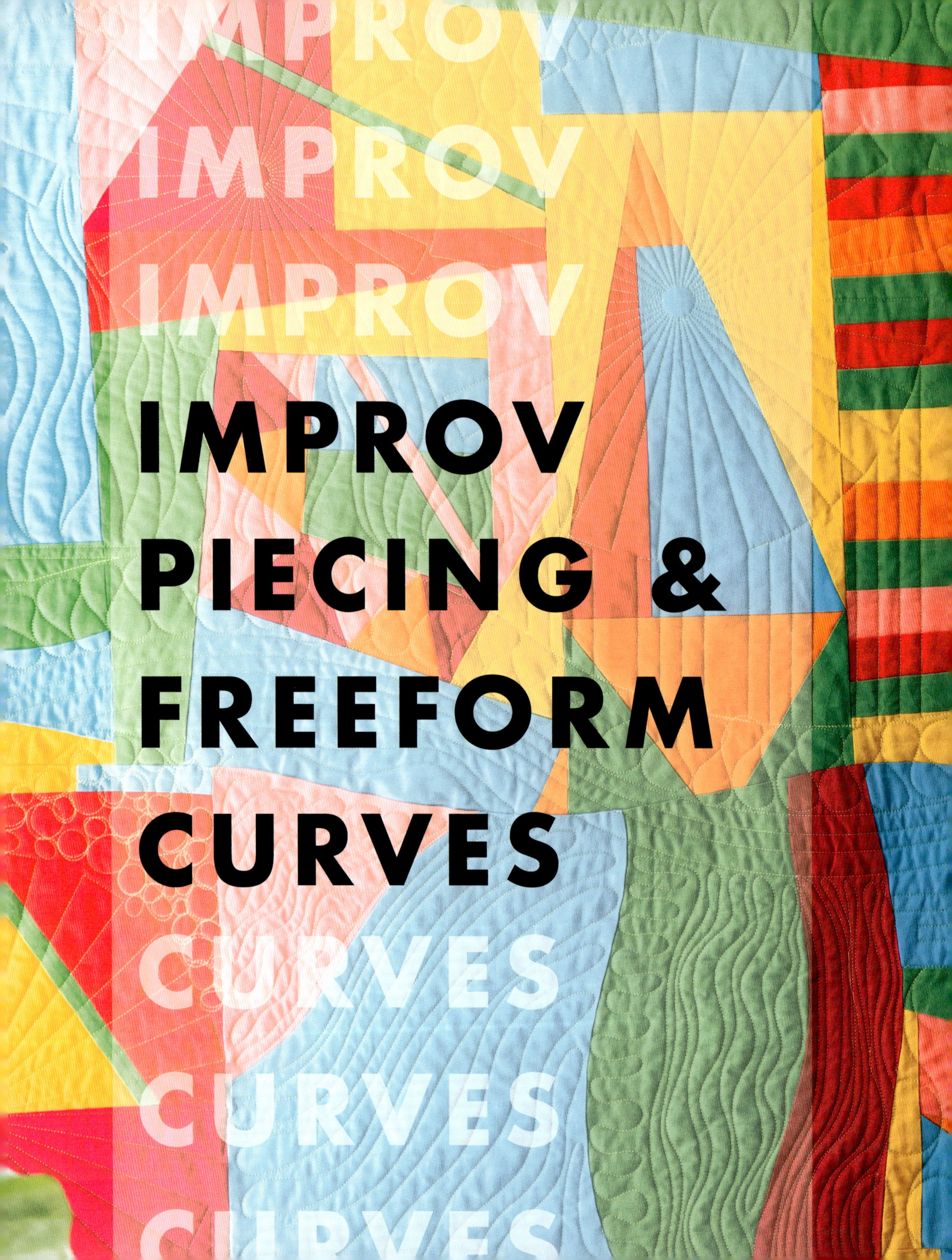

IMPROVISATIONAL PIECING

When I first tried to come up with quilt designs for this book, I struggled. I usually start a new project with a person or idea in mind and use that as my jumping-off point, but with this book I had to come up with ideas without my usual inspiration. I couldn't feel my creativity flowing until I began imagining I was actually designing *for* a specific person.

Improvisational quilting can be a little like that as well. Most of us are used to following a quilt pattern, and the unrestricted freedom improv piecing affords may feel overwhelming. Improv can be intimidating when you're used to structure. Obviously we want to be comfortable in the knowledge that we will like our finished project. If a quilt will be made "on the fly", where should I start? What if I mess up? What if this whole thing turns out to be a waste of time and money? These are all great questions. Although it feels unfamiliar, I encourage you to relax and focus on the positives. Like any quilting technique, improvisational piecing may be your cup of tea, or it may not, but I encourage you to try it, you might be surprised. Like anything, it takes practice. As you become more comfortable, you'll be more proficient.

First and foremost, you are the master of your domain, meaning that literally anything you want to do, you *can* do. You've always wanted to make a quilt with pinks, purples, electric yellow, and lime green? Go for it! You've entertained the idea of mixing straight lines and curves? Give it a shot! You sew something together then want to cut it up and add more? This is the time to do it! One of the things I truly love about improv piecing is how a project constantly evolves; it may start off going in one direction, only to end up somewhere else entirely. Quilting without restraint can be a roller coaster of exploration, but letting your mind have the freedom to simply *create* is really valuable artistically.

JUMP IN AND START

Ok, so you've picked your colors. Double check that the fabrics have a variety of value (light, medium, and dark) and scale (small and large prints), if you've decided to use printed fabric. Read through Piecing Basics: *Fabric and Design*, pages 53–58, for ideas and tips for picking fabrics.

Now what??? *Just start.* That's right, go ahead and sew something together. You don't need a plan.

- Start with your favorite fabric or color.
- Cut a piece of it to a reasonable size. (What's reasonable? Make it easy on yourself and choose something manageable to handle.)
- Pick another piece and sew them together. Don't overthink this, pick what seems right on first glance.
- Pick a third piece and keep going.
- Add pieces at whatever angle you like, precise 45- or 90- degree angles are not required. In fact, random angles enhance the design.

BUT, WHAT IF? If you just can't get into an improvisational headspace, start with scraps and start small. Build a single block or section. Play with the fabric. Try some of the ideas in this chapter and remember—there are NO RULES!

IMPROV PIECING

ADD SOME STRUCTURE (MAYBE)

TRIANGLES

Whether wide, narrow, tall, or squat, use triangles as trees, for flying geese, or simply as they are. They're a versatile shape and it's simple to make a triangle block.

- Place two fabrics directly on top of each other, *right* sides up on your cutting mat.
- Through both layers, cut one angled side of the triangle, pull away the cut fabric slightly. It'll be the background.
- Cut the other angled side of the triangle for the second background wedge.
- Switch the fabrics for the two triangles. Sew the 1st background to the 2nd triangle and vice versa.
- Press, trim the dog ears, and—voila, you now have two triangle blocks!
- Alternately, if you have a square or rectangle block that isn't working for you, cut the shape on a diagonal to get two triangles to work with.

REPEATED MOTIFS

The seams for these motifs don't have to be straight. Cut your strips freehand and sew them together "wonky". Trim the results freehand, too. This technique gives the motifs a beautiful, organic feel.

- Checkerboard strips add interest. Sew together two strips of different fabrics, then cut the joined strips into sections. Sew the sections together alternating colors so a checkerboard look results.

- To create a striped motif, sew strips of varying widths together. Cut shapes of random sizes and with differing angles from your striped "fabric".
- A triangle strip adds extra pizzazz when it's made from a striped motif. Cut the striped strips you've made on the diagonal to make triangles. Sew them back together randomly and you've got an improvised triangle strip.
- Insert any (or all) of these kinds of improvised motifs into a block by cutting through the block and sewing the strip into it. This is a great way to introduce an accent color or a focal point into your quilt.

WHERE TO NOW?

After you've got a block or section going, step back and take a look. Do you like where it's headed? This may sound hippy dippy, but how does it make you *feel*? If you don't like the *vibe*, change it. Above all, put away your seam ripper. When you're tempted to "un-sew" something, *add* something instead. Remember this is just like improv comedy. Focus on "yes, AND." You've got this!

- Cut the block up and add another color or more of a color that's already there.
- Add some smaller or larger pieces of fabric to balance what's already there.
- Add a curve to one of the edges or cut the block anywhere and add a curve there. There's a whole section and project for improvisational curves in this chapter. That's not because they're hard; it's because people sometimes feel intimidated by them. Refer to *Freeform Curves,* page 148, for techniques and tips.
- Add some specific motifs. Although improvisational piecing implies that there is no direction to anything (and that truly may be the way you decide to improvise), there can be some structure. You might want to create improv flowers or trees or leaves or waves.

HOW DO YOU KNOW YOU'RE DONE?

As your blocks get bigger, look at them and check for balance in color, piece size, shapes, and value.

- Squint your eyes and stand back to see if colors need more balancing.
- Take a photo. Looking at a small image on a camera phone lets you see the overall effect of the design.
- Convert the photo to black and white. Most camera phones have a monotone option. This helps you see if light, medium, and dark values are balanced (or not) in the quilt.
- Ask yourself: Does the quilt look heavy somewhere? Do you need more bigger or smaller pieces in a section? Does the design need more visual interest in a certain area? Are there areas that are too busy and need a place for the eye to rest?
- Where you see a need for change, cut into that section and add something. It's improv, you're not done until you say you're done.
- Once you have a bunch of improv sections or blocks, put them on your design wall and start looking at how to join them. This is like putting a jigsaw puzzle together.
- Consider how the colors blend and contrast, as well as which shapes look best next to each other.
- Fit the shapes together by cutting them so they do. Or add a strip to make it work.
- Continue to add, trim, cut, and design as you go. As you join the blocks, your quilt will grow and become more and more interesting. You can always add or take away. Your quilt is not done until you're happy with it.
- When joining large pieces of fabric together, hide long seams by using a straight seam then changing to a curving seam. Overlap the sections and cut a line that is both curved and straight, then pin and stitch as for sewing curves. This results in a long seam that doesn't look obvious or continuous. For more details on this technique, refer to *Freeform Curves*, page 148.
- Another improvisational freedom you have? Add appliqué over the piecing later. (There are two chapters in this book on appliqué: Machine Appliqué, starting on page 98, and Hand Appliqué, starting on page 116.)
- If you're stuck, walking away from a project like this and "sleeping on it" can really help, too. A fresh eye and rested mind always bring a new perspective and an ease to the process. If you feel frustrated, can't make a decision, or feel like you're out of ideas, take a break. It will all work out in the morning. Trust me on this.

IMPROV PIECING

HOW I SEE IT

I can't emphasize enough that this is *your* improvisation and what *your* eye sees and what *your* gut tells you about the design are the most important factors to consider. These are some examples of changes I would make because of what *my* senses tell me. Remember though, "you do you".

A black-and-white photo makes it easy to see the heaviness in this section.

Adding some lighter-value fabric changed the feel.

This section feels frantic with all the small pieces.

The larger pieces add a bit of breathing room.

Too many large pieces added together need to be broken up.

Adding this striped piece creates more interest.

WINGING IT

Winging It is a totally improvisational quilt. I used all the techniques and suggestions in this chapter and kept going until I was happy with the finished product. I encourage you to do the same. Let your inner artist have free reign to piece, cut, add, cut again, and add more until you have a quilt you love.

Fabrics are by Alison Glass for Andover Fabrics: Poppy, Shrimp, Sunflower, Dragonfly, Grass, and Carrot from the Kaleidoscope collection

FINISHED SIZE This is an improvisational quilt and there is no pre-determined size. I've given you the dimensions of *Winging It* but . . . whenever you decide yours is done, that's *your* finished size!

FINISHED SIZE 57" × 64"

MATERIALS

Use fabrics from your stash, buy something new, or both. Check out *Fabric and Design* in Piecing Basics (pages 53–59) for ideas. This is your place to create and shine.

CUTTING

Cutting will be random and different for every free-form quilt that you make. Use the techniques and tips on pages 139–145 to get you started and keep you going as you cut and sew, add and subtract.

PROJECT INSTRUCTIONS

1. Collect a few fabrics that you want to include in the quilt.

2. Sew together your favorite two.

3. Add a third fabric.

4. Trim a side and add another piece.

5. Maybe make some triangles and repeated motifs (pages 140 and 141) and piece them in.

6. Or randomly cut a gentle curve through the fabrics (page 149) and piece something new in between.

7. Keep going. Only you can decide when you're done.

FREEFORM CURVES

Can we talk? I can't tell you how many times I've heard a fellow quilter say, "I don't sew curves." Curves can feel intimidating, even for seasoned quilters. I have a friend who has been quilting for over 30 years and has never sewn one! Freeform curves are the place to start. They may take a bit more finesse than sewing a straight line, but they're not inherently difficult. I personally love them because they add a softer, graceful feeling to projects. Not only are curves beautiful, but gentle curves add an interesting element to improv quilts. Cutting up a pieced block and adding a curved insert is a quick way to add design details. Being able to sew a curve opens up myriad quilt design possibilities.

The project quilt, *Riding the Waves* (page 152), is a good introduction to freeform pieced curves.

- Place 2 fabrics *right* side up on your cutting mat; overlap them by no more than 3" to keep the curve gentle. Eyeball the overlap or use a ruler to make sure that it's consistent down the length of the fabric.
- Use a rotary cutter to cut gentle curves through both layers of fabric.
- Keep the curve within the overlap, cutting through both fabrics at once.
- Remove the narrow strips of fabric that you've cut away.
- You now have two pieces of fabric that fit together perfectly.
- Flip one piece of fabric *wrong* side up and align the fabrics *right* sides together.
- Align the centers of the peaks of each fabric with the corresponding valleys of the other.
- Pin the raw edges together at the peaks and valleys to hold them in place.
- A lot of additional pinning isn't necessary for gentle curves. Just pin enough to prevent stretching on the bias edges of the curves. Perfection isn't paramount here. Gentle, smooth curves can be matched and eased while stitching.

AVOID BULK WHEN STITCHING When sewing curves, fabric can become uneven and bulky in front of the sewing machine's presser foot. This is because the convex side of the curved seam is being bunched slightly while the concave side is being stretched slightly to match each other.

After you've sewn a bit of a curve, if you get a buildup of fabric in front of the presser foot, raise the presser foot *with the needle down*. Smooth and shift the bulky part of the fabric to behind the foot.

When you resume stitching, carefully align the stitching direction with the part of the curve you've already sewn to avoid putting a small jog in the curve.

- Sew the pieces together, removing the pins as you advance the fabric.
- Take your time around the turns and smooth the fabric out as you go. Backstitch at the beginning and end of the strip to provide extra stability.
- Press the seams toward the darker fabric from the *wrong* side.
- Turn to the *right* side and press again. Gently pull the fabrics away from each other as you press to get flatter seams but don't be forceful. If you pull too strongly, the stitches will show on the front.

Stitches show on the front from pulling when pressing

A gently pressed, smooth seam

IMPROV PIECING

WHAT COULD GO WRONG?

ISSUE I pieced too many like-colors together and now there is too much color saturation in one area.

SOLUTION Cut it apart and add different colors. Add anything you want!

Even a small strip of contrasting fabric will completely change the look of a quilt.

ISSUE This is hard. My brain doesn't work this way.

SOLUTION Switching from structured patterns to complete freedom is tough. I get it. While improv quilting is completely different from what you are used to, we learn from trying new things. I encourage you to let go of what you expect to happen, and simply enjoy the journey.

Take breaks when you get frustrated. Coming back to it later with fresh eyes can sometimes make all the difference.

RIDING THE WAVES

Visually intriguing and quick to make, this quilt is assembled using curved piecing techniques. The curves can be as thick or thin as you like, and can be constructed with any variety of colors. The result is an interesting and attractive, non-traditional quilt.

Seam allowances are ¼"

WOF=Width of Fabric

Fabrics are by Alison Glass for Andover Fabrics: Strawberry, Citrus, Goldenrod, and Lichen from the Kaleidoscope collection

FINISHED SIZE I've given the size of my quilt but because this is improvisational, yours will be different. It depends on how much your strips overlap and how steep your curved cuts are.

MATERIALS

Accent fabric 1 (Citrus): ⅝ yard

Accent fabric 2 (Goldenrod): ⅝ yard

Accent fabric 3 (Lichen): ⅝ yard

Background fabric (Strawberry): 2⅝ yards

Backing: 3⅜ yards

Batting: 60" × 75"

Binding: ½ yard (for 2¼"-wide, double-fold, diagonally pieced binding)

CUTTING

Accent fabric 1: Cut 2 strips, 10" × WOF.

Join the strips at the short ends and subcut 1 strip, 10" × 54".

Accent fabric 2: Cut 2 strips, 10" × WOF.

Join the strips at the short ends and subcut 1 strip, 10" × 54".

Accent fabric 3: Cut 2 strips, 10" × WOF.

Join the strips at the short ends and subcut 1 strip, 10" × 54".

Background fabric: Cut 6 strips, 15" × WOF.

Join the strips at the short ends and subcut 4 strips, each 15" × 54".

Backing: Cut 2 pieces, 60" × WOF.

Join along the long edges using a ½" seam allowance and trim to 60" × 75".

Binding: Cut 7 strips, 2¼" × WOF.

FINISHED SIZE **54" × 69"**

PROJECT INSTRUCTIONS

Use the techniques and tips in *Freeform Curves*, pages 148–150, to guide you through this process.

Assembly

1. Pair an accent strip with a background strip and overlap the strips 3". Both fabrics should be *right* sides up.

2. Cut a gentle curve staying within the 3" overlap. (Fig. 1)

3. Place the strips *right* sides together, aligning the centers of the peaks and valleys. (Fig. 2)

4. Join the strips, backstitching at the beginning and end of the seam. Press. (Fig. 3)

5. Repeat this process to add a background strip.

6. Continue to alternate the remaining two accent strips with the remaining two background strips.

7. End with a background strip.

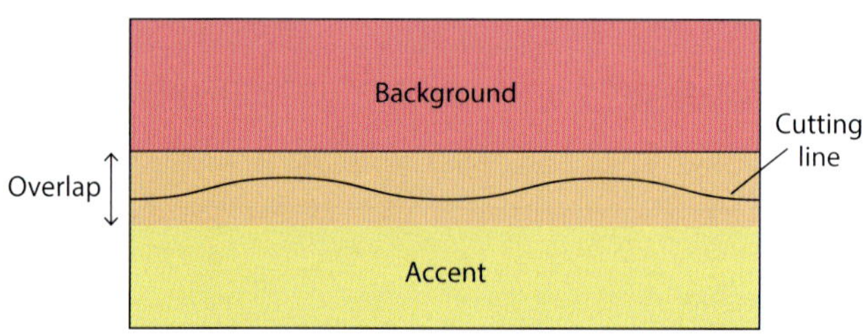

Fig. 1

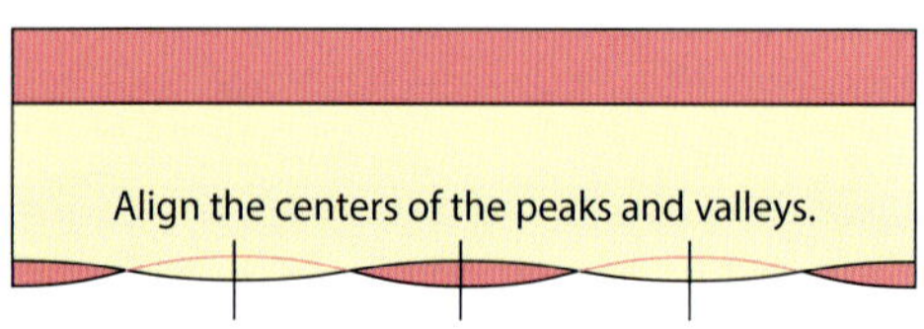

Fig. 2

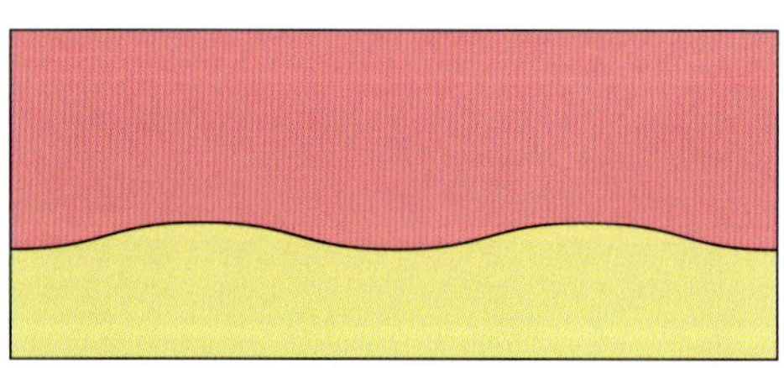

Fig. 3

Finishing

The piecing in *Riding the Waves* is organic and flowing and I wanted the quilting to be, too. So I quilted gentle curves from edge to edge across the width of the quilt to complement the curves in the quilt. This design provides a great opportunity for quilting on a domestic machine. The quilt is small enough to fit through the throat of many machines and the smooth curves are manageable and uncomplicated. If you're not into free motion quilting, you can use a walking foot for this type of relaxed curved line.

To allow the background to appear to flow off the edges, I bound the quilt in the background fabric.

Binding the quilt with one of the accent fabrics, instead of the background, would give the impression that the "waves" are flowing out.

Of course, when you decide how to quilt and bind your quilt, go for whatever *your* eye wants to see.

Don't forget your label!

FROM ONE CURVE TO ANOTHER Before cutting lines of curves, pay attention to how new cuts correspond to curves you've already sewn. Cut with an eye for your vision of the design and what you're aiming to achieve.

Do you want the width of the accent strips to be balanced across the quilt, wide at some spots and narrow at others?

Will one accent strip only have wide sections and another have narrow ones?

Are you aiming for uniformity or wonkiness? Will the curves be similar on the top and bottom or more random?

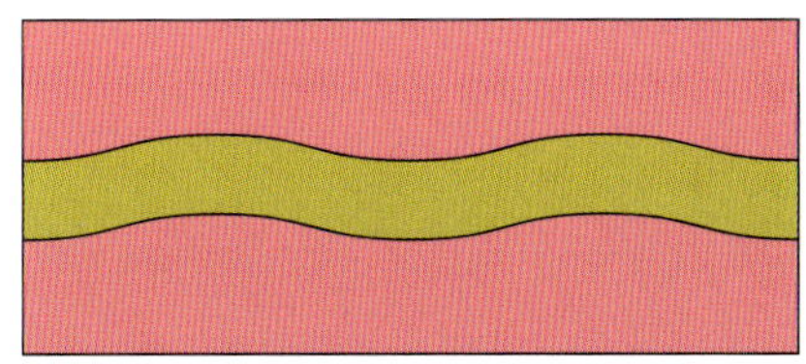

Uniform width from edge to edge

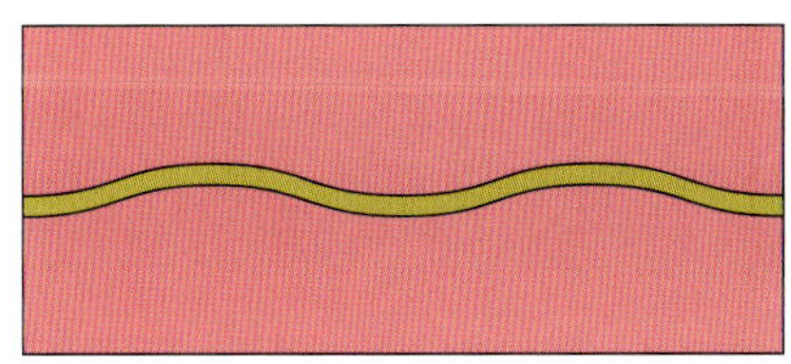

Narrow

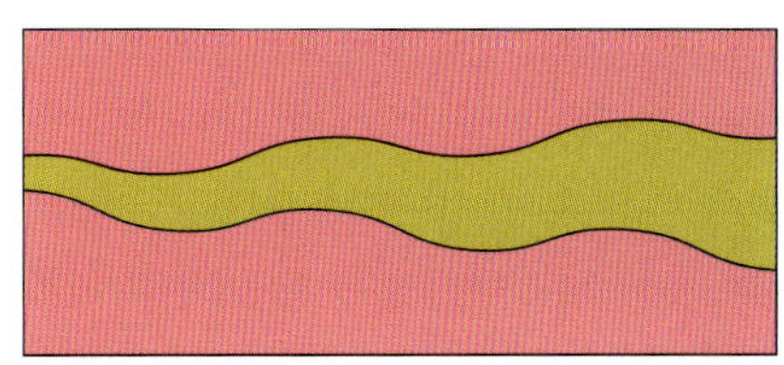

Narrow to wide

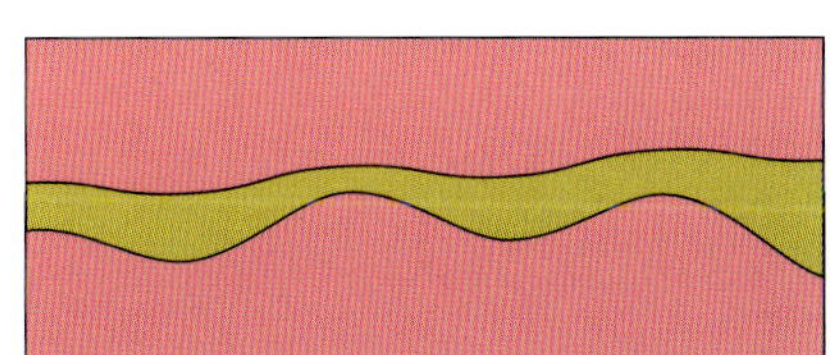

A little more wonky

ENGLISH PAPER PIECING

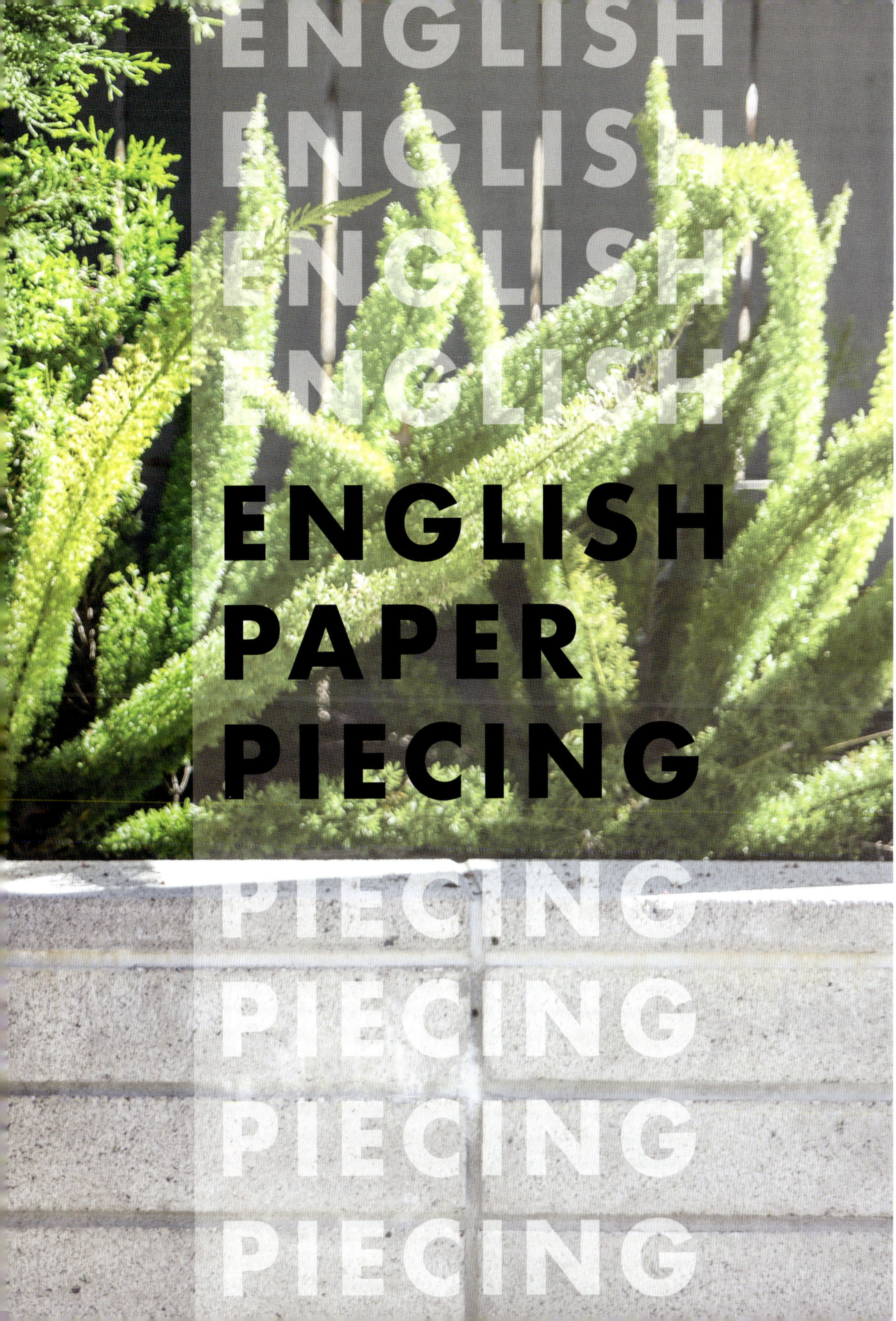

ENGLISH PAPER PIECING

If you love the meditative aspect of handwork, enjoy the process of creating, and want to work on your projects anywhere, English paper piecing (EPP) is for you! EPP consists of wrapping fabric around templates made from heavy paper or acrylic, then sewing those pieces together by hand. EPP templates are often reusable and can usually be found at quilt shops. Many people bring their EPP projects on road or plane trips because they can be worked a little bit at a time, no sewing machine necessary.

EPP lends itself beautifully to fussy cutting, page 56, and some spectacular EPP quilts are entirely fussy cut. Many fabric and pattern designers sell acrylic templates and papers for large EPP quilt projects. English Paper Piecing is slow going, so if you're looking for a quick weekend project, this isn't it. What EPP projects lack in speed, they make up for in beauty and relaxation.

SUPPLIES

Papers

Piecing papers are the foundation of every EPP quilt. They can be found in a variety of sizes at quilt shops, craft stores, or online. Often there's a hole punched in the center. Some folks think the papers are easier to remove when they have a hole.

- Hexagons (hexies) and diamonds are the most common EPP shapes.
- Quilts require a lot of papers. *Hex Key,* the pillowcase project in this chapter, is 18" × 18". It required 76 hexie papers. Sometimes papers can be reused and you can get by with fewer.
- If you decide to make your own papers, paper weight is important. Lightweight cardstock works well. Printer paper won't support the fabric or hold up to fabric being folded over it. Heavy cardstock will be too rigid to bend when it comes time to sew pieces together.
- EPP hexie sizes are determined by the length of one of the hexagon's six sides. For instance, if the side measures 1½" long, the hexie size is 1½".

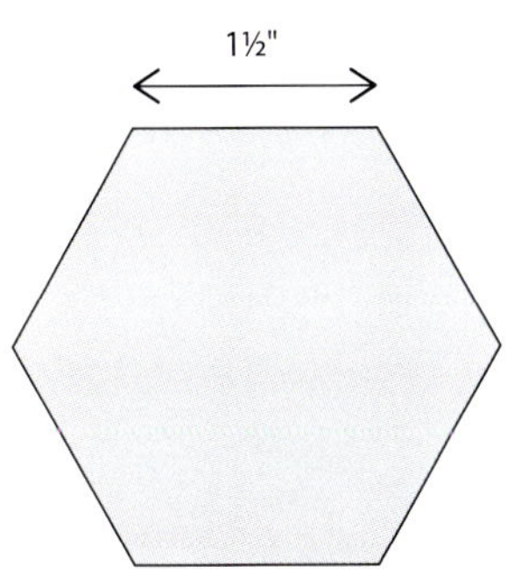

1½" hexie

Cutting Templates

Acrylic Templates

- Acrylic templates aren't necessary, but definitely come in handy. They already have the seam allowance added, so tracing the shape and cutting are simplified.
- They're especially good for fussy cutting, because you can see through them to center over the fabric designs.
- Acrylic templates hold up to wear and I recommend them for a project with a lot of pieces.
- Acrylic templates usually come in pre-packaged EPP quilt kits with the EPP paper templates.

Homemade Templates

- You can always make your own templates. It's pretty simple. Heavyweight cardstock is a great option and found easily at craft stores.
- Trace around one of your papers. Then add a ¼" to ⅜" seam allowance around it.
- Cut out the template on the seam allowance line and, there you go, you've got a template.
- These templates don't last as long as acrylic ones. Once you get hooked on EPP, I predict you'll start buying those!

Needles

- My favorite needle for EPP is the Tulip Hiroshima Big Eye Appliqué #10. They are made from nickel-plated steel which gives them flexible strength that resists warping. The eye is longer for easier threading, and the needles are strong and stay sharp. I used to deal with bent needles all the time. These steel needles stay straight and can be used over and over.
- Other good EPP needle options are milliners, sharps, and other brands of appliqué needles.

Thread

- When choosing a thread color, try and match the fabric of the pieces. If your choices are either one shade too dark or one shade too light, go with the lighter color. If the fabric has many colors and matching isn't possible, use a light-to-medium gray or taupe thread.
- Aurifil 50wt is what I use for hand piecing. This thread doesn't tangle, holds up to being pulled in and out of the fabric, and won't break if it is accidentally pulled through an EPP paper (whoopsie!).
- Aurifil is 100% cotton and has a matte finish which doesn't have the shimmer of some polyester thread, so it disappears into the design. It comes in a large array of colors, so matching thread to fabric is a breeze.
- 60wt and 80wt thread are other good options. They're lighter than the 50wt and often come in polyester. Check that it doesn't have a sheen.
- 100wt silk thread will be almost invisible. It's strong, lightweight, and comes in a lot of colors.
- Don't use the lightest weight threads for projects that will get a lot of wear. Choose 50wt or 60wt for those.
- Monofilament thread, available in clear and smoke, disappears into the fabric but I don't recommend it. It can stretch while stitching which pulls the fabric together too tightly and causes puckers. It tangles around itself and can also slip out of the needle.

TECHNIQUES AND TIPS

Cut the Fabric Pieces

Before cutting, double check that your cutting template is ⅜" larger on all sides than the piecing papers. This extra is for the seam allowance.

- I use a ⅜" seam allowance to ensure there is enough fabric to wrap around the piecing paper. A quarter inch of fabric isn't quite enough. Acrylic templates that come with the papers are usually made with a ¼" seam allowance so I cut a little outside the template to get the size I want.
- To fussy cut a fabric motif, use an acrylic template and center the template over the motif.
- Place the template on your fabric and trace around it with a thin, light pencil line.
- Stack several layers of fabric (unless fussy cutting) and cut out the shape using scissors or a small (28mm) rotary cutter. Large rotary cutters aren't a good choice as they are too cumbersome.
- A rotating cutting mat makes this easier, but is by no means necessary.
- Precision isn't paramount when cutting your fabric. The fabric piece can be rough cut because the seam allowance will be folded around the paper before sewing. Just make sure you have enough fabric for the seam allowance.

Baste the Fabric Around the Papers

There is no right or wrong way to do this. Some folks prefer glue basting (me!), and others prefer thread basting. Try both and see what feels best to you.

BASTING AROUND SHARP CURVES Sharp curves need special treatment when basting fabric around a paper. Gently pleat the seam allowance around convex curves to get a smooth folded edge. For concave curves, snip into the seam allowance to get the stretch you may need. Snip no closer than ⅛" away from the paper.

Glue Basting

Elmer's glue sticks are what I have readily available at home. I purchased an attachment that extrudes the glue out of a narrow tip. It has quickly become indispensable when I'm EPP-ing. Specialty quilting glue sticks are also available. I like the Sewline brand. They're slim, easy to use, and come in colors, making it easier to judge how much glue you're using. The color disappears when the glue dries. If you are going to be doing a lot of glue basting, consider investing in these slimmer, colored glue sticks.

- With piecing paper centered over the *wrong* side of the fabric piece, swipe a thin line of glue on the paper about ⅛" away from the edges. Alternatively, put the glue on the outer edge of the fabric's seam allowance.
- Keep the glue away from the edge of the paper. If the glue gets too close to the edges, it's hard to only pick up the 2 or 3 threads you want to keep your stitches invisible and the seams flat.
- Don't use a lot of glue! A light swipe is usually enough.
- Fold the fabric over onto the paper and press firmly to adhere.
- Repeat on all edges of the paper.
- Go clockwise or counter clockwise around the paper; don't change directions from edge to edge. Use a hot, dry iron to set the glue.

Pros

- *This is the fastest and easiest method I know.*
- *You get crisp, precise edges.*
- *Glue's inexpensive and easy to find.*

Cons

- *A flat surface is necessary to apply the glue so it's not as portable. You can bring along a small rotating cutting mat for this.*
- *It's a bit difficult to remove the papers from the fabric after the pieces are sewn together. This is rougher on the papers than thread basting, so they can't be reused as often.*
- *Despite these cons, it's still my favorite method! Once you master applying the glue, you're good to go.*

Thread Basting

Use a contrasting thread color so it's easy to see when you're removing it later.

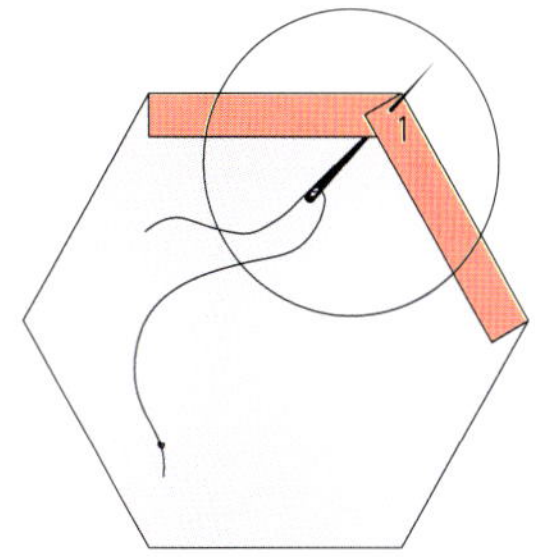

See inset details below.

- Center the paper over the wrong side of the fabric.
- Start with the seam allowances of two adjacent edges folded over the paper and finger-pressed.
- Bring the needle up through the overlap of the folded seam allowances (Fig. 1)
- Insert the needle on the other side of the fold and bring it out close to the first stitch (Fig. 2)
- Insert the needle again on the far side of the fold (Fig. 3)
- Bring the needle up through the next pair of folded seam allowances (Fig. 4) Take 2 small stitches here; continue basting around the hexie.
- Go in one direction around the paper so the folds all face the same way. Don't change directions.
- When complete, pull the thread through the fabric toward the center of the hexie; clip leaving a long tail. No knot necessary. (Fig. 5)
- If you use large papers, take a basting stitch or two through the seam allowance *and* the paper before moving on to the next corner. (Fig. 6)

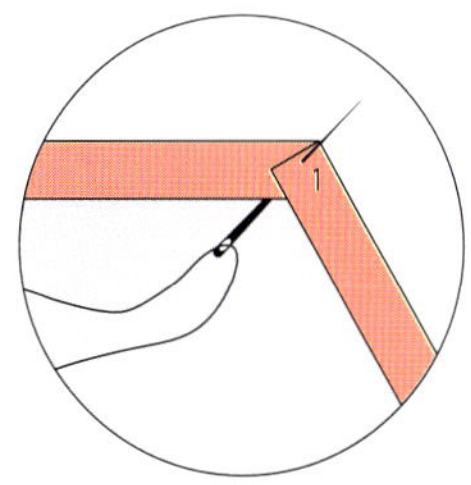

Fig. 1

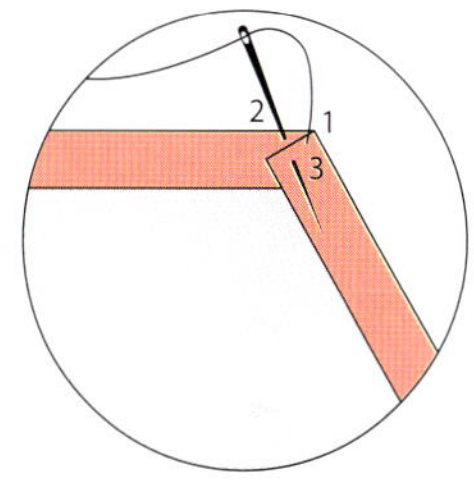

Fig. 2

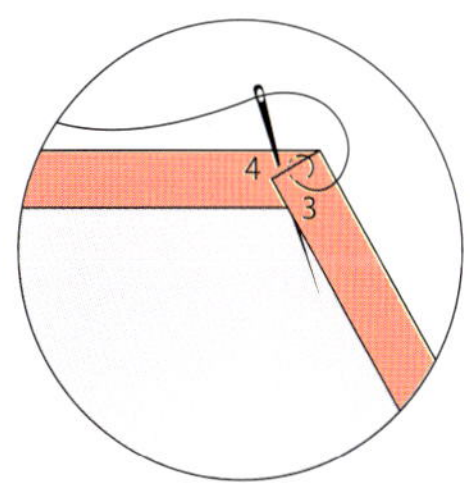

Fig. 3

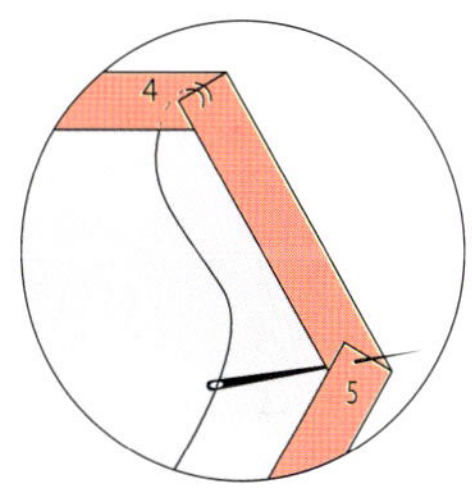

Fig. 4

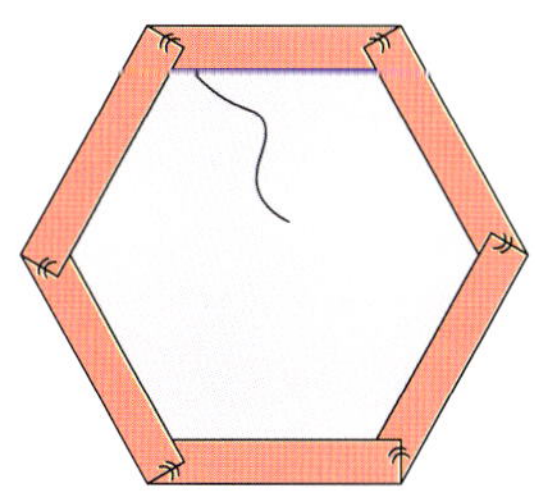

Fig. 5

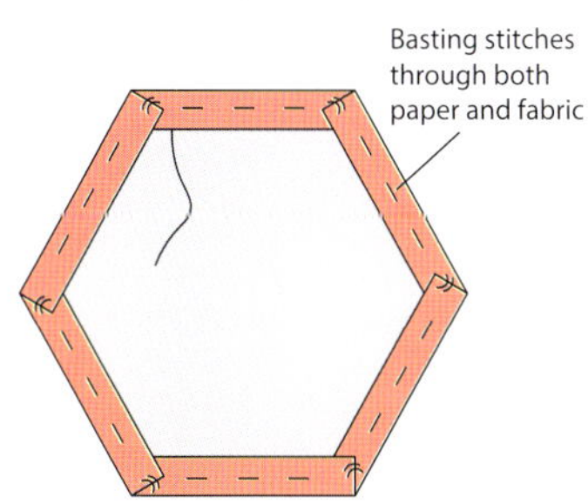

Fig. 6

Pros

- *This technique can be done anywhere (airplane, couch) with minimal supplies.*
- *There isn't much wear and tear on the paper templates so they can be reused more often.*
- *The templates are easy to pull out, no glue to "un-glue".*

Cons

- *More time consuming than gluing and takes slightly longer to master.*

Sew the Pieces Together

Some folks sew toward themselves, some sew away. I don't believe there is a "correct" way to EPP. Your body will tell you what feels most comfortable.

Basics

The basic stitch, as well as anchoring your thread at the beginning and end of a line of stitching, is the same whether you use the Traditional Method or the Flat Back one (page 166).

- Take 2 or 3 stitches in place at the beginning of the seam to secure the thread. Hide the tail between the basted seam allowance and the paper.
- Stitch down the seam line. Shoot for a stitch every 1⁄16" or 15–20 stitches per inch.
- Make 2 or 3 stitches in place at the corners to reinforce them as these are the weakest sections.
- Finish a line of stitching in the same way you started, taking a few basting stitches in the seam allowance and hiding the tail.
- With this method, knotting is not necessary at either the start or the finish of stitching.
- If you prefer to knot, use a small quilter's knot, page 223.
- Both stitching methods use a variation of the whip stitch. Whatever method you choose, don't sew through the papers!

Traditional Method

The large majority of EPP tutorials both online and in print will teach this method. It's a quick and easy method that's perfect for joining straight edges, but a little more difficult for curves.

- Place fabric-covered papers right sides together with one edge aligned. (Fig. 1)
- Start at a corner where the pieces meet. Anchor your thread by taking 2 or 3 stitches in place to secure it. (Fig. 2)
- Move down the seam line about 1⁄16" for each new stitch and pick up 2 or 3 threads from each fabric at the edge of the papers. (Fig. 3) The thread tail left at the beginning of the seam line can easily be "buried" under these first few stitches.
- Keep stitching until you get to the end of the seam line. Anchor your thread by taking 2 or 3 stitches in place, as you did at the start. Pull the needle through the seam allowance, bury the tail, and clip the thread. That seam is done!
- As you join subsequent pieces, fold the papers of the prior pieces, as needed, to keep the current pieces aligned properly. (Fig. 4)
- To reduce strain on your hands and keep the pieces aligned, use binding clips or Sewtite® Mini magnetic pins to hold pieces together as they are being stitched. (Fig. 5)

Fig. 1

Fig. 4

Fig. 2

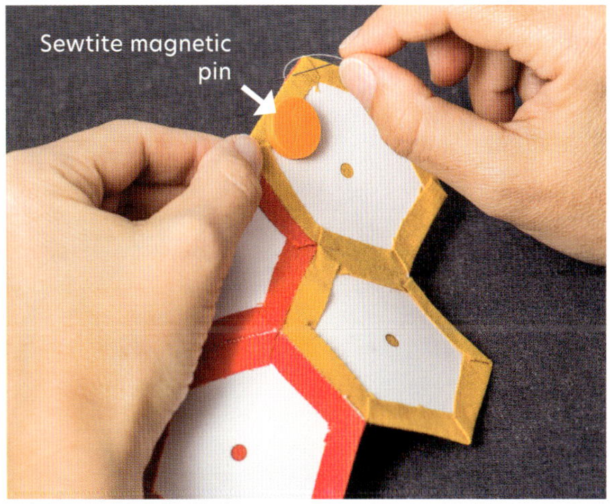

Fig. 5

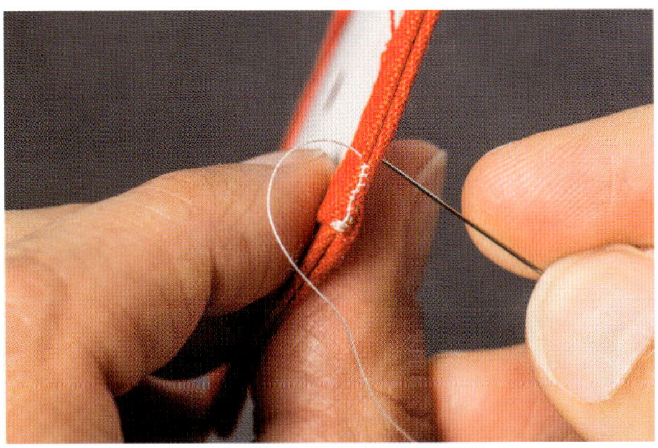

Fig. 3

Flat Back Method

This method is fantastic for curves and creates truly invisible stitches. The seams are not stressed and the papers don't have to be bent for adjacent edges. Coordinating thread color isn't as important, as long as it's a neutral.

- Place two adjacent fabric-covered paper pieces on a flat surface, *right* side up.
- Butt the pieces against each other and secure in place with washi or blue painter's tape. This keeps the pieces from shifting as you sew. (Fig. 6)
- Painter's and washi tape are safe for fabrics and don't transfer adhesive or pull color out. Don't leave on for more than 12 hours or expose it to heat; that may cause some color to transfer.
- Sew from the *wrong* side with the pieces flat. Only grab threads from the back of the fabrics. (Fig. 7)
- Start at a corner and take 3 stitches in place to secure.
- Move down the seam line about 1⁄16" for each new stitch and pick up 2 or 3 threads from each fabric. (Fig. 8)
- Gently tug the stitches secure but don't pull them too tightly; that may pucker the fabric.
- Keep stitching until you get to the end of the seam line. Anchor your thread and bury the tail. (Fig. 9)

Fig. 6

Fig. 7

Fig. 8

Fig. 9

ENGLISH PAPER PIECING

? WHAT COULD GO WRONG?

ISSUE You've finished a section of a quilt and realized one of the fabrics is in the wrong place or a fussy-cut piece is upside down.

SOLUTION This may be a heart-stopping moment, but don't worry, it's fixable.

Re-insert a template into all of the pieces that surround the mistake piece. This gives the section stability.

Next, snip the stitched seams all the way around the mistake piece. Snip from inside the back of the mistake piece to avoid accidentally cutting the fabric of the "good" pieces.

Remove the mistake piece. This will leave a hole in your project.

Baste fabric around a new template with the fussy cut in the correct orientation.

Insert it into the correct spot and sew it into place. Use the Flat Back Method, page 166.

ISSUE Hand trauma from overuse. This actually happened to me, and it stank. I got tendonitis because I was holding my paper pieces too tightly and at a weird angle.

SOLUTION Take your time, make sure you aren't stressing your wrist. Find a comfortable angle to hold your pieces as you sew.

Take a break every 20 minutes or so and do very gentle stretches. Look for a video online for hand yoga.

HEX KEY

This bright and fun project is a great introduction to English Paper Piecing. Its small size makes it a "quick" EPP finish. It can be customized using your preferred colors, and becomes functional art—perfection!

Seam allowances are ¼"

WOF=Width of Fabric

Fabrics are by Alison Glass for Andover Fabrics: Shrimp, Salmon, Strawberry, Peony, Poppy, Tomato, Persimmon, Carrot, and Sunflower from the Kaleidoscope collection

FINISHED SIZE 18" × 18" pillow

MATERIALS

9 different fabrics for the pillow front: 1 fat quarter of each

1½" hexagonal English Paper Piecing papers: 76 (or fewer if you plan to reuse them)

A cutting template for the hexies (with seam allowance)

Batting: 24" × 24"

Muslin or other light-value fabric: 24" × 24"

Fabric for pillow back: ⅜ yard

Pillow form: 18" × 18"

THE PILLOW FRONT

Use the techniques and tips on pages 161–167 to guide you through the process for this project.

1. Double check that your template has a seam allowance added. I use a ⅜" seam allowance.

2. Trace around the template and cut 8 hexies from each of 5 fat quarters; cut 9 hexies from each of 4 fat quarters.

You should have 76 fabric hexies, 8 for each odd-numbered row and 9 for each even-numbered row.

3. Baste the fabrics to the hexie papers. Either baste all of them at once or baste one row at a time.

4. Hand stitch together 1 edge of 2 hexies of the same color. I used the Traditional Method for this project because the edges are all straight. (Fig. 1)

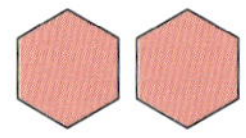

Fig. 1

5. Add another hexie of the same color to the opposite edge.

6. Continue adding hexies of the same color until you have a row of them. (Fig.2)

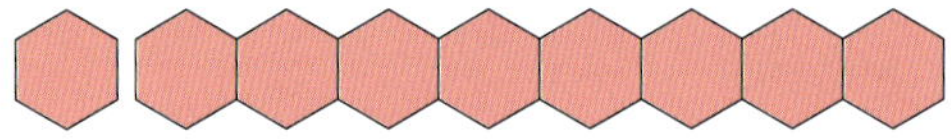

Fig. 2

7. Make 4 rows with 9 hexies and 5 rows with 8 hexies. (Fig. 3)

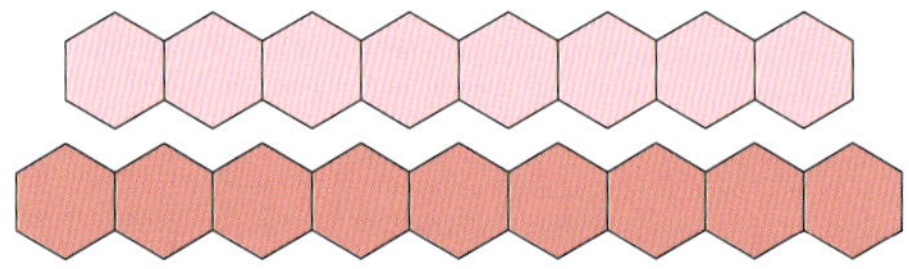

Fig. 3

8. Join 2 adjacent rows. Fold the sewn hexies as needed as you sew along the row to get the proper joins.

9. Continue to add adjacent rows until you've sewn together all 9 rows. (Note that the beginning of each alternate row shifts from left to right). (Fig. 4)

Fig. 4

10. Remove the papers from the back of the hexies.

11. Center the batting on the muslin.

12. Center the completed pillow front, *right* side up, on top of the batting.

13. Pin baste this sandwich.

14. Quilt the pillow front as desired. I quilted a simple crosshatch pattern of diamonds to enhance the modern feel of the design.

15. Trim the quilted pillow front to 19" × 19", centering the design. (Fig. 5)

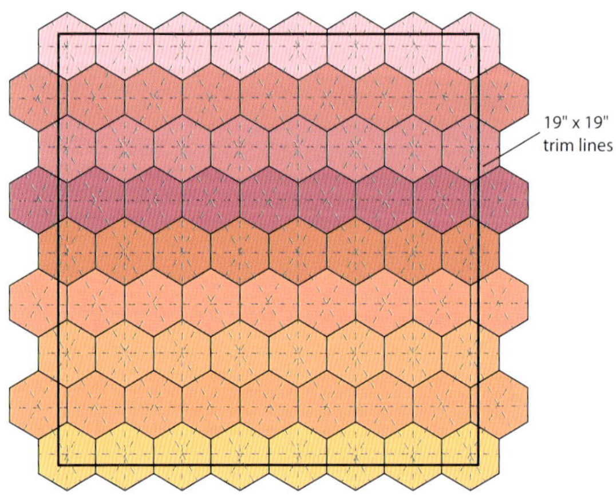

Fig. 5

PILLOW ASSEMBLY

1. From the backing fabric, cut a strip, 12" × WOF. From this strip, subcut 2 rectangles, each 12" × 19".

2. Make a ½" fold along the 19" side of both rectangles. Press.

3. Fold again another ½" and press. You now have a double fold on one long edge of both rectangles.

4. Topstitch the fold on both rectangles. (Fig. 1)

5. Align the raw edges of one of the rectangles with the raw edges of the trimmed pillow front, *right* sides together.

6. Pin, then sew together with a ½" seam allowance. Backstitch at the start and end of stitching. (Fig. 2)

7. Align the other rectangle with the remaining raw edges of the pillow front, again *right* sides together. This rectangle will overlap the first one.

8. As with the first rectangle, pin, then sew together with a ½" seam allowance. Backstitch at the start and end of stitching.

9. Trim the corners. (Fig. 3)

10. Turn the pillowcase right side out.

11. Gently push out the corners from the inside using a chopstick or other quilting tool.

12. Last but not least, insert the pillow form. You're done!

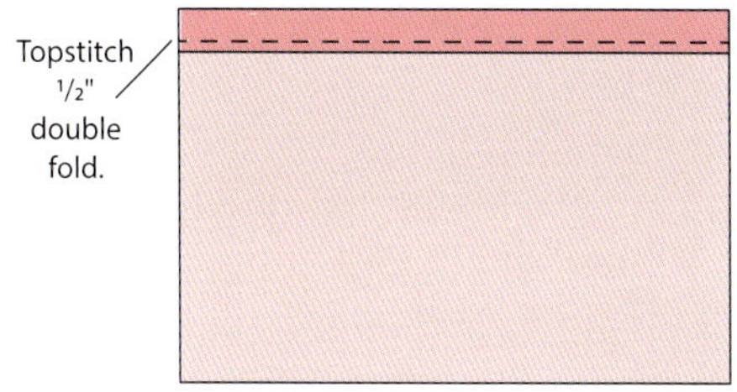

Fig. 1

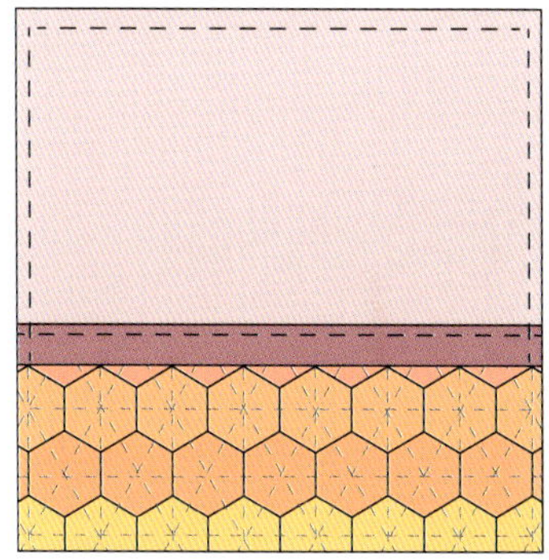

Fig. 2

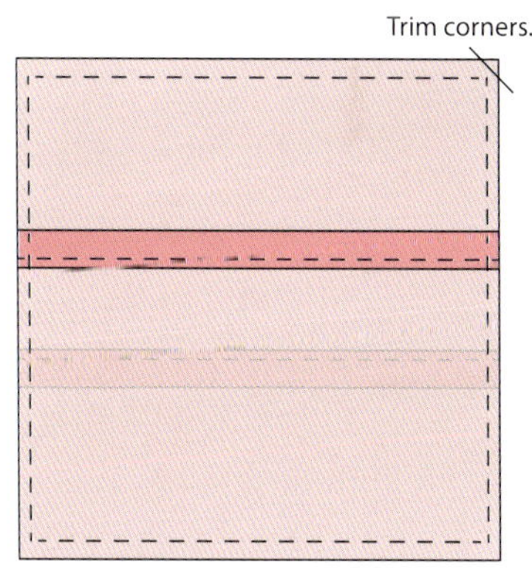

Fig. 3

HEXIE PAPERS When can you remove the papers from your hexies? You could wait until the whole pillow front is done. If you prefer to remove the papers as you go, leave them in until all six edges of the hexie have been stitched to another.

T-SHIRT QUILTS

EXTRA
CHEESE

T-SHIRT QUILTS

Anyone else have a bunch of old t-shirts you don't wear but can't bring yourself to pass on? T-shirts from favorite sports teams, concerts, family reunions, races, events, college, conventions, sentimental shirts, shirts your child has long grown out of, or clothing from a family member who has passed on . . . it's hard to know what to do with them. T-shirt quilts are a really wonderful way to reuse and repurpose what you already have. They are super simple to put together, and make great sentimental gifts.

Our neighbors and good friends had a bunch of shirts their 5-year old had grown out of. One night while at their house, they pulled out a bag of shirts and asked if we wanted any of them before they passed them on. They seemed a little sad that their son was no longer able to wear them. (There were lots of cute shirts!) Me being me, I told them they needed to keep the shirts and have a quilt made out of them. I didn't immediately volunteer to make the quilt, but they hung on to the shirts.

When I started thinking about a t-shirt quilt project for this book, I knew exactly where I could find the shirts I needed to complete it. Now my neighbors have a quilt that reminds them of when their kiddo was small, and also a useful, cuddly, functional quilt. Remember to add a label to this quilt to make it even more meaningful, and maybe a hanging sleeve!

TECHNIQUES AND TIPS

Prep the Shirts

The simplest way to make a t-shirt quilt is to cut every shirt to the same size.

1. Using the smallest shirt or design as a starting point, decide how big to cut the other shirts.

2. Iron the shirts inside out. Avoid ironing them right side out. Hot irons may melt the design of the shirt and stick to the plate of your iron.

3. Cut along the side seams of the shirt straight up to the shoulders. Kids shirts may need to be cut through the sleeve cap to get all of the design.

4. Decide if you're using the front or back of the shirt. Or both! Cut across the preferred side of the shirt just under the neck hole and cut off the hem of the shirt bottom.

5. Press the shirt, *right* side down.

6. Cut lightweight, single-sided, fusible interfacing to the size of the shirt. I use Pellon SF101 Shape-Flex. Iron the interfacing to the *wrong* side of the shirt.

7. Trim each interfaced shirt to the desired size.

8. Arrange the shirts on a design wall, floor, or bed and consider how they look together. Distribute dark and light shirts evenly around the quilt so that the quilt looks balanced.

9. Take a picture of the layout for future reference. This is helpful if your prepped shirts mistakenly get out of order.

10. Number the horizontal rows in the order you plan to sew them. This provides a roadmap for sewing. If you want, you can label each individual shirt (ex: row 1, block 1), but I find that with simpler quilts like this, labeling just the row and having a photo to refer to is enough.

THAT ITTY BITTY SHIRT If there's a shirt that's a lot smaller than the others but you *really* want it in the quilt, never fear! Put a border around it after it's interfaced. Add strips of fabric to the sides, top, and bottom to enlarge it to the size you want.

SASHING

Decide if you want to use sashing between your shirts or simply sew them to each other. I much prefer the separation that sashing provides. It's like a little frame for the shirts so each looks individual, and it makes the overall quilt look more cohesive and professional.

If using sashing, choose a color that will coordinate with the shirts. Most times this means choosing a neutral color. I chose a blue/gray because my t-shirt quilt has lots of black, blue and gray. Although I'm a big fan of bright, bold colors, using something that really pops will take away from the focus of your quilt: the shirts.

Choose the finished width you want for your quilt's sashing. I typically choose sashing that finishes between 1" and 1½". Just enough to provide separation for the shirts, but not so wide it looks chunky or out of place.

Cut the sashing strips ½" wider than the finished width to accommodate the ¼" seam allowances.

Vertical Sashing

1. Cut the vertical sashing the same height as the prepped shirts.

2. Cut sashing only for the interior sides of the prepped shirts, no sashing is needed for the left and right edges of the quilt.

3. Stack the prepped shirts from your first row starting with the leftmost shirt on the top of the stack. Bring the stack to your sewing area.

4. Align one short end of a sashing strip with the top right corner of the prepared shirt, *right* sides together, and secure using pins or binding clips.

5. Sew together using a ¼" seam allowance. Backstitch at beginning and end of the seam.

6. Repeat to sew sashing to the right edge of each shirt in the row, *except* the last one. (The right edge of the last shirt is an exterior edge; we don't need to attach sashing there.)

7. Press seam allowances toward the sashing.

8. Sew each shirt to the sashing of its adjacent shirt, *right* sides together, until the row is sewn together.

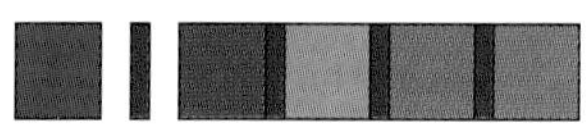

9. Press toward the sashing.

10. When all the prepped shirts in the row are sewn together with sashing, carefully trim any sashing "tails" so the row has even straight edges.

11. Repeat for the remaining rows.

Congratulations, you've completed all of your vertical sashing!

Horizontal Sashing

1. Measure the width of each row of your quilt after you've added the vertical sashing. Take the average of these widths and cut the horizontal sashing that long.

2. Sew horizontal sashing, *right* sides together, to the bottom edge of all the rows, *except* the bottom row. (The bottom edge of the last row is an exterior edge; we don't need to attach sashing there.)

3. Press toward the sashing.

4. Sew each row to the sashing from its adjacent row, *right* sides together, until all the rows are sewn together.

5. Press toward the sashing.

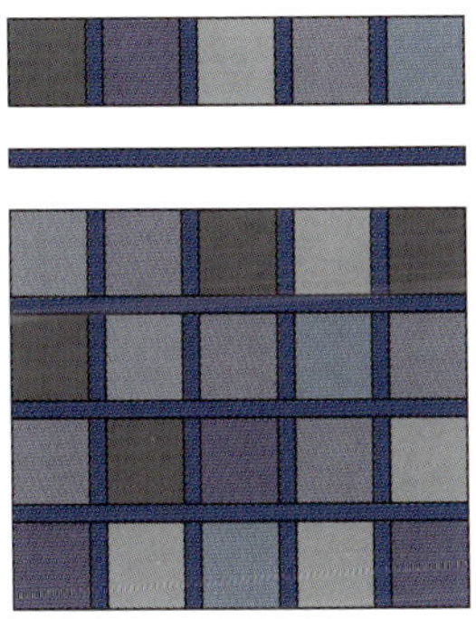

You've finished your quilt top!

QUILTING AND FINISHING

- Before quilting, stay stitch around the edge of the quilt. Even though the shirts are stabilized, they may stretch a little.
- If quilting on a domestic machine, use a walking foot to quilt.
- Choose thread that complements the shirts in the quilt. For this quilt I chose medium gray because there are both light- and dark- colored shirts. Thread nestles into t-shirts, so the quilting isn't as obvious as on quilting cotton.
- I like simple quilting, like parallel lines, for t-shirt quilts, because I don't want the quilting to take the focus away from the shirts.
- Use one of the horizontal seams as a guide for the first line, or mark a line with painter's tape or a Hera marker. Use a guide bar to keep the distance consistent between the lines. Refer to Types of Quilting: *Guide Bars*, page 226, for more information on quilting parallel lines.
- When you come to the end of a quilting line, do not turn the quilt around and sew back in the opposite direction. This causes rippling in the quilt. Pull the quilt back towards you and start quilting in the same direction as the previous line.
- Use a denim needle to quilt. It may be necessary to get through the thicker screen printing or decals on t-shirts.
- Stitch slowly to avoid skipped stitches.
- Finish by binding and labeling the quilt in whatever way suits your style!

A SASHING TUTORIAL

I chose sashing to finish at 1". Here is how I figured out how much fabric I needed:

VERTICAL SASHING

The prepped shirts in my quilt were 13" tall, so each vertical sashing strip should be cut at 1½" × 13".	Vertical sashing cut size = 1½" × 13"
Each row of my quilt has 5 shirts. I needed 4 sashing strips per row. (Remember, we don't add sashing to the left and right exterior edges.)	4 sashing strips per row x 5 rows = 20 sashing strips
Sashing strips are 13" long. Divide 42" (usable WOF) by 13". Round down for the number of sashing strips you can get from each WOF strip.	42" (WOF) ÷ 13" = 3 sashing strips (round down)
I needed 20 sashing strips. Divide that by 3 (the number I'll get from each WOF strip). Round up for the number of WOF strips to cut.	20 sashing strips ÷ 3 = 7 WOF strips (round up)
Subcut the sashing strips from the WOF strips.	Subcut 20 sashing strips, each 1½" × 13"

HORIZONTAL SASHING

After I sewed the vertical sashing to the shirts, the average row width was 57", so each horizontal sashing strip should be cut at 1½" × 57".	Horizontal sashing cut size = 1½" × 57"
My quilt has 5 rows so I needed 4 sashing strips to sew the rows together.	4 x 57" = 228" total length
My fabric had a 42" usable WOF, so I needed to cut 6 WOF strips, 1½" × WOF, to get 228".	228" ÷ 42" (WOF) = 6 WOF strips (round up)
I needed 4 sashing strips, so I joined the WOF strips at the short ends and subcut the sashing.	Subcut 4 sashing strips, each 1½" × 57"

TOTAL SASHING FABRIC

For all sashing, I needed 13 WOF strips, 1½" × WOF, or ⅝ yard. Buy a little extra—when cutting narrow strips, the fabric may need frequent squaring up. (See *Square It Again?*, page 62.)	13 WOF strips × 1½" = 19½" or ⅝ yard (round up)

WE CAN ALL BE HEROES
IRON MAN
EXTRA CHEESE
BATMAN
CAPTAIN AMERICA
STRONGER TOGETHER
i will save the world
SPIDER-MAN
A LONG TIME AGO IN A GALAXY FAR, FAR AWAY...
STAR WARS
AVENGERS
STAR WARS

SMALL
SMALL
SMALL

SMALL PROJECTS

PROJECTS
PROJECTS
PROJECTS
PROJECTS

SMALL PROJECTS

To start, I'll confess I'm not a super generous quilt giver. Let me explain: If I'm going to gift you a handmade quilt, I love you. A lot. In addition, I have to really feel like you will *value* a quilt. Let's face it, quilts take a good amount of time (and money!). to make. Sometimes, I just don't have the time to make an entire quilt, but still want to gift something handmade and personal. Small projects are perfect for this. They can be customized and are great practical gifts. (They're also good for those of us who love to procrastinate!). Don't forget, you're not limited to placemats and coasters. Wall hangings, table runners, pot holders, and trivets can all be made using the same techniques.

Small projects really show off your fabric choices, as well as your design and quilting skills. They are a good place to experiment with new techniques and color combos. Placemats are ideal for practicing free motion quilting!

Whether you're fussy cutting, using a strip of impactful fabric, or practicing new skills, these little projects can pack a big punch. Up 'til now in this book, the projects were made with solid fabrics, so I took the opportunity to play with pattern here. I paired a patterned fabric from my stash with a complementary solid. I added a bright pop of color for the backing fabric, so these are reversible. I encourage you to experiment with your fabrics to find fun and interesting combinations.

TECHNIQUES AND TIPS

- Prewash all fabrics for coasters and placemats. Prewashing helps prevent shrinking or distorting when the projects are washed.
- Spray baste small projects like these for simplicity and speed. Placemats and coasters are lightweight, easy to handle, and small enough to be spray basted on a cutting table. (Be sure to follow the manufacturer's directions for the spray baste, especially the cautions about having adequate ventilation.)
- Spray one side of the batting. Gently place the backing or top of the project, *wrong* side down, over the sticky batting, smoothing from one edge to the other as you go. This will prevent and eliminate wrinkles, stretching, and puckering.
- If you prefer not to use spray baste or don't have any on hand, pin or thread baste the projects. (Refer to The Quilt Sandwich: *Layer and Baste,* page 214, to see the various types of basting).
- Batting scraps are great for small projects! Save the leftovers from bigger projects and use them up in these.
- Binding small projects can be a challenge because the short edges of the project mean the space for joining the binding tails is short. On a coaster, the tails are especially short. Sew the tails together with a straight seam, not a diagonal one. Bend the coaster and manipulate it to comfortably sew the binding tails together. Refer to the chapter Finishing: Binding, Facing, and More: *Binding Tails—Straight Seam,* page 244, for more information.

ROAD TRIP PLACEMATS

Custom placemats add vibrant style to any table. The design and color possibilities are endless, and your friends will be in awe of your skills. Seriously, when I have people over for dinner, they oooh and ahhh over handmade placemats. How fantastic to be able to make something quickly that elicits such an appreciative response!

Seam allowances are ¼"

WOF=Width of Fabric

Fabrics are by Alison Glass for Andover Fabrics: Flip Quarter from the Road Trip collection and Beetle from the Kaleidoscope collection

TRIVETS If you will be making trivets intended to be placed under hot items, use a specialty batting that provides heat protection.

FINISHED SIZE 18" × 14"

MATERIALS AND CUTTING FOR SIX PLACEMATS

MATERIALS

Solid fabric: ¾ yard

Patterned fabric: ⅝ yard

Batting: 1 piece 38" × 45"
OR 6 pieces, each 19" × 15"

Backing: 1⅓ yards

Binding: ⅞ yard

CUTTING

Solid fabric: Cut 6 strips, 4¼" × WOF

Subcut 12 strips, 4¼" × 18"

Patterned fabric: Cut 1 strip, 18" × WOF

Subcut 6 strips, 18" × 6½"

Batting: Cut 6 pieces, each 19" × 15"

Backing: Cut 3 strips, 15" × WOF

Subcut 6 pieces, each 15" × 19"

Binding: Cut 12 strips 2¼" × WOF. Join the short ends with diagonal seams.

Subcut 6 lengths, each 2¼" × 72", one length for each placemat

PROJECT INSTRUCTIONS

1. Place a solid strip *right* sides together with a patterned strip, aligning the long edges.

2. Sew together, along a long edge.

3. Sew another solid strip to the other long edge of the patterned strip.

4. Press both seams toward the patterned fabric. This raises it a bit more than the solid fabric to feature it on the placemat.

5. Apply spray baste to one side of a piece of batting. Adhere the *wrong* side of the backing to it. Gently smooth the fabric to be sure it is flat but not stretched.

6. Apply spray baste to the other side of the batting and adhere the *wrong* side of the placemat top to it. Again, smooth any wrinkles without stretching.

7. Quilt the placemat, as desired. I machine quilted horizontal lines across the placemats to keep the focus on the patterned fabric. Refer to Types of Quilting: *Quilting Parallel Lines,* page 227, to get started.

8. Trim the batting and backing even with the placemat.

9. Bind the edges.

10. Repeat these steps to make 6 placemats.

To get maximum design impact in minimal time, fussy cut a section from a print you love. There are many gorgeous fabrics out there that are perfect for this. Piecing fabrics is another artistic way to make placemats. Use scraps that have been piling up and it's a double win.

SIMPLIFIED DESIGN Make your placemats from a single fabric to simplify the design. Six can be made from one yard of fabric that has a 42" usable WOF. Buy 1⅛ yards to allow for squaring the leading edge of the yardage.

HAPPY HOUR MUG RUGS

Coasters (or "mug rugs") are functional and common, but how often do you really *notice* the coasters you use? One of my favorite things when visiting a new place is finding unexpected treasures. Handmade coasters are just that—unexpected treasures! I'm thrilled when I discover everyday items that have real style or whimsy; they delight me and I love making them as gifts.

Small, practical, and quick to make, these coasters pack a big design punch. To coordinate these with my *Road Trip* placemats, page 184, I fussy cut a design from the same patterned fabric.

Fabrics are by Alison Glass for Andover Fabrics: Flip Quarter from the Road Trip collection and Beetle from the Kaleidoscope collection

QUILTING ON SMALL PROJECTS Scale down the quilting for smaller projects. A large pattern won't have much impact on a small piece.

FINISHED SIZE 4½" × 4½"

MATERIALS AND CUTTING FOR ONE COASTER

Fabric for the top of the coaster*: 4½" × 4½"

*If fussy cutting, center your chosen design in the square before cutting.

Backing: 5" × 5"

Batting: 5" × 5"

Binding: 2¼" x approximately 20"

PROJECT INSTRUCTIONS

1. Apply spray baste to one side of a square of batting. Adhere the *wrong* side of the backing square to it. Gently smooth the fabric flat without stretching it.

2. Apply spray baste to the other side of the batting and adhere the *wrong* side of the coaster top to it. Again, smooth any wrinkles without stretching.

3. Quilt the coaster as desired. To coordinate with the placemats, I again machine quilted horizontal lines. Note that I spaced the lines closer together on the coasters than on the placemats because of the coaster's smaller size. Refer to Types of Quilting: *Quilting Parallel Lines*, page 227, to get started.

4. Trim the batting and backing even with the mug rug.

5. Bind the edges.

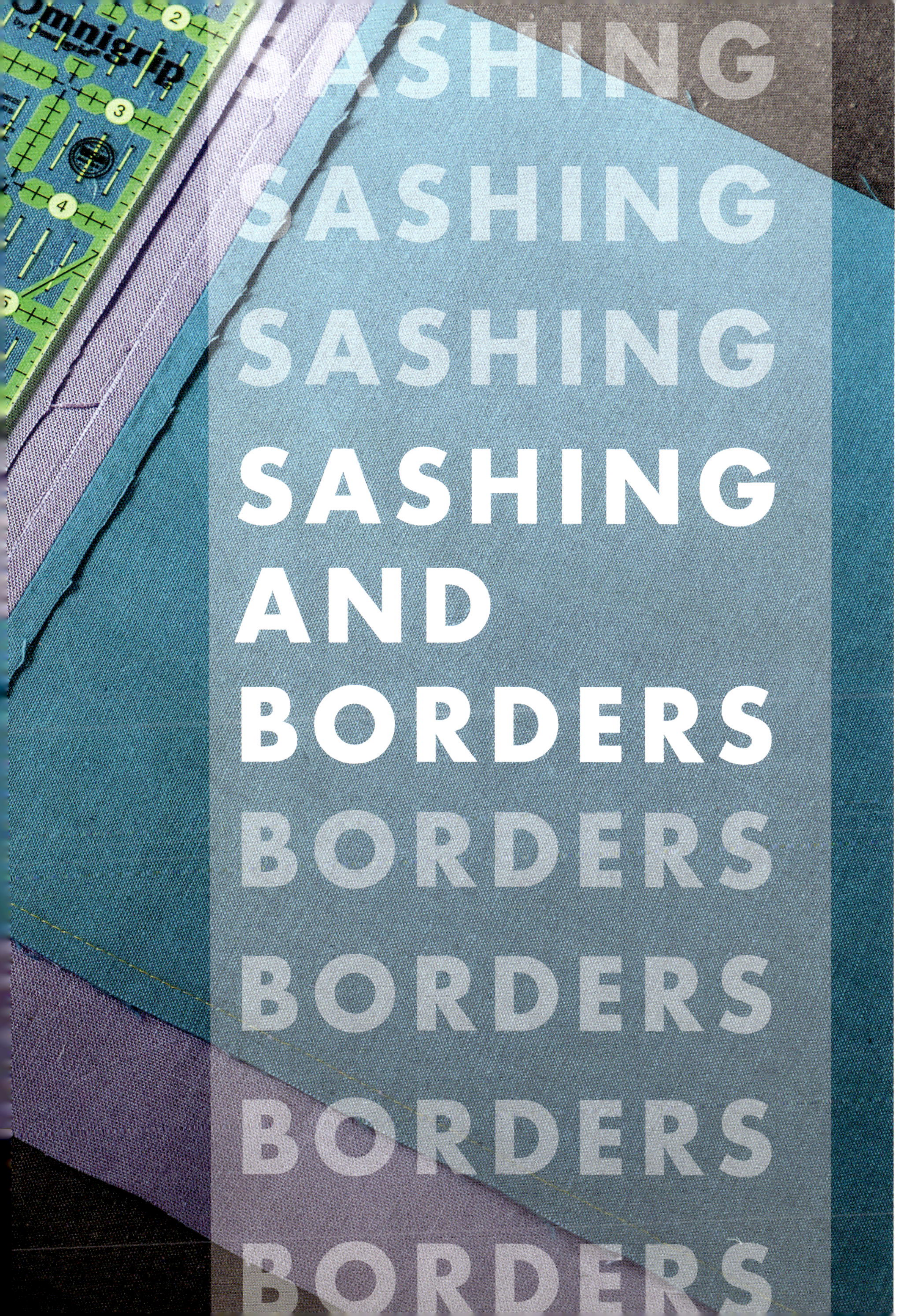

SASHING AND BORDERS

SASHING AND BORDERS

Adding sashing and/or borders can turn a jumbled, hectic quilt into a cohesive, organized one. Sashing refers to strips of fabric sewn between quilt blocks to provide separation. Sashing frames the individual blocks. Borders frame the entire quilt after the blocks are sewn together (with or without sashing). While there is no rule that a quilt needs both sashing and a border, they often go hand in hand.

Sashing frames the blocks

Borders frame the quilt

PINNING

Use this technique for sashing strips and borders. It's hard to evenly distribute long strips of fabric without careful pinning, especially since blocks and quilt edges may have slight variations in size. Even distribution ensures a square quilt in the end.

- Finger crease or pin the center of the block or the center of the quilt edge.
- Next, pin the ends of the strip to the corners of the block or quilt, then pin the centers together.
- Add pins along the strip as needed to ensure the strip is evenly distributed across the block or quilt edge.
- Ease and/or stretch the strip, as you pin. Easing the strip is needed when the strip is slightly too long. Stretching is needed when the strip is slightly too short.
- If possible, use a walking foot on your sewing machine. It pulls both layers of fabric under the needle at the same rate.

DIAGONAL SEAMS

Long sashing or border strips may need to be pieced to get the needed length. Piece them on the diagonal instead of with a straight seam. A straight seam across the strip might be a little quicker to sew, but it will add more bulk to that part of the quilt and might even distort the seam a little, when it's pressed. A diagonal seam distributes that bulk and allows the seams to lie flatter.

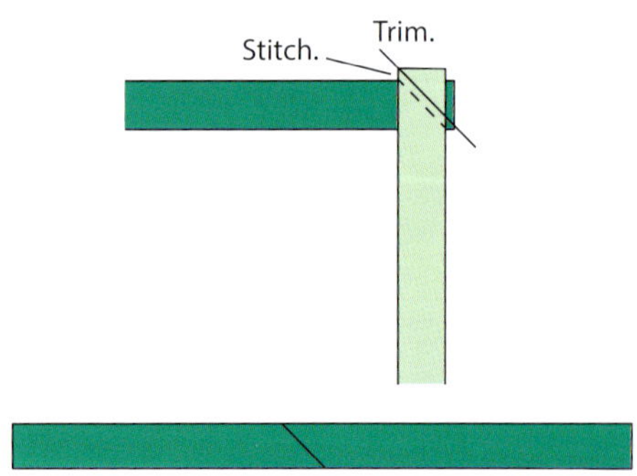

SASHING

A few years ago, I made a rainbow scrap quilt. My original intent was to piece 6" blocks that, when joined, would slowly transition from color to color through the rainbow. The plan was to sew the blocks together and have a quilt entirely bursting with color. As I hung the blocks on my design wall, it became apparent that they needed separation to really shine. I decided on white sashing, and it immediately changed the entire look of my quilt.

Sashing Considerations

Sashing can change a quilt for the better. Before adding sashing to quilt blocks (Fig. 1), decide what the function of the sashing is.

Fig. 1

- Sashing frames the individual block so the blocks are not massed together. The design and color choices within the blocks are highlighted.
- Sashing provides rest for the eye. White strips of fabric separate the bright colors without taking away the motion in them. The sashing lets the eye relax as it scans over the quilt. The result is a calmer, more cohesive quilt. (Fig. 2)

Fig. 2

- After sewing all the blocks for a quilt, you may want a larger finished size. The sashing makes the quilt larger without creating a lot more work. (But size alone is not a good reason to add sashing; be sure it's a good design decision, too.)
- Sashing provides a unifying element. Although it physically separates the blocks, the quilt looks more coordinated as a whole because of the uniformity of the sashing.
- Sashing width determines the amount of separation for the quilt blocks. Before cutting your strips, use a design wall or the floor to audition different sashing widths. Place a large piece of the sashing fabric on the wall and arrange blocks on it. Do you want lots of space between the blocks (Fig. 3) or simply a narrow strip (Fig. 4)?

Fig. 3

- Take a photo of each width that you try; that'll make it easier to compare your options.
- Cut your sashing pieces ½" wider than the desired finished sashing width. This extra is for the ¼" seam allowances. For example, if you want the sashing to finish at 2" wide, cut the sashing strips 2½" wide.

Fig. 4

- Fabric is another important design choice for sashing. A contrasting fabric separates and frames the quilt blocks. (Fig. 5) A coordinating fabric gives the illusion the quilt blocks are "floating" on the quilt top. (Fig. 6)

- The same fabric as the sashing *between* the blocks may be added as a border *around* the outermost ones. Replicating the sashing adds to the cohesiveness of the quilt. (Fig. 7)

- Sashing isn't limited to a simple strip of fabric. Sashing can be a pieced strip such as flying geese. Get as creative as you like with sashing designs. (Figs. 8 and 9)

- Cornerstones, also known as "posts", are squares of contrasting fabric at the sashing intersections between quilt blocks. (Fig. 10)

- Cornerstones do not need to be simple squares of fabric; they can be pieced to add a further design element to the quilt. (Fig. 11)

Fig. 5

Fig. 6

Fig. 7

Fig. 8

Fig. 9

Fig. 10

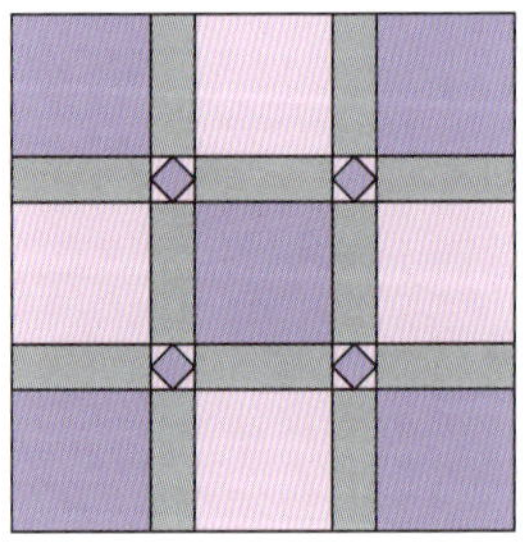

Fig. 11

SASHING TUTORIAL

Seam allowances are ¼″.

For this tutorial, assume there are 20 quilt blocks, 4 across and 5 down, that finish to 10" x 10".

Vertical Sashing

Measure the center height of several blocks. Take the average of these to determine the length of the vertical sashing. If any block's dimensions are more than ⅛" different than the others, remake it. A large difference is hard to ease or stretch to fit the sashing.

- Sashing width is up to you. For this example, use 2½"-wide strips that finish at 2".
- In this example, the blocks' unfinished measurement is 10½" × 10½". Cut the vertical sashing 10½" × 2½".
- This quilt has 4 blocks across and 5 blocks down. Sashing is only necessary on the interior edges of the blocks, so you need 3 sashing strips per row. For 5 rows, you need a total of 15 strips, each 2½" × 10½".
- Pin and sew together 4 blocks and 3 sashing strips. Press.
- Make 5 rows.

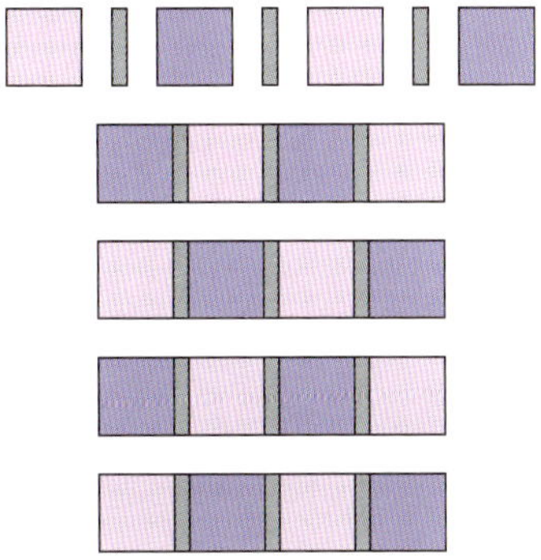

Horizontal Sashing

To determine the length of the horizontal sashing, either take the average of the width of the rows or calculate it, as described below.

- In this example, the blocks finish to 10" wide and there are 4 of them per row. That's 40".
- The sashing finishes to 2" wide and there are 3 vertical sashing strips per row. That's 6".
- There is a ¼" seam allowance at each end of the rows, totaling ½".
- 40" + 6" + ½" = 46½".
- There are 5 rows. You need 4 sashing strips, each 2½" × 46½".
- Cut 5 WOF strips, each 2½" × WOF. Join the short edges. Subcut 4 sashing strips, each 2½" × 46½".
- Pin and sew together the 5 rows and the 4 long sashing strips. Press.

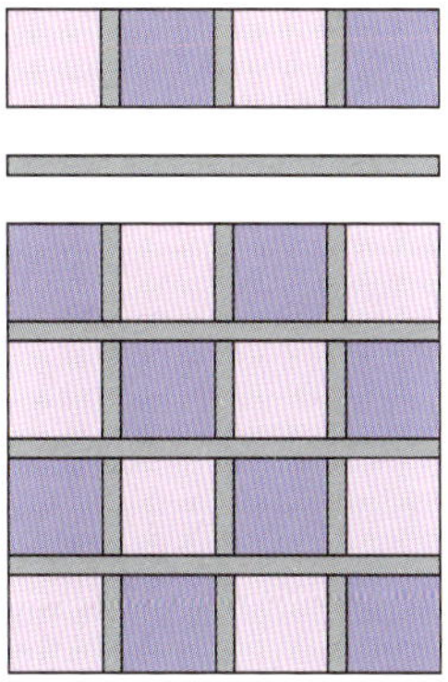

Aligning the Blocks

If you are not careful when adding horizontal sashing, the blocks may be misaligned. Here's a way to prevent that.

- Sew the horizontal sashing to the bottom edge of all the rows, except the final row. Press.
- *Before* sewing the rows together, align a ruler with each vertical sashing strip and lightly mark the horizontal strip at each vertical seam. Mark within the seam allowance so it will not show on the quilt top.
- These marks are a guide for pinning together the two rows. Pin the sashing seams of the next row at each of the marks.

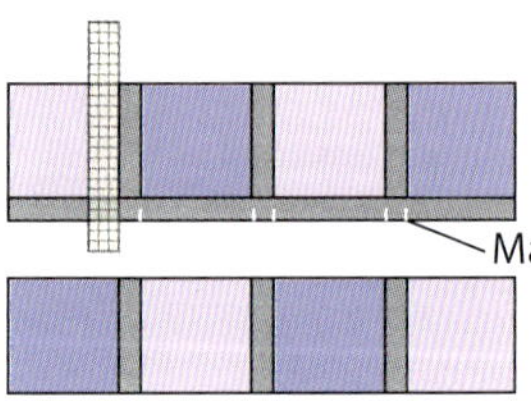

Sashing with Cornerstones

Cornerstones are pieced into the horizontal sashing before it is sewn to the rows. The horizontal sashing is cut the same length as the unfinished blocks' width. In this tutorial, that is 10½".

- Cut 16 sashing strips, each 2½" × 10½".
- Cut 12 cornerstones, each 2½" × 2½".
- Join 4 sashing strips and 3 cornerstones to make a long sashing strip. Make 4.
- Sew horizontal sashing between the finished rows, aligning the seams of the cornerstones with the seams of the vertical sashing.

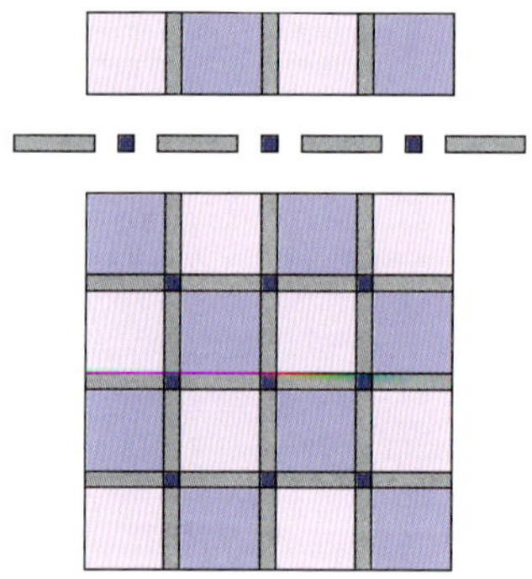

BORDERS

I think of the border as the frame for my quilt. Although borders aren't necessary, they can provide a finished look for a quilt top. A simple border can bring a calming effect, or a jazzy one can add some pizzaz. If you really want to get fancy, add multiple borders in varying widths and colors.

My road to Bordertown was not without potholes. Years ago, I put together a quilt top for a friend's daughter. This quilt had flowers, it had unicorns, it had... all sorts of stuff. I decided to add a border to calm it down a bit. What did I do? I sewed a really long strip to one side of the quilt, trimmed it, then did the same on the other three sides. I was so proud of myself until I laid the quilt on the floor prior to basting it. *Oh my*. The quilt had the waviest of wavy borders. My waves were so big, they were tsunamis! The border fabric sewn to the quilt top was perfectly flat, but the outer edge was rippling to a degree that I simply could not get it to lie flat. I ended up removing all of the borders and searching online for what it was that went wrong.

Here is the correct way to do it; it all comes down to measuring and pinning.

BORDER TUTORIAL

Seam allowances are ¼".

For this tutorial, the quilt top (without borders) is 80" wide × 100" long.

Side Borders

- Attach borders to the longest edges first. This saves fabric and minimizes waviness.
- Measure the length of the quilt top in 3 places: along the left edge, through the middle, and along the right edge. (Fig. 1)
- Take the average of these measurements to determine the length of the border strips. For this quilt, the length is 100".
- Border width is up to you; in this tutorial we will cut 5½" border strips for a border that finishes at 5" wide. So the side border strips must be 5½" x 100".
- Cut 6 strips, 5½" × WOF. Piece the short edges of the strips together diagonally. Subcut 2 strips, each 5½" × 100".
- This next pinning process may seem tedious but it goes a long way toward having a square quilt and preventing waves in the borders.

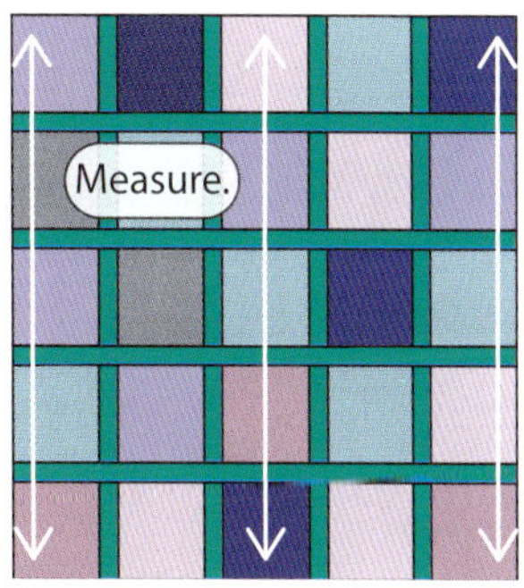

Fig. 1

- Fold a border strip into quarters and finger press or pin to mark the 3 folds.
- Do the same for one long edge of the quilt top.
- Place the border strip on the quilt top, *right* sides together, matching the pins or creases. Pin the strip and quilt top together at each of these points.
- Match the ends of the border strip with the edges of the quilt top. Pin.
- Pin the remainder of the border strip to the quilt top making sure the fabric is distributed evenly. (Fig. 2) (Refer to *Pinning*, page 190.)
- Sew the border strip to the quilt, gently easing or stretching the strip as you go. Press.
- Repeat this process to attach the other side's border strip.

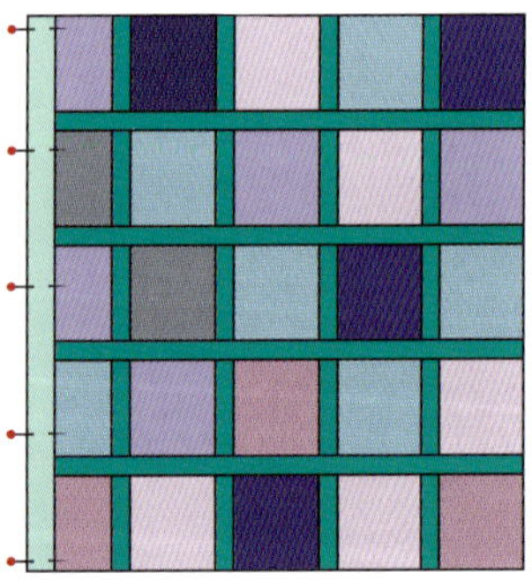

Fig. 2

Top and Bottom Borders

- Measure or calculate the width of the quilt. In this tutorial, the quilt width plus side borders and seam allowances is 90".
- The border cut width is 5½". So the top and bottom border strips must be 5½" × 90".
- Cut 6 strips, 5½" × WOF. Piece the short edges of the strips together diagonally. Subcut 2 strips, each 5½" × 90".
- Use the same process as for the side borders to pin and sew the top and bottom borders to the quilt top.

Borders with Cornerstones

Border cornerstones add color and style to your quilt without investing a lot of time. They are usually a contrasting color to the border fabric. Border cornerstones can be solid squares of fabric or pieced blocks.

- Cornerstones are pieced onto the ends of the top and bottom border strips before they're sewn to the quilt.
- Add the side borders to the quilt (refer to *Side Borders*, page 195). Press.
- The cornerstones measure the same as the unfinished border width. In this tutorial, that is 5½". Cut or piece 4 cornerstones, each 5½" × 5½".
- Measure the quilt's width *without* the side borders, using the 3-point measuring technique described in *Side Borders*, page 195.
- In this tutorial, the quilt width is 80". So you need 2 border strips, each 5½" × 80".
- Cut 5 strips of border fabric, 5½" × WOF. Piece the short edges of the strips together diagonally. Subcut 2 border strips, each 5½" × 80".
- Attach a cornerstone to each end of both border strips. Press.

- Add one border/cornerstone strip to the top edge of the quilt and the other border/cornerstone strip to the bottom edge. Align or nest the seams before stitching to ensure they match.

Borders with Mitered Corners

Mitered corners are another border option. The borders are attached to the quilt and the corners are joined with a 45-degree angle instead of a 90-degree one.

- For mitered corners, the length and width are measured *before* adding any borders.
- The formula for the border strip lengths is: quilt measurement plus 2 times the border cut width.
- Add an extra 2", just to be safe.

STRIPED FABRICS Striped fabrics need finesse in the miter process. When pinning together, check the right sides of the fabric and align the stripes from one strip to the other. Stitch first with a basting stitch. Open and check the alignment of the stripes. Adjust as needed. Restitch with a standard stitch length when the stripes look just the way you want them.

Cut Side Strips

- Measure the quilt's length, using the 3-point measuring technique described in *Side Borders*, page 195. This quilt's length is 100".
- The border cut width is 5½". Multiply that by 2 and you get 11".
- 100" + 11" + 2" extra = 113". So you need 2 side border strips, 5½" x 113".
- Cut 6 strips, 5½" × WOF. Piece the short edges of the strips together diagonally. Subcut 2 strips, each 5½" × 113".

Cut Top and Bottom Strips

- Measure the quilt's width, using the 3-point measuring technique described in *Side Borders*, page 195. This quilt's width is 80".
- The border cut width is 5½". Multiply that by 2 and you get 11".
- 80" + 11" + 2" extra = 93". So you need 2 strips, each 5½" x 93", for the top and bottom borders
- Cut 6 strips, 5½" × WOF. Piece the short edges of the strips together diagonally.
- Subcut 2 strips, each 5½" × 93".

Miter the Corners

- Use the pinning process described in *Side Borders*, page 195, to pin a side border to a side edge of the quilt. Leave the excess border fabric free.
- Sew the border strip to the quilt; gently ease or stretch the border strip as you go.

- Start and stop ¼" from the edges of the quilt top. (Fig. 3) Backstitch at both places to secure the stitching. Press.
- Repeat this process to attach the other side border strip and then the top and bottom strips. Press.
- The beginning and ending stitches of each strip should *meet* the stitches of the adjacent strip but *not* overlap.
- After you've sewn and pressed all 4 borders, fold the quilt top onto itself diagonally *right* sides together to make a triangle. (Fig. 4) Match up the quilt's edges.
- Smooth the border strips and align the raw edges of the 2 adjacent strips.
- Align a ruler with an edge of the quilt and draw a diagonal 45-degree line on the wrong side of one strip of border fabric.
- Pin together the 2 border strips at that corner. Sew on the drawn line. Backstitch at the start and stop.
- Start stitching at the point where the 2 border stitch lines end, without stitching over them.
- Open the seam to check the miter. If you're happy with the result, trim the excess seam allowance to ¼". (Figs. 4 and 5) Press.
- Repeat the process for the remaining 3 corners.

Fig. 3

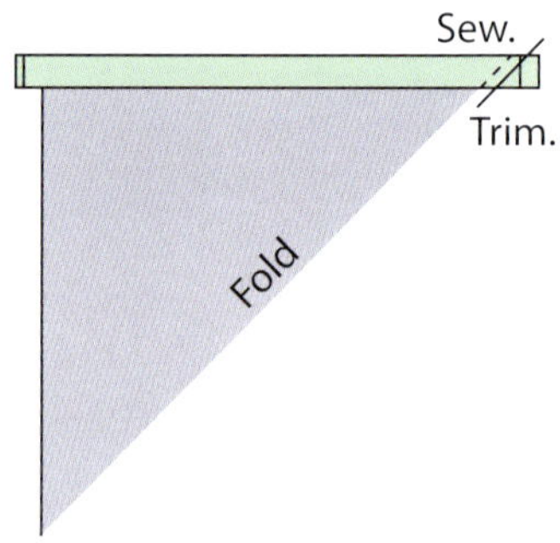

Fig. 4

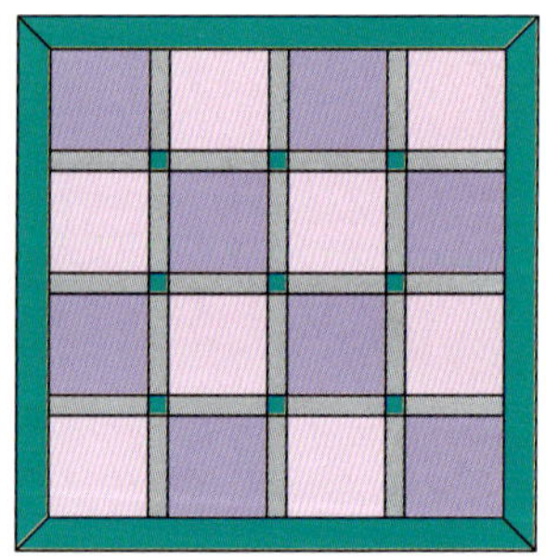
Fig. 5

Border Considerations

- Whenever possible, cut the border fabric strips on the lengthwise grain, that is, parallel to the selvage. This has the least stretch and minimizes waviness in the borders.
- Place the quilt top on a design wall, bed, or floor and audition borders. Your own design aesthetic comes into play in every step of quilt making, and this is no exception.

- Quilt tops can have multiple borders. Maybe one border is enough for your quilt, or maybe not. Consider a narrow inner border with a wider outer one. Or add three borders and make the middle one a pieced design.
- Another option is to add the borders in a clockwise order instead of sides first, top and bottom second.
- Another idea is to use different fabrics for the sides than for the top and bottom.
- What if you joined the borders with 45-degree angles at the corners instead of the standard 90-degree ones? These are mitered corners and are great for striped fabrics.
- Brainstorm and try anything you can think of. The sky's the limit.
- Take a photo of each border combination along the way. It's easier to compare the different designs this way.

Border Examples

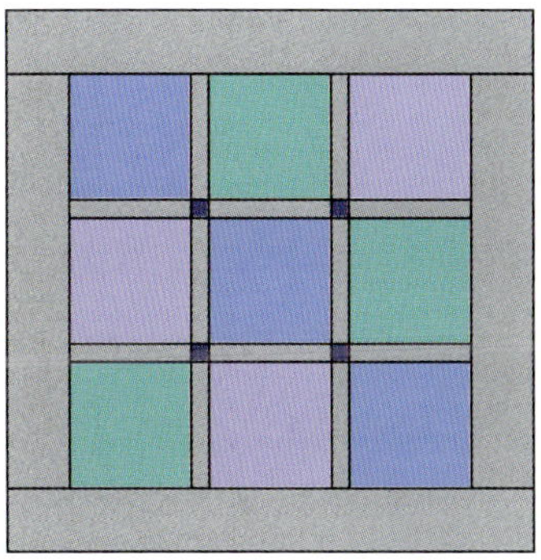

One border

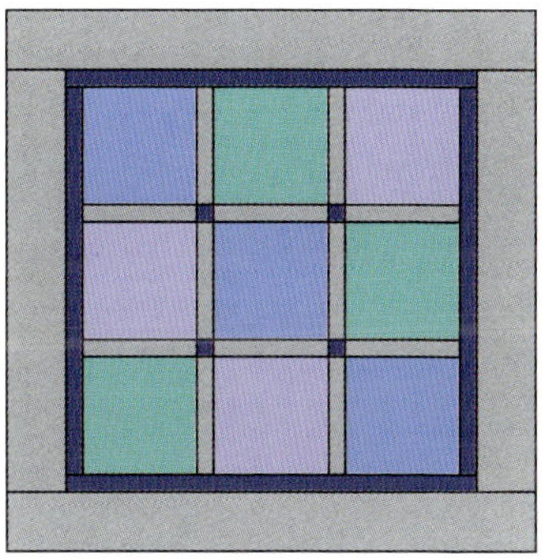

A narrow inner border combined with a wider outer border

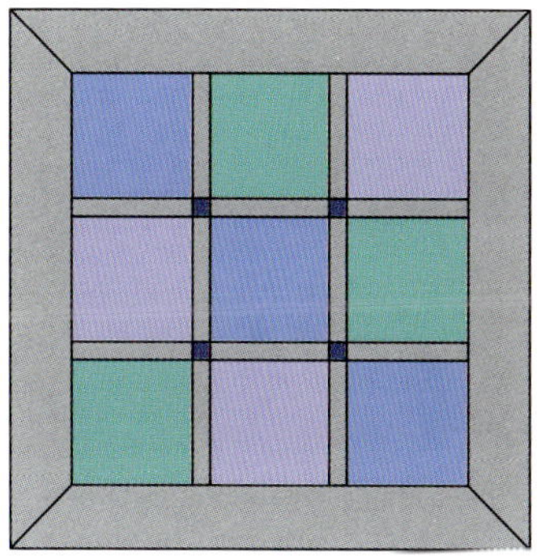

A border with mitered corners

An inner border with an outer border added counter-clockwise

An inner border, a middle pieced border, and a wider third border

THE QUILT SANDWICH

THE QUILT SANDWICH

A quilt has 3 layers: the quilt top, the batting, and the backing. Baste these 3 layers together and you have what's known as "the quilt sandwich". This chapter gives you, the quilter, the information that will help you get that sandwich prepared so you can finish your quilt, whether by hand, by machine, or simply taking it to someone who will do this part for you. We'll cover preparing each layer and basting them together with techniques and tips along the way.

When I began quilting, I didn't know what my finishing options were and I found myself wanting more direction. Most books had minimal information on what to do after a quilt top was completed. So, what did I do? First, I researched and found there is no one-size-fits-all solution for finishing a quilt top. Then I experimented and practiced. I've found that the more care you take to prepare each layer, the easier it will be to actually quilt it. Let me explain. Trying to quilt a wrinkly top with lots of stray threads and uneven seams will not be a fun or rewarding experience. Whether you plan to tie, hand quilt, use a domestic machine, or send your quilt to a longarm quilter, here are a few tried and true ways to make sure your quilt is ready.

THE QUILT TOP

This first layer is the star of the show—your finished project or quilt top. Careful prep will make your life simpler and lead to a beautiful, finished piece.

- Press the top and make sure it is free from wrinkles. Quilting on a wrinkly top is as difficult as trying to draw on a wrinkled sheet of paper.
- Press the seams flat on the wrong side of the top. This eliminates bulk and makes it easier for the needle to move over the seams when quilting.
- Press the right side of the quilt, too. Check that the seams are flat and none are folded over on themselves.
- Snip any errant threads on both the front and back of the quilt top. Pay special attention to dark threads that will show through lighter fabric.
- Fix any loose seams. If a seam has opened, it's a perfect place for the sewing machine's presser foot to snag the quilt top, making your stitches irregular and possibly even snagging and tearing a hole in the top.
- Make sure the quilt top lies flat. An easy way to do this is to place it on the floor and smooth it out. If it doesn't lie flat it will be very difficult to quilt. Whether the problem is in the piecing or the borders, it can result in puckering, tucks, or uneven quilting. "Un-sew" the offending sections and correct the problem before going any further.
- Trim (square up) your quilt top so the sides are straight and the corners are right angles. Be sure to leave ¼" around all the edges for the seam allowance of the binding. Starting with a squared top goes a long way toward ensuring your quilt will be square after being basted and also after quilting.
- Stitch around the outside of the quilt top about ⅛" from the edge to reinforce the seams. These outside seams are subjected to more stress and can easily pull apart if there isn't reinforcement. Use a slightly longer stitch length than usual so the edges stay flat and don't get distorted.

THE BATTING

Refer to Equipment and Materials: *Batting*, page 36 for more information.

Batting is available in a variety of materials, both natural and synthetic. Select one that matches the intended use of your quilt. For instance, do you want it super warm or lightweight? Machine washable and dryable? Sometimes when I choose a heavier backing, I leave the batting out altogether. This is another place where what's right for you is what's right for your quilt.

- Make sure the batting is free from wrinkles. Just as the quilt top and backing should be wrinkle-free when you get ready for quilting, the batting should be, too. A wrinkle-free batting won't bunch or fold between the quilt top and backing.
- Check batting for stains, holes, or thin areas. High-quality batting shouldn't have any, but it's always a good idea to check. Fix any issues prior to quilting.
- For smaller quilts that you plan to hand quilt, quilt on a domestic sewing machine, or hand tie: Trim the batting about 4" larger than the quilt top. That gives you 2" extra on all sides. For example, if your quilt is 50" × 50", trim the batting to 54" × 54".
- For a quilt that's twin size or larger, trim the batting about 6" larger than the quilt top. That gives you 3" extra on all sides. For example, if your quilt is 90" × 90", trim the batting to 96" × 96".
- For quilting on a longarm, trim the batting 8" larger than the quilt top. That gives you 4" extra on all sides. For example, if your quilt is 50" × 50", trim the batting to 58" × 58".
- If you plan to give your quilt to a professional longarm quilter, ask them *before* you trim. Each quilter has their own size preference.

THE QUILT BACKING

We all know the quilt top is the main event, but a good quilt backing is important, too. It has the same surface area as the top, and therefore has as much potential to impact overall design. A carefully chosen backing can bring your design to the next level. While the quilt top is almost always quilting cotton, the backing fabric doesn't have to be. Different choices allow you to use a quilt in different ways and there are a lot of options. Where and how the quilt will be used are guides for the type of backing to select. The backing will determine the weight and style of the quilt, too. Here are specific considerations to get you going.

Backing Considerations

Where and how will the quilt be used? Are you wanting something cuddly and soft for a baby or small child? Do you want to keep a picnic quilt in the car for outdoor use at the park? Do you need a lightweight quilt for summertime? Would you like to hang a quilt on the wall for display?

- What style of backing will complement the design of the quilt top?
- Do you want the quilt to be reversible?
- What fabric texture do you want for the backing? (Cotton, flannel, Minky?)
- How large does the quilt backing need to be?
- Do you want a pieced backing? Will it be simple or intricate?
- Are there leftover blocks from the quilt top that you want to incorporate in the backing?
- Do you want the quilt to be extra warm, extra light, or somewhere in between?
- What kind of batting are you using? Coordinate this with the backing.
- Don't forget—the backing is the part of the quilt that touches your skin when you're snuggling under it—make sure it has the feel you want!

Backing Basics

- Remove the selvages from the fabric prior to piecing the backing. (See Equipment and Materials: *Fabric Know-How*, page 82.)
- Use a ½" seam allowance for a pieced quilt backing and press seams open. This reduces bulk that might show on the quilt top after quilting. This is especially important with heavier fabrics.
- Press the backing and iron out all wrinkles prior to layering it in the quilt sandwich.
- If the quilt top is pieced with light-colored fabrics and a lightweight batting is used, make sure the backing fabric won't show through. This can happen when using a very busy or dark backing fabric.

BULKY SEAM ALLOWANCES Minky and fleece do not lie flat when ironed, so ½" seam allowances can get bulky. If the seam allowances fold over on themselves, this bulk bunches up and makes bulges that can be hard to sew over in the quilting process. I recommend swiping a bit of glue under the seam allowances and ironing with a hot, dry iron to secure them in place. This guarantees they will stay put through the quilting process, whether on a domestic or longarm machine.

Backing Options

Quilting Cotton

- Hands down quilting cotton is the most popular backing fabric. It has a soft, lightweight feel, can be found in a huge variety of colors and prints, and is readily available at fabric stores and online.
- Cutting and piecing quilting cotton is simple and straightforward.
- Using fabric that is 42" to 44" wide is the most common. Fabric lengths are sewn together to create a backing large enough for the quilt top.
- Wider fabrics are available, made especially for quilt backs. They range from 104" to 120" wide with 108" being the most common. With these, one length can be cut that will be wide enough for most quilt tops, so piecing usually isn't necessary.
- If you have a few extra blocks that weren't used in the quilt top, piece them into the backing as a design element.
- Some quilt backings are as complex as the quilt top. I know quilters who use intricately pieced designs for both the top and back of their quilts.

Flannel

- Flannel is a great choice to add weight and warmth to a quilt.
- Often used for baby quilts, flannel comes in a lot of wonderful patterns.
- High-quality flannel is available at many local quilting stores, making it easy to find.
- It's easy to rotary cut clean edges and piece the same way as quilting cotton.
- Pre-wash and dry your flannel because it may shrink more than quilting cotton and batting.

Minky

- Minky is plush microfiber fabric that is lightweight but super soft and warm. I love it and use it all of the time, but it is more difficult to piece than other fabric.
- Minky sheds a ton of fluff when cut and stretch more easily than quilting cotton.
- When cutting Minky, use a piece of painter's tape on the cutting line to minimize the shedding. Remove the tape before sewing.
- If you plan to quilt a Minky-backed quilt on a domestic machine, stabilize the wrong side of the fabric with a lightweight fusible interfacing first. Why? Minky can be incredibly stretchy and difficult to piece or quilt effectively without stabilizer. Stabilizer allows the fabric to pass through the sewing machine without bunching, creasing, or stretching. My stabilizer preference is Pellon SF 101 Shape-Flex. Stabilization is not necessary if the quilt is being quilted by a longarmer.
- *Always* use a walking foot to sew together pieces of Minky.

Fleece

- Fleece is very cuddly and warm, making it perfect for cold weather quilts. It's available in a wide variety of prints.
- Use an anti-pill luxe fleece as it wears better over time.
- Fleece can be tricky to piece because sometimes the edges will curl after being cut. Placing a line of painter's tape on the cutting line of the fleece will help prevent curling. Remove it right before you sew.
- Use a walking foot to sew together pieces of fleece to prevent pulling or bunching.

Denim

- A denim backing will make a quilt utilitarian and heavy.
- Denim is great for backing picnic blankets or quilts that will see rougher use.
- Use a walking foot and a denim needle to piece.

ALTERNATIVE BACKING FABRICS The ready-made backing options and the heavier fabrics like fleece and denim require special treatment for quilting. Always make a sample quilt sandwich with the fabric and batting you're considering. Quilt it to see what presser foot, needle, thread, and stitch length work best. Adjust the tension of your machine and the presser foot pressure as needed.

Ready-Made Options

When choosing a ready-made backing, keep in mind that it may not wear evenly, it may not shrink at the same rate as quilting cotton, and it may not last as long. Also, pre-wash it to remove excess dyes that might bleed onto the quilt top.

Flat sheets

I like using flat sheets because they require no cutting or piecing, they're easy to find, are relatively inexpensive, and available in lots of great prints. Buy sheets made from 100% cotton, but not stretchy or jersey ones. Many quilters don't use sheets as backing because of the high thread count, but I've never had an issue. Low thread-count sheets are better; the looser weave of the fibers allows the sewing machine needle to pass through more easily. Lower quality sheets won't wear as long as quilting cotton. Keep that in mind when choosing.

Throw blankets

I love using super soft plush throw blankets as backings. They're inexpensive and I have found them at a variety of home-goods stores. Some have fun prints that are perfect for holiday or juvenile quilts.

Waterproof tablecloths

Waterproof tablecloths are ideal as backings for quilts that will be used as picnic blankets. They're great for use on damp grass and can be wiped clean.

How Much Backing You'll Need

- Calculating how much fabric you'll need for a quilt backing can seem intimidating, but it doesn't have to be. Of course, the easiest way to determine backing yardage amounts is to go online and search "quilt backing calculator". Plug in the quilt top measurements and voila! You've got what you need. But if you don't have immediate access to a computer or you just want to do it yourself, here's how to figure it out.

- Measure the quilt top and add 6" to both the width and length. That gives you an extra 3" on each side. For example, for a top that is 72" × 82", you need a backing that is 78" × 88".

- For a small wall hanging, having only an extra inch or two on each side would probably be enough. It depends on your comfort level in centering the quilt top and batting over the backing.

- Next, decide whether you want a horizontal or a vertical seam. This will affect the amount of fabric needed. Check out the yardages in the examples on pages 210 and 211.

- If you chose a directional fabric, decide how you'd like the pattern to be oriented. That will determine the seam direction.

- Remove the selvages (Equipment and Materials: *Fabric Know-How*, page 28) before piecing the backing. If you're using a ready-made option, remove any edge treatments.

LONGARM QUILTERS If you are giving your top to a professional longarm quilter, ask them *before* you decide on a backing size and fabric. Most longarm quilters require at least 4" to 5" of extra backing fabric on *all sides* of the quilt. That means adding 8" to 10" to the quilt dimensions. For example, if your quilt is 72" × 82", the backing needs to be at least 80" × 90". Also, some longarm quilters prefer horizontal seams on quilt backings. Consult with the quilter when making this decision, too.

Vertical Seams

Assume a 40″ WOF to allow for ½″ seam allowances and selvage removal.

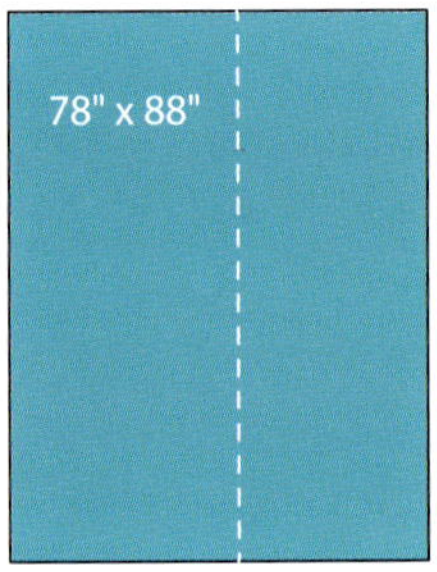

Quilt Backings with Vertical Seams

BACKING WIDTH	WOF PIECES NEEDED
Up to 40" wide	1 (no seam required)
41" wide to 80" wide	2
Over 80" wide	3 or more

1. Refer to the table above to determine how many WOF pieces you need for the width of the backing.

> Our example quilt backing width is 78" and requires 2 WOF pieces.

2. Multiply the number of WOF pieces you need by the *length* of the backing.

> 2 x 88" = 176"

3. Divide this by 36" to get yardage.

> 176" ÷ 36" = 4.89 yards

4. Round up to the next ⅛ or ¼ yard to account for fabric possibly being skewed off the bolt. This is the amount of yardage you need to buy.

> Round up ⅛ yard. You need 5 yards of fabric.

Horizontal Seams

Assume a 40″ WOF to allow for ½″ seam allowances and selvage removal.

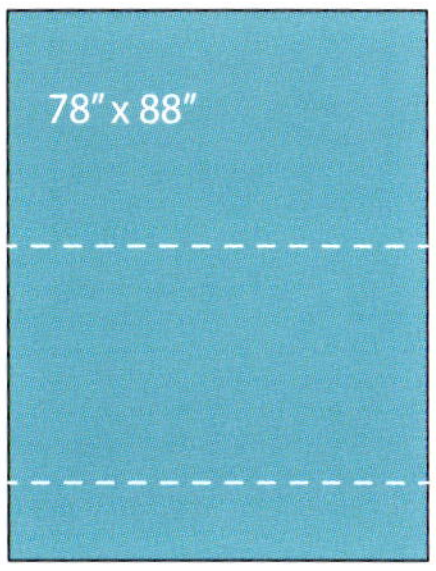

Quilt Backings with Horizontal Seams

BACKING LENGTH	WOF PIECES NEEDED
Up to 40" long	1 (no seam required)
41" long to 80" long	2
Over 80" long	3 or more

1. Refer to the table above to determine how many WOF pieces you need for the length of the backing.

Our example quilt backing length is 88" and requires 3 WOF pieces.

2. Multiply the number of WOF pieces you need by the *width* of the backing.

3 x 78" = 234"

3. Divide this by 36" to get yardage.

234" ÷ 36" = 6.5 yards

4. Round up to the next ⅛ or ¼ yard to account for fabric possibly being skewed off the bolt. This is the amount of yardage you need to buy.

Round up ⅛ yard. You need 6⅝ yards of fabric.

Pattern Match at the Seamlines

Imagine you've chosen the perfect backing fabric. You trim the selvages, sew it together and... it looks totally wonky and mismatched! The designs are cut off in the middle or the seam is super obvious. This is where pattern matching comes into play. Taking the time to do this is not difficult, and results in a quilt back that looks amazing.

- Cut the lengths of fabric needed for the backing.
- Trim the selvages, making sure that the trim line is as straight as possible along the pattern.
- Place the first backing piece on your ironing board, *right* side up.
- On the second piece of backing fabric, fold a straightened edge under ½" to the wrong side (*wrong* sides together).
- Press to create a crisp edge.
- Using a washable glue stick, run a light line of glue along the folded ½" of fabric. Keep the glue away from the crease edge so it doesn't gum up your needle later. (Fig. 1)
- Place this folded fabric *right* side up (*glue side down*) onto the fabric on the ironing board, lining up the print as you go. (Fig. 2)
- Be sure to overlap at least ½" of the first piece to guarantee a sufficient seam allowance.
- Ensure the prints are matching, the fabric placement is correct, and there is at least ½" overlap. (Fig. 3)
- Using a hot, dry iron, adhere the folded fabric to the bottom fabric.
- Carefully unfold the top fabric and smooth it over the bottom fabric, right sides together. (Fig. 4)
- Pin, if needed.
- Sew along the creased line.
- Trim the seam allowance to ½".
- Peel the glued fabric apart and press the seams open.

EXTRA FABRIC NEEDED

Directional fabrics have distinctly repeating pattens. Depending on the distance between repeats, you will likely need extra fabric to ensure you have enough to match the patterns.

Fig. 1

Fig. 2

Fig. 3

Fig. 4

LAYER AND BASTE THE QUILT SANDWICH

- Make the quilt sandwich by layering the top, batting, and backing. Basting holds the layers together so they can be quilted.
- Pin basting is my go-to method. I find with practice, this method is the quickest and cleanest way of basting a quilt. I use curved basting pins made specially for quilters. They look like standard safety pins but have a curved shaft. These make pin basting a snap.
- On a solid surface (floor or table), place the quilt backing right side *down*. Smooth the fabric with your hands and forearms. Remember, you'll be pin basting through the layers, so choose a surface that can take a little scratching without damage.
- Tape the edges of the backing fabric to the surface with painter's tape so the fabric is smooth but not stretched.
- Center the batting over the quilt backing and starting at the center of the quilt, smooth outwards until the batting is flat. Hopefully, the batting is slightly smaller than the quilt backing so you can see exactly where you are placing it.

LONGARM QUILTING

If you are planning to have your quilt quilted by a longarm quilter, do not layer and baste it! Once your quilt top, batting, and backing are prepared and trimmed to the right dimensions, you are good to go.

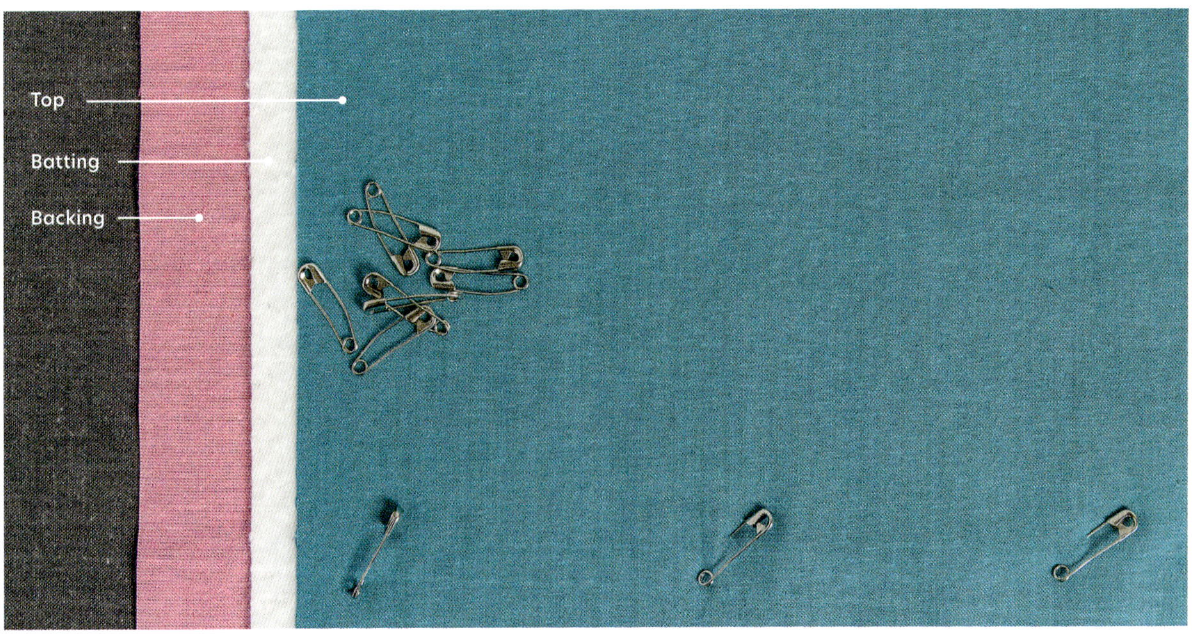

- Center the quilt top right side *up* over the batting. Starting at the center of the quilt and moving out, again smooth any wrinkles.
- Starting at the center of the quilt top and moving out toward the sides, use basting pins to pin through all three layers of the quilt sandwich.
- Pin every 3–4" over the entire quilt top, smoothing the fabric as you go.
- Take care not to push or stretch the top as you smooth it.
- Although it may be tempting to space the pins further apart, resist the urge. More space between the pins increases the chances of the fabrics or batting shifting while quilting.
- Your quilt is ready to be hand quilted, quilted on a domestic machine, or hand tied!

LARGE QUILTS The layering process can be hard with large quilts. Getting the batting and then the quilt top centered without shifting the layers underneath is really tough. So, after the backing is taped down, fold the batting in half. Place it over half the backing and then unfold it over the other half of the backing and smooth. Do the same for the quilt top. This helps keep the backing and batting from shifting.

Take Care of Your Body

- Basting on the floor can be difficult and rough on your body. Kneel on a pillow, take breaks, and stretch often.
- A large table is another good option. It's easier on your back than the floor. Some quilters buy bed risers to put under the legs of a table, which raises the table to a height that reduces bending and strain on their backs.
- Some quilt shops let their customers use the large tables in their classrooms to pin baste quilts. Check with your local shop to see if this is an option.
- If kneeling on the floor or working on a table won't work for you, spray basting on a design wall is an alternative. I don't prefer it because of the chemicals and messy overspray. It doesn't hold the quilt sandwich together as well as pin basting and can be expensive. That being said, if you need to, spray baste away! I know plenty of quilters who do. Always have good ventilation when spray basting and carefully follow the manufacturer's directions.
- Closing the basting pins can stress a quilter's hands and sometimes one of us breaks a fingernail. There are specialty products made just for this! The Kwik Klip™ is one of these. It has grooves that stabilize the pin while closing it.

TYPES OF QUILTING

TYPES OF QUILTING

If you've ever seen an exquisitely stitched quilt, you understand how much quilting can enhance a project. Quilting can magnify, highlight, and bring your piecing to the next level. Quilting is functional as well. Without it, the 3 layers of the quilt sandwich would fall apart. Quilting serves both as a visually appealing element and as a practical one. Its importance cannot be overstated.

When I first began quilting, I hand quilted my projects. It was all that I knew, and I enjoyed it. Years (years!) later, I switched almost exclusively to quilting on my domestic sewing machine. A few years further down the line, I bought my longarm and I switched to quilting that way. I found joy in each quilting technique, and I'm grateful to have them all in my arsenal. There is value in knowing which type of quilting works best for your projects, and how to achieve that result. This chapter features four quilting techniques and why each would be used.

HAND TYING

When I was born, my Aunt Nancy made me a baby quilt. I loved that quilt, and slept with it well into high school. It was pieced simply, and hand tied with embroidery floss. It was a staple of my childhood, and held up through years of use.

Hand tying a quilt doesn't officially count as quilting, but tying functions the same as quilting and so has a place in this chapter. Tied quilts are soft, have a lovely drape, and feel cuddly.

Tying quilts is especially popular for baby quilts; it's a quick way to finish a quilt and the homey look of a tied quilt always works in a crib or stroller.

Hand-Tying Supplies: A Needle and Thread

Embroidery floss and Perle cotton – are the two most common types of thread used for tying quilts. Embroidery floss has a sheen to it and Perle cotton has a matte finish.

Use all 6 strands of the embroidery floss. Don't separate the Perle cotton fibers, either.

An embroidery needle– is the best choice for this hand work. Choose one with an eye large enough for your choice of thread. Refer to Equipment and Materials: *Needles*, page 18, for more information.

Hand-Tying Techniques and Tips

- Thread an embroidery needle with 18" of your chosen thread.
- Look at the basted quilt and choose where you'd like your ties to be. Plan to keep the ties about 4–5" apart. For instance: Do you want ties at the corners of each block or square? The centers? Both?
- To make a tie, push your needle through the quilt sandwich, then pull it back up again about ¼" away from the first spot.
- Cut the excess thread, leaving each tail about 2" long.
- Tie a square knot to secure and cut off the excess so there are ½" tails.
- Repeat all over the quilt.

HAND QUILTING

Hand quilting holds a special place in my heart. There is something wonderful about the repetition, and the slow, methodical progression of a hand-quilted project. My favorite thing is how hand-quilted stitches look entirely different from those done by machine. Unlike the solid stitching line a machine produces, hand quilting looks like dashed lines. These lines have character because they are not completely uniform, and that complements any quilt.

The most important part of hand quilting is consistent stitch length and spacing. Keep in mind that teeny tiny stitches won't be very visible on a project and the quilting will take forever. Long stitches will not hold the quilt sandwich together effectively and will likely snag.

Which batting you choose will affect the length of your stitches, too, and how they will look. Low-loft batting allows you to take smaller, more precise stitches. High-loft batting requires longer stitches and hides them a little but showcases the quilting design with a puffier look. Polyester and wool batting are popular among hand quilters.

Hand-Quilting Supplies

Thread

Traditional hand-quilting thread is between 12wt and 40wt. Aurifil 12wt or 28wt is perfect for this. The line of stitching will have definition without being heavy. If you'd like the quilting to really stand out as a major part of the design, use Perle cotton or embroidery floss.

Choose a complementary color thread or a contrasting one, solid-color or variegated, based on your design goals.

Needles

Choose a needle with an appropriate eye size for the thread being used. A between or quilting needle is the perfect size for hand quilting. Always use a sharp needle.

Thimble

A thimble is necessary in hand quilting to push the needle through the quilt sandwich. There are many options out there made from metal, silicone and leather, including stick-on dots. The thimble usually goes over the tip of your middle finger.

Hera marker

Use a Hera marker to mark where you'd like to stitch. A fabric marker or chalk also work well, but marks are not guaranteed to disappear, so use caution.

Hoop

To hoop or not to hoop? I don't use a hoop for hand quilting, although many quilters do. I prefer to be able to quilt different parts of my project without having to move a hoop around. Some folks keep their hand under the quilt to guide the needle and a hoop makes that easier. Since I like to hand stitch while watching television, I usually work on my lap.

I find that a pillow with a hard surface on top makes a perfect place to stitch. (I use one of my son's books.)

Needle grippers

Pulling the needle through the quilt sandwich is much easier when using needle grippers. They not only help your fingers grab the needle, but also prevent overuse injury. They protect the skin on your fingers as well, when you hand quilt for long periods of time. A small set of pliers works perfectly for this, too.

Hand-Quilting Techniques and Tips

- Once the quilt is basted, mark a section of the stitching lines with a Hera marker. (Fig. 1)
- Thread your needle with about 18" of thread. Tie a quilter's knot, page 223, at one end.
- Bring the needle up from the back of the quilt where your first stitch will begin. (Fig. 2)
- Pull the thread through and use a little bit of force to pull the knotted thread through the backing. You'll hear a "pop" sound as it pulls through. Don't pull so hard that the knot pulls up through the quilt top. You want it to be nestled in the batting so it isn't visible on the top. Use a fingernail to scratch away the blemish left where the knot pulled through the quilt backing.

Fig. 1

Fig. 2

- Make stitches by rocking the needle up and down through the quilt sandwich and advancing forward. Start by picking up 2 or 3 stitches at a time on the needle, until you feel comfortable picking up more. (Fig. 3)
- Pay attention to the length of the stitch as well as the distance between stitches.
- Pull the thread through, but don't pull the stitches too tightly. It will bunch the fabric. Continue picking up stiches on your needle, following your design line.
- When you're at the end of a section or running out of thread, bring the needle and thread up through the quilt top and tie a knot about ⅓–½" from where the thread emerged from the fabric. (Fig. 4)
- Keeping the needle parallel to the quilt sandwich, push the tip through the quilt top and batting, but not through the backing fabric. Guide the needle tip back up through the top about an inch away, and pop the knot through the fabric into the batting.
- Hold the thread taut and trim the thread, using a set of snips. (Fig. 5)

SECURE THE TAIL OF THICK THREAD If using thick thread to hand quilt, you may not be able to pop a knot through the quilt top to secure the tail at the beginning and end of stitching. In this case, start a couple of stitches ahead of the starting point on the line where you plan to stitch. Take a long stitch *backwards* through the top fabric and batting, not through the backing, and come up at the starting point. Repeat this in the opposite direction to end stitching.

Fig. 3

Fig. 4

Fig. 5

THE QUILTER'S KNOT

This is a helpful skill to have when hand stitching, whether quilting, appliquéing, or sewing down a binding. The knot is secure but not bulky so it won't show beneath your fabrics.

- Thread a needle and keep the lead section of the thread shorter than the tail section.
- Hold the threaded needle and anchor the end of the tail section of thread between your thumb and pointer finger.
- Wrap the tail thread around the needle 2 or 3 times. (Fig. 1)
- Pull the wrapped thread down over the needle between your thumb and pointer finger, and down the whole length of thread. (Fig. 2)
- The thread will knot just at the end of the tail, leaving you with a small knot perfect for hand sewing. (Fig. 3)

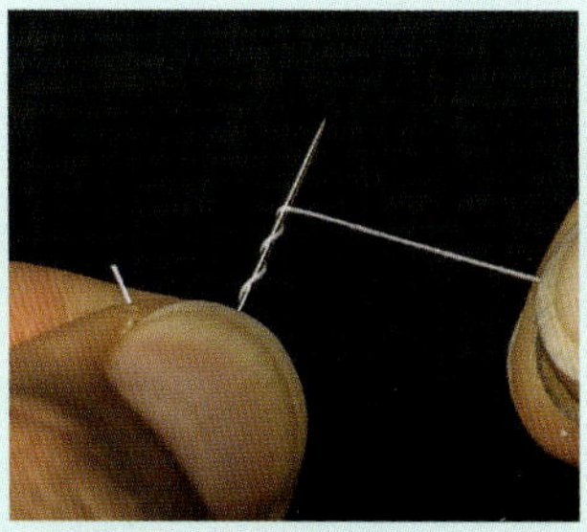

Fig. 1

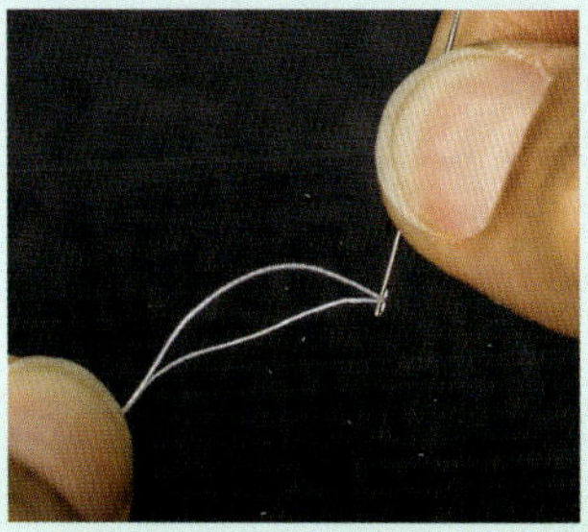

Fig. 2

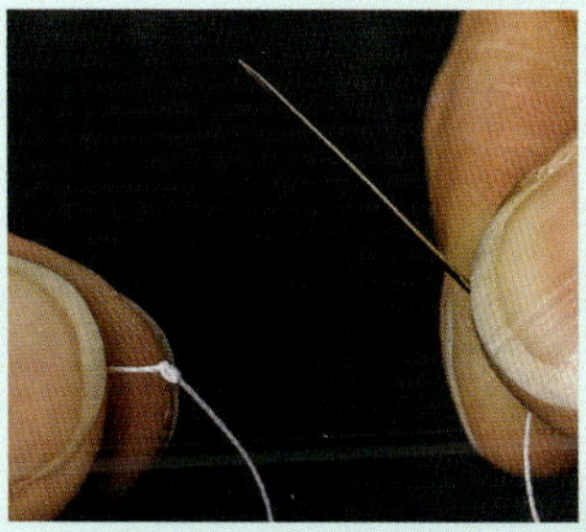

Fig. 3

DOMESTIC-MACHINE QUILTING

Quilting on a domestic sewing machine is a great option. You likely have a sewing machine for piecing; try using that machine for quilting, too! Not only can you save money by doing the quilting yourself, but you can quilt on your own time, at your own pace, and with your own design sense. There are two main ways to use your domestic machine for quilting: straight-line quilting and free motion quilting.

Straight-Line Quilting

Using a walking foot, a quilter can stitch straight or gently curved lines on a quilt. Channel quilting, crosshatch, and stitching along the seam lines (known as "in the ditch") are a few of the simpler designs for a walking foot. In addition, straight-line quilting can be used to create complex patterns.

There are many books out there with beautiful patterns. Check out both *WALK: Master Machine Quilting with Your Walking Foot* and *WALK 2.0: More Machine Quilting with Your Walking Foot* by Jacquie Gering.

Some sewing machines have a dual-feed system that works similarly to a walking foot. Experiment with it to see if it quilts as smoothly as a walking foot. Many quilters who have dual-feed use it for piecing but still prefer a walking foot to manage the three layers of a quilt sandwich.

Free Motion Quilting

The feed dogs under the stitch plate on your sewing machine keep your fabric moving straight ahead. Lowering them lets the quilt move in any direction, known as "free motion". This enables you to stitch a design "drawn" by the way you slide the quilt under the needle. This is a great technique for swirls, pebbles and other organic shapes.

Free motion quilting on a domestic machine requires patience and practice. The goal is to move the fabric at an even speed under the needle so that the stitches are a consistent length. Don't be intimidated if your first attempt doesn't yield the results you were hoping to see. With practice you'll see improvements.

Some newer machines come equipped with a stitch regulator that adjusts the speed of stitching in relation to how quickly or slowly you are moving the quilt under the needle. This makes it easier to keep your stitch length consistent.

Domestic-Machine Quilting Supplies

Presser feet

There are two basic sewing machine presser feet for machine quilting. Use a walking foot for straight-line and gentle-curve quilting. A walking foot feeds the layers of the quilt through the machine evenly, ensuring the layers won't shift or pucker while being quilted.

Use a free motion foot for free motion quilting. This foot has a spring to give it more motion and lighten the pressure on the foot so you can move the quilt smoothly under the needle.

Thread

Depending on the look you want, there's a variety of thread to pick from. Many quilters use a standard 50wt thread. Other quilters prefer a slightly heavier weight to give the quilting more definition. Thread comes in solid colors and variegated colors which add more pizzazz, if that's what you're looking for. It's all a part of making your project reflect your own design sense.

Needles

True to their name, quilting needles are perfect for machine quilting. If using a heavier weight thread, use a larger size needle. Some quilters prefer a top-stitch needle for machine quilting with a 40wt or heavier thread because it has a longer groove to guide the thread through the needle's eye.

Quilting gloves

Wearing quilting gloves helps your hands grip the quilt top as you slide it under the needle, providing more control. The nubby dots on the gloves do some of the work, saving your hands and shoulders from overuse.

Marking Tools

Marking your quilt ahead of time provides a map for the quilting, making it easier to know where to stitch. Quilters use a variety of marking tools including Hera markers, disappearing fabric markers, and painter's tape. Always use caution with markers, sometimes they don't truly "disappear". Refer to Piecing Basics: *Fabric Markers*, page 52, for more information.

Guide bars

By attaching a guide bar to your walking foot and using your previously stitched lines as guides, you'll be able to sew evenly spaced, parallel lines. Every sewing machine I've owned has come with the right-side guide bar, but not the left. (Why don't they give you both?!) If you need a left guide bar, just insert the right-side guide bar upside down on the left of the presser foot and use it that way.

Domestic-Machine Quilting Techniques and Tips

While you're practicing and getting up to speed on your machine-quilting skills, consider these ways to make your life easier.

- Use a machine with a large throat space. I cannot stress this enough. The simplest way to make quilting on your domestic machine easier is to do it on a machine that can accommodate your quilt. A small throat space will not have enough room to comfortably maneuver the quilt. A larger throat space can fit the rolled-up part of the quilt that isn't currently being stitched. That being said, there are people (magicians!) who quilt very large quilts on their domestic machines.
- Distribute the weight of the quilt. Let the quilt drape into your lap so the entire weight of the quilt is not pulling down on the section being stitched.
- Use an extension table, both in front of and to the side of your machine, to further distribute the weight of the quilt. An extension table supports the quilt so there is less drag while you're maneuvering it under the needle. That in turn makes it easier to stitch smooth curves and have a consistent stitch length. (The table will also save your shoulders and arms from having to support the weight of the quilt).
- Use a walking foot when quilting straight lines and gentle curves. This is an absolute must for me!
- Always bring the bobbin thread up before starting to quilt. If you don't do this, there will be a matted nest of thread on the back side of the quilt.
- To secure the thread at the beginning and end of a line of stitching, take a few stitches in place. Another way is to knot the thread tails by hand and bury them in the batting.
- Roll the excess fabric up neatly. Having the quilt sandwich in a tidy roll makes maneuvering it through the sewing machine much easier.
- Remove the basting pins as you quilt. When you come to a basting pin, remove it and continue to stitch. Sewing over a safety pin is not fun and hard to remove (ask me how I know!).
- Plan out your quilting ahead of time. Mark your design on the quilt before you begin quilting. This will give you a plan and a blueprint to follow as you quilt. I like to use a Hera marker which creates a small crease.

QUILTING PARALLEL LINES Quilting straight, parallel lines gives a quilt a streamlined, modern look and it's easy. Start by finding the center of your project. Mark a center line across it and quilt that line first; then use that line as a guide for the adjacent lines. Continue using each previous line as your guide until you've completed the quilting.

LONGARM-MACHINE QUILTING

While the needle on a domestic sewing machine is stationary and the quilt moves under it, the needle of a longarm machine moves and the quilt is stationary. Longarms are specifically made just for quilting and have a deep, wide throat space which allows a large area of the quilt to be stitched before repositioning it. This space, and the resulting ability to see a large section of the quilt, allows longarm quilters to create intricate designs that would be difficult or impossible to create with a domestic machine.

To start, a quilt is loaded onto the frame of the longarm. The horizontal section that is visible in the throat space is stitched. When that first section is finished, the quilt is advanced and work begins on the next section. This continues until the entire quilt is stitched.

The size of the visible and "quilt-able" area depends on the depth of the machine's throat. An 18" throat won't allow as much space for quilting as a 26" throat. In general, a larger throat space is advantageous for the longarm quilter because more of the quilt can be quilted on each pass. There are two main types of longarms, hand-guided and computer-guided.

Hand-Guided Longarm Machines

Hand-guided longarm machines are "driven" by the longarm quilter, either by free motion quilting, using a pantograph, or doing ruler work.

Free motion on a longarm

In free motion longarm quilting, the quilter is not following a pattern and stitches how and where they like. There may be a general motif, but the quilter is not bound to a specific pattern. Free motion can be as simple as an all-over meander, or as difficult as a dense, highly complex design.

Longarm quilting using a pantograph

Pantographs are paper patterns the quilter follows to replicate designs onto a quilt. Pantographs are usually purchased by a longarmer who often has quite a few. Customers can choose their desired quilting motif by browsing through the selection the quilter has on hand.

Longarm ruler work

Ruler work takes longer and requires more skill than using pantographs or creating simple free motion designs. This is completely customized quilting where the longarmer uses rulers to achieve a specific look or design. Some longarmers are highly skilled and create amazing works of art with rulers.

Computer-Guided Longarm Machines

Computer-guided longarm machines allow the quilter to stitch out almost any pattern. A computer-guided longarm is controlled by a computerized tablet containing a large number of patterns. It is able to stitch out highly stylized and accurate patterns without being driven by the quilter. Additional patterns are easily purchased online and downloaded to a memory stick inserted into the tablet. These patterns can be resized, flipped, rotated, and duplicated to achieve the desired look, so there is versatility in quilting design. Many modern quilters like the precise quilting a computerized machine affords. They love the fact that they don't have to drive the machine to create beautiful stitching. I love that I can set up my design, press a button, and the machine stitches out the pattern while I stand back and watch.

One of the best features of a computerized system is its flexibility. If I don't have a pattern that appeals to my client, I can easily do a search online, find one that works, buy it, and download it. It's so fast. If my client isn't sure what they want, I can pull up a bunch of designs that they can compare side by side. I'm able to modify and crop out parts of a design, or insert patterns into specific areas. The versatility is amazing!

WHY USE A LONGARM QUILTER?

Many quilters send their quilts to a longarm quilter to have them quilted. Years ago I sent a quilt to one, and honestly, it was simply because I had no idea how to quilt it myself. Someone I met early in my machine-quilting journey told me quilters just handed their quilts over to a professional, and I went along with it.

I remember not really understanding what a longarm quilter did, other than put some stitching onto the quilt sandwich. Now that I have lots of experience with quilting on a longarm, I understand why it's a popular way to have your quilts finished.

There are plenty of reasons you would utilize longarm quilting services. These are some I've heard from my clients:

- I only enjoy piecing my quilt tops; I don't enjoy the quilting.
- I like the intricate designs a longarm can achieve.
- I'm not interested in getting on the floor to baste my quilt.
- I hate trying to quilt on my domestic machine.
- My hands hurt when I try to quilt.
- It's way easier for me to have someone else quilt it.
- My domestic machine isn't big enough to handle my quilt.
- I just want to be done with this project.
- I appreciate the patterns my longarm quilter suggests to me.
- I want custom quilting on my project.
- I don't feel creative with the quilting; I want someone else to do that part.
- I trust my longarm quilter to make my quilt look amazing.

Consult with your longarm quilter ahead of time to hear their preferences for batting and backing sizes and prepping your quilt for them. Have a talk about your heart's desire for your quilt, to be sure you're on the same wavelength. Then relax and let them work their magic.

FINISHING: BINDING, FACING, AND MORE

If you've made it this far, congratulations! You are *this close* to finishing your quilt. Most of the hard work is done and all that remains is finishing the edges, which usually means applying a binding. Some people love the binding process; it can be relaxing and feel satisfying because it is the very last part of the quilt. Other people hate it because it is another step that needs completing when all they want to do is use the quilt and move on to the next project. I fall somewhere in the middle. While I'm anxious to get my quilt finished, I don't mind the binding step. Whether you're a take-your-time-and-enjoy-the-process person, or an I-want-this-done-NOW person, there is a technique for you here.

There are a few common ways of finishing a quilt: traditional binding, facing, and self binding (using the backing as binding). One is not inherently better than another, but there are practical uses for each.

FINISHING: BINDING, FACING AND MORE

BUT FIRST...TRIMMING

This may seem obvious: Trimming is an important step toward getting your quilt ready for binding. Now that the quilting is done, trim the excess batting and fabric using a rotary cutter. This ensures you have straight edges and square corners to sew the binding to.

Note: If you will be using the backing as the binding, do not trim this way. Refer to Self Binding, *page 250, for instructions.*

- Use two rulers: an 18" × 18" square for the corners and a 6" × 24" rectangle for the long edges.
- When trimming, always leave ¼" outside of any piecing for the binding's seam allowance.
- If you are using a wider binding that you want to show as wider on the front to get a "chunky" look, leave enough of the quilt sandwich *past the ¼" seam allowance* to fill the finished width of the binding.
- Start at one corner and align the edges of the square ruler with the edges of the quilt. See *Split the Difference*, page 235, for a tip about trimming.
- Trim the quilt's edges with a rotary cutter. Leave the ruler in place.
- Next, align the long ruler with the edge of the quilt and the side of the square ruler.
- Continue to trim down the side of the quilt.
- Move down the quilt, aligning the ruler with the quilt's edges and continue trimming.

- Overlap each section to be trimmed with a small section of the previous one to ensure that the line of trimming is continuously straight. Or, if you have another long ruler, align it with both the edge of the quilt and the edge of the first ruler to continue trimming.
- At the next corner, use the square ruler again, aligning it with the corner and the previous trimmed edge. Trim.
- Continue in this way around the rest of the quilt.

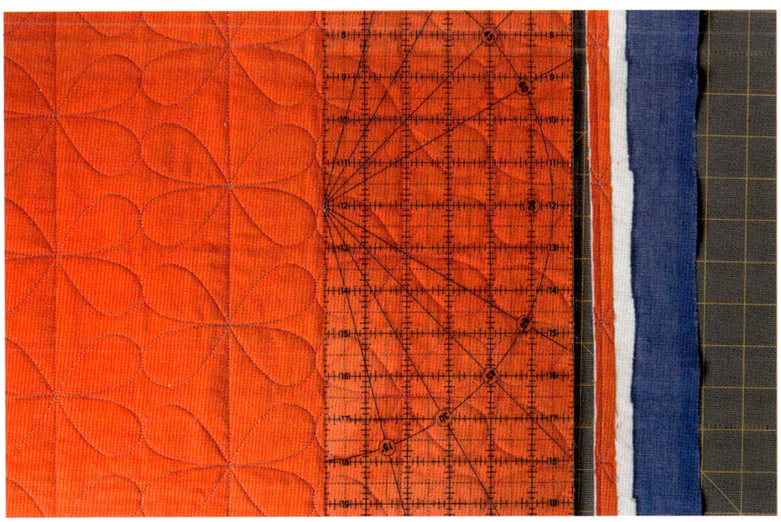

SPLIT THE DIFFERENCE

When aligning a ruler's edges with the quilt's edges, also align some of the ruler lines with seamlines on the quilt. This is not always easy because many quilts will never be *exactly* square. But if you don't at least try to do this, you may end up with a quilt that looks a little wonky because it has square corners and straight edges that aren't square with the piecing seamlines of the quilt. (Of course, this doesn't matter with freeform, improvisational quilts! See my quilt, *Winging It*, page 146, for an example of this.) Do your best and split the difference, usually less than ⅛", between the quilt's edges and the seamlines.

BINDING

Binding is a band of folded fabric that covers the raw edges of a quilt. It acts as a frame for your quilt top, protects the edges of the quilt sandwich, feels soft to the touch, and gives the quilt a finished look. In addition, binding adds a design element to your project.

How to Make Binding

There are two types of binding I use regularly. Binding made with WOF strips cut on the straight-of-grain, and binding made with strips cut on the bias. Straight-of-grain strips are the standard. They are quicker and easier to cut and use less fabric. While bias-cut binding wears a bit longer, the difference is negligible.

Bias-cut strips have more stretch. Definitely use them for curved and scalloped edges. If you're using a directional print you'd like to show on the diagonal, such as a stripe, cut bias strips for that too.

I cut binding strips at 2¼" wide if my quilt backing is quilting cotton, or 2½" wide if I'm backing my quilt with thick fabrics, like Minky or fleece. If you prefer a chunky binding, cut your strips wider.

Straight-of-Grain Binding

- Use width-of-fabric (WOF) strips, cut from selvage to selvage. Strips cut from the lengthwise grain have almost no give to them and make the binding more difficult to fold smoothly over the quilt's edges and corners.

- Determine the perimeter of the quilt and add 10". Why add 10"? Having some extra length when you join the ends of the strips makes that part of the process just a little easier, too. If your project is a small wall hanging, add less.

For example, if the quilt is 50" × 60", the perimeter would be
50" + 50" + 60" + 60" which is 220".
Add 10" to that to get 230".
For this example quilt, you need 230" of binding.

- Divide the length of binding by 42" minus the cut width of your binding. Round up to figure out how many strips of fabric you need. Why 42" minus the binding width? First, WOF is usually around 42". Second, if you use diagonal seams to join the binding strips, like I do, the strip length loses the amount of the binding width with each join.

For this example, 42" minus 2¼" is 39¾".
You need 230" of binding.
230" ÷ 39¾" is 6 strips (rounded up).

- Use a ruler and a rotary cutter and cut your binding strips at your preferred width across the WOF.

Cut 6 strips, 2¼" × WOF.

- Put strips *right* sides together at a 90-degree angle. Mark a 45-degree (diagonal) line and stitch across, joining the strips with a diagonal seam. (Fig. 1)
- Open and check that the seam is stitched correctly, then trim the seam allowance to ¼". Press the seams open. Join all your strips. (Fig. 2)

Fig. 1

Fig. 2

WHY DIAGONAL SEAMS? Diagonal seams aren't as visible or as bulky in the finished binding. There are already enough layers for the machine's needle to pierce with the two layers of binding and the three of the quilt sandwich. A diagonal seam minimizes bulk and is easier to stitch down than a straight seam. Diagonal seams are also more flexible to fold to the back later, because they're sewn across the bias.

Bias Binding

There are different methods for cutting bias binding and the "tube method" is my favorite. When I first learned about this technique, it seemed overly fussy to me. Math? An offset tube I have to create and then cut with scissors? My brain kind of turns off when something gets too technical, so it wasn't love at first sight. I'm glad I tried it, though. It's not difficult, and it *works*. I don't make bias binding for every quilt, but when I *do* make it, this is my preferred method. I've taken the math out of the equation here (pun intended, har, har) by giving you a table with various lengths and widths of binding (see opposite page) so you can simply cut and sew.

Start with a Square

- Measure the perimeter of the quilt and add 10".

For example, if the quilt is 50" × 60", the perimeter is
50" + 50" + 60" + 60" = 220".
220" + 10" = 230".
For this example quilt, you need 230" of binding.

- Next, consult the table "Square Sizes for Bias Binding Tube Method", (opposite), for the size square to cut.

Or, if you'd rather do the math yourself, here's how.

- Multiply the binding length by the cut width of your binding strips. Find the square root of that number.

230" x 2¼" = 517½". The square root of 517½" is 22¾".

- Multiply the binding width by 1.414 and add that number to the square root. (This accounts for the fabric lost in the seam allowance.) Round up and now you have the size square of binding fabric you need to create enough binding for your quilt.

2¼" x 1.414 = 3¼".
22¾" + 3¼" = 26".
You need a 26" x 26" square of binding fabric.

WHY THE TUBE METHOD? This method is my favorite for a few reasons. First, there's less wasted fabric because there's a mathematical formula to get exactly the length of binding needed. Second, it's a time saver because there's no need to sew together individually cut binding strips. And third? For diagonal prints, like stripes, matching the pattern is super easy. It's the absolute best way to do it!

Square Sizes for the Bias Binding Tube Method

BINDING LENGTH NEEDED	SQUARE SIZE FOR CUTTING 2"-WIDE STRIPS	SQUARE SIZE FOR CUTTING 2¼"-WIDE STRIPS	SQUARE SIZE FOR CUTTING 2½"-WIDE STRIPS
100"	18" × 18"	19" × 19"	20" × 20"
125"	19" × 19"	21" × 21"	22" × 22"
150"	21" × 21"	22" × 22"	23" × 23"
175"	22" × 22"	24" × 24"	25" × 25"
200"	23" × 23"	25" × 25"	26" × 26"
225"	25" × 25"	26" × 26"	28" × 28"
250"	26" × 26"	27" × 27"	29" × 29"
275"	27" × 27"	29" × 29"	30" × 30"
300"	28" × 28"	30" × 30"	32" × 32"
325"	29" × 29"	31" × 31"	33" × 33"
350"	30" × 30"	32" × 32"	34" × 34"
375"	31" × 31"	33" × 33"	35" × 35"
400"	32" × 32"	34" × 34"	36" × 36"
425"	33" × 33"	35" × 35"	37" × 37"
450"	33" × 33"	36" × 36"	38" × 38"
475"	34" × 34"	36" × 36"	39" × 39"
500"	35" × 35"	37" × 37"	39" × 39"

Bias Binding Tube Method

- Cut the fabric square in half diagonally from corner to corner.
- Place the resulting triangles *right* sides together, aligning short sides. Leave ¼" of each triangle free on the sides. Sew together using a ¼" seam allowance. (Fig. 1)
- Open the fabric up to a parallelogram shape and press the seam open.
- Using a ruler and fine-tipped pen or pencil, measure and mark parallel lines on the *wrong* side of the fabric. The distance between the lines should be the width of your binding. For example, if you want 2¼"-wide binding, mark lines 2¼" apart. (Fig. 2) After marking the lines, trim any excess fabric.
- Make a short snip along the line at Point A. Bring the short ends of the parallelogram *right* sides together and offset the marked lines by one strip, matching Points A and B. (Fig. 2) Pin. *Note: the marked lines should intersect at the ¼" seamline. (Fig. 3)*
- Sew with a ¼" seam allowance. Press open.
- Start at the offset line and cut along the uninterrupted drawn lines until you have your long bias fabric strip. Use scissors, *not* a rotary cutter. Voilà—bias binding!

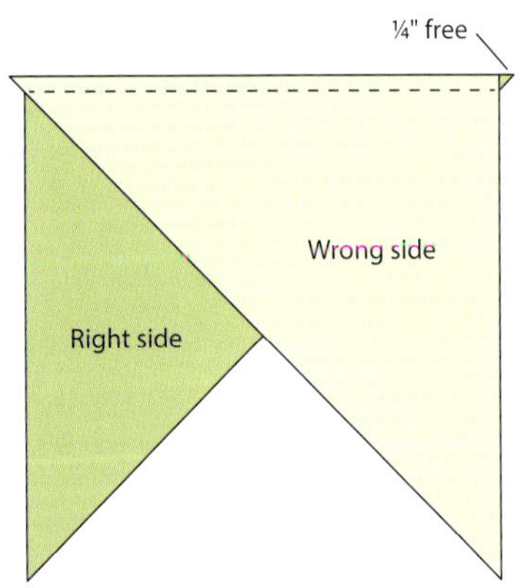

Fig. 1

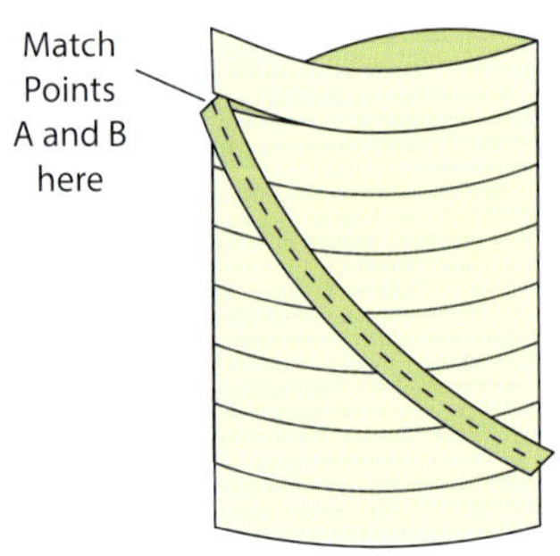

Fig. 3

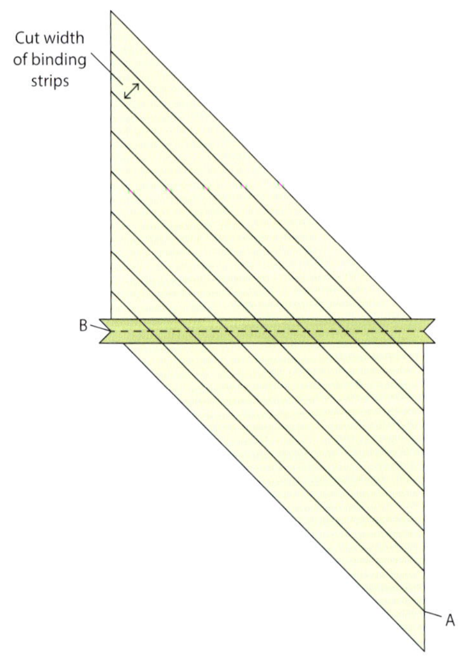

Fig. 2

MANAGEABLE CUTTING

CUTTING LARGE SQUARES

Trying to cut large squares can be difficult if you don't have a big cutting table. To make this step more manageable, first cut a width of fabric (folded selvage to selvage) the size you need for the square. Leave the fabric folded. Divide the size square you need by 2. Measuring from the fold, trim the fabric down to that size. (Trim the selvage edges; don't cut off the fold.) Open and press.

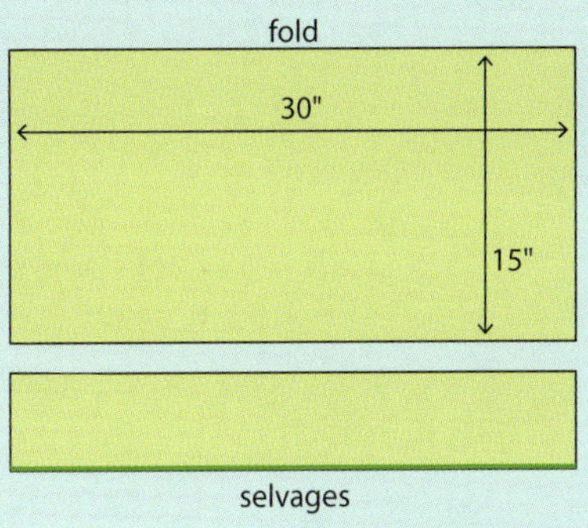

To get a 30" square, trim the folded fabric to 15".

CUTTING ON THE DIAGONAL

Cutting a large square on the diagonal can be awkward and imprecise. To make it easier, fold the square in half diagonally to make a triangle. Place a ruler across the triangle through the point of the 90-degree corner and aligned with the fold of the triangle. Cut through the fold and the point. Unfold the resulting triangles and you have the large squares you need.

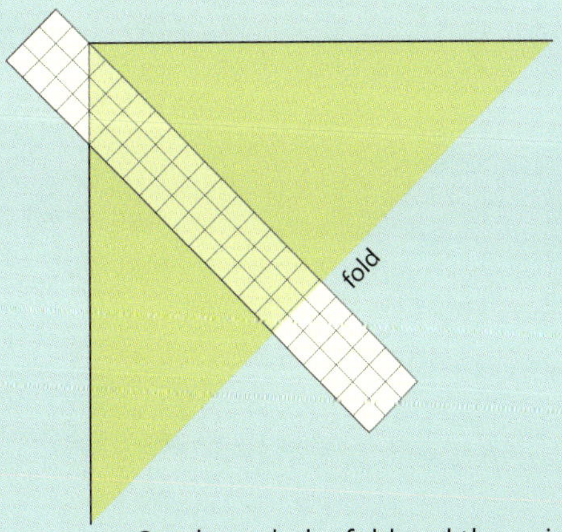

Cut through the fold and the point.

Attach the Binding to the Quilt

Sew the binding to the front of the quilt with a sewing machine. Use a walking foot or, at the very least, a dual-feed system. This greatly reduces the likelihood of wrinkled, stretched, or uneven binding. If you get skipped stitches while attaching or finishing the binding, switch to a heavier needle. Denim needles are great for sewing through multiple layers of fabric and batting.

Start Binding

- Fold the binding *wrong* sides together so the long raw edges are aligned.
- Press with a steam iron. Some quilters use a starch alternative to keep the fold crisp, especially with a bias binding. It keeps the bias from stretching during the process.
- You may choose to attach the binding to the quilt with pins or binding clips prior to stitching. This ensures the strips stay put while they're being sewn.
- Use a walking foot and set your stitch length a little longer than usual, 2.4 or more, because you are sewing through many layers.
- Starting in the middle of one edge of the quilt, align the raw edges of the binding with the raw edge of the quilt.
- Leave a 10" section of binding free and backstitch to start sewing the binding to the quilt. Use a ¼" seam allowance.

THE EXCEPTIONS TO THE RULE These are two reasons for you to start by machine sewing the binding to the *back* of the quilt, not the front. (See *Finishing by Machine*, page 246.)

1. If you are using a fluffy fabric for the backing, like Minky or fleece, sew the binding to the back and wrap it to the front for both hand finishing and machine finishing. Here's why: If you hand finish the binding, it's difficult to hand stitch to the fluffy fabric. If you machine finish the binding, glue is used and it's less effective with fluffy backings.

2. If you want the absolute fastest method, machine sewing the binding to the back and then to the front skips the gluing step. Use a decorative stitch that crosses the fold to hold it down on the front. Or, if you've got a precise eye and a steady hand, topstitch along the edge of the fold to secure.

Turn the Corners

- As you near the corner of the quilt, stop stitching ¼" away from the edge. Backstitch to secure.
- Rotate the quilt and fold the binding strip up at a 45-degree angle over the previously sewn side. (Fig. 1)
- Then fold the binding strip down over itself and align it with the second side of the quilt. (Fig. 2)
- Backstitch to start and stitch down the second edge of the quilt.
- Repeat this process at all 4 corners.

PLAN AHEAD If the seams in the binding strip hit at the corners of the quilt, the extra fabric will result in a bulky corner. To avoid this, check before stitching that none of the binding's seams will be at a corner. If they are, reposition the start point until that is avoided.

Fig. 1

Fig. 2

Three Ways to Join the Tails

As you approach the point where you started stitching the binding to the quilt, stop about 15" short and backstitch. Leaving this space will allow you to easily join the binding tails.

Believe it or not, I have talked to long-time quilters who say they hate joining the binding tails so much that they just avoid binding their own quilts. This is totally unnecessary! There are multiple ways to join binding tails and there is truly a simple and understandable way for every quilter to do it without frustration.

Binding Tails—Diagonal Seam

This technique requires accuracy and can be a little fussy but it is the most commonly used. It matches the other diagonal seams in the binding, is less visible than other methods, and minimizes bulk.

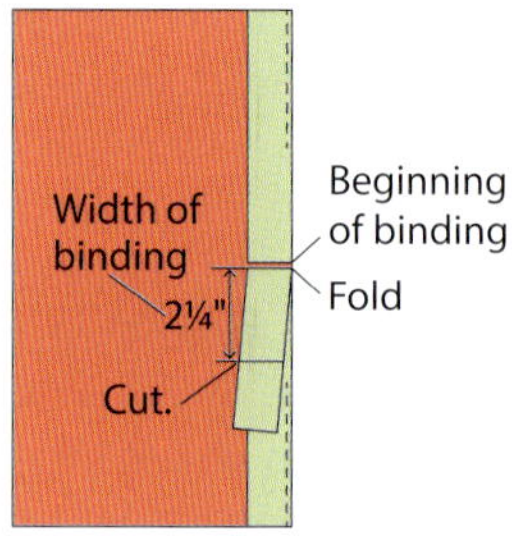

Fig. 1

- Fold the tails back on themselves so the folds meet. Crease the fabric at the folds.
- Trim the tails so one overlaps the other by the width of the binding. (Fig. 1) For example, if you started with a 2¼"-wide binding strip, you want the tails to overlap 2¼". (Use a ruler to measure this or open a trimmed excess piece and measure with that.)

Fig. 2

- Unfold the binding tails and place the ends *right* sides together at a 90-degree angle. (Fig. 2)
- Join with a diagonal seam. (Fig. 3)

Fig. 3

- Open the seam and check that the tails are joined correctly. Trim the excess fabric and finger press the seam. (Fig. 4)
- Re-fold the binding strip and finger press.
- Sew the last section of the binding strip to the quilt using a ¼" seam. Backstitch at the beginning and end.

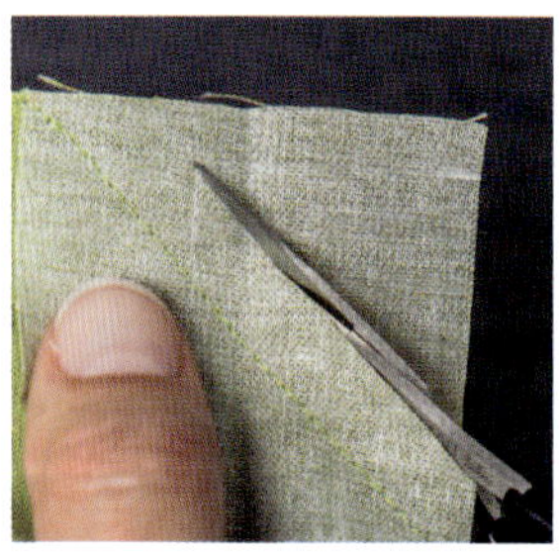

Fig. 4

Binding Tails—Straight Seam

This is a quick and easy way to connect the binding tails. It's especially good for small projects where there isn't room for a diagonal seam.

Note: while this method is simpler than the diagonal one, it's bulkier and more visible.

- Fold excess length of the tails back on themselves so the folds meet. Crease the fabric at the folds.
- Trim tails ¼" beyond each of the folds. (Fig. 5)
- Place fabric *right* sides together matching the folds.
- Sew with a straight stitch using a ¼" seam allowance. Finger press the seam. (Fig. 6)
- Re-fold the binding strip and finger press.
- Sew the last section of the binding strip to the quilt using a ¼" seam allowance. Backstitch at the beginning and end.

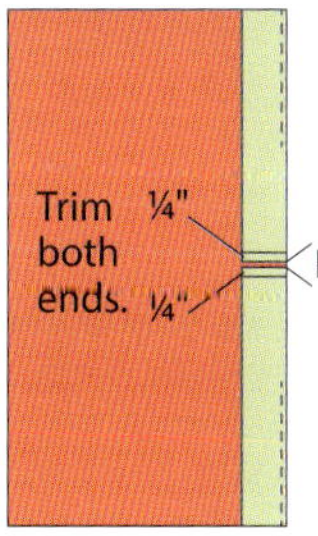

Fig. 5

Fig. 6

Binding Tails—Taco Method

This is a simple way to join binding tails with no measuring. Be aware that this method has the most bulk of the three and includes some hand sewing.

- Open one binding tail. Fold it *wrong* sides together at a 45-degree angle. Finger press to create a crease.
- Unfold the tail and trim ¼" from the crease. (Fig. 7)
- Place the second binding tail inside the trimmed tail. (Fig. 8)
- Trim the second tail ¼" longer than the first. When the tails are folded together, the second should be completely covered by the first. (Fig. 9) It's as if the first is the "taco" and the second is the "filling". (Fig. 10)
- Sew this last section of the binding strip to the quilt using a ¼" seam. Backstitch at the beginning and end.
- There is an unsewn section where the second tail goes inside the first one. The end of the taco is open! Hand sew it closed.

Fig. 7

Fig. 8

Fig. 9

Fig. 10

Finish the Binding

The binding now needs to be wrapped to the other side of the quilt and sewn down. There are two main finishing methods: by hand and by machine.

Finishing by Hand

Hand finishing the binding is the traditional method. The stitches are almost invisible, giving the quilt a handmade look and feel. Some people really enjoy the process, despite it taking longer than finishing by machine. It's a peaceful, repetitive motion that has a Zen-like relaxing quality to it. If you plan to enter the quilt in a competition or are intentionally making an heirloom-quality quilt, choose hand binding. (That being said, I have seen machine-bound quilts hanging in judged shows.)

- Thread a bunch of needles. I usually start with six. Use thread that matches the binding.
- Tie a quilter's knot, page 223, at the end of the tails.
- Wrap the binding strip over the raw edge of the quilt. Make sure the folded edge of the binding covers the machine stitching where the binding was attached. (Fig. 1)
- Secure with binding clips.
- Check that the width of the binding on the front is consistent.
- Hide the thread's knot under the binding before beginning to stitch.
- Blind stitch the binding down by stitching up through the crease in the fold and down hiding the stitch under the binding's edge. The stitching should not go through to the front of the quilt.
- At the corners, take a stitch or two in the fold of the mitered turn on both sides of the quilt. (Fig. 2)

Finishing by Machine

Machine finishing the binding is much faster than finishing by hand and, depending on the quality of your hand stitching, may result in

Fig. 1

Fig. 2

stronger stitches. Use a straight stitch or one of your machine's decorative stitches. It's also a good method for people who have hand pain. Quilting traditionalists may tell you hand finishing is the only way to bind, but I disagree. I machine bind 95% of my quilts because of ease and speed. After experimenting for years with different methods, my favorite way to bind is by glue basting the binding before finishing by machine. It is a secure, accurate, and durable way to bind a quilt. (Binding clips or pins can be used instead of glue, but I find glue basting keeps the binding in place more precisely.)

- Place the quilt on your ironing board with the unsewn binding side up.
- Apply a thin bead of glue to a small section of the stitching where the binding was sewn to the other side. A specialty fabric glue can be used for this, but I find white washable school glue works just as well.
- Wrap the binding over the raw edge of the quilt and onto the glue. Make sure the folded edge of the binding overlaps the stitching by about ⅛". (Fig. 1)
- Use a hot, dry iron to secure the binding to the quilt. It should hold very well.
- Continue to wrap and glue the binding down all the way to a corner.
- To start the next edge of the quilt, fold the next section of the binding strip down over the glued section at a 45-degree angle. Press this well before moving on. (Figs. 2 and 3)
- Continue to wrap, glue, and iron all the way around the quilt.
- Turn the quilt over to stitch from the sewn side of the binding; the glued side will be face down. Stitch in the ditch of the seamline where the binding was machine sewn to the quilt. Use a coordinating thread to help your stitches disappear.
- Backstitch at the beginning and the end of stitching.
- Note that you won't be able to see the binding that you've glued down and are securing. If you have done a good job glue-basting, your stitching will fall exactly where it's supposed to. (Fig. 4)

Fig. 1

Fig. 2 Fig. 3

Fig. 4

FACING

Facing is used when you do not want to see a binding "frame" around the outside edges of the front of the quilt. To face a quilt, sew binding strips to the front and fold them at the seamline to the back. The strips are only visible on the back of the quilt. Facing is often used with modern quilts, wall hangings, art quilts, and projects that require a clean, minimal look.

- Measure the quilt width and length.
- Cut 2 strips of facing fabric, 2½" × the width of the quilt.
- Cut another 2 strips, 2½" × the length of the quilt minus 1".
- For example, if your quilt measures 50" × 60", cut 2 strips that are 2½" × 50", and 2 strips that are 2½" × 59".
- Fold the strips in half *wrong* sides together with the long raw edges aligned.
- On the *front* of the quilt, place the *width* strips across the top and bottom edges of the quilt, aligning the raw edges and the corners.
- Again, on the *front* of the quilt, place the *length* strips on the side edges of the quilt, aligning the raw edges. The ends of these strips will be about ½" from the corners of the quilt.
- Secure the facing strips to the quilt with binding clips. I use binding clips because the quilt sandwich is thick and pins tend to distort the edges.
- Stitch the facing down around the perimeter of the quilt, using a ¼" seam allowance. Backstitch at the beginning and end of sewing.
- Sew a diagonal line at each corner to add stability, backstitching at the beginning and end. Trim outside the diagonal stitch line to reduce bulk. (Fig. 1)
- Turn the facing to the back of the quilt precisely on the seamline. The goal is that the facing doesn't show at all on the front of the quilt. (Fig. 2)
- Push out the corners using a point turner. If you don't have one, don't fret—I've used a pointy chopstick and had great results. (Fig. 3)
- Press with a hot, steam iron.
- Stitch the facing down by hand to the backing with a blind stitch, using a matching thread color.

Fig. 1

Fig. 2

Fig. 3

Facing with Corner Triangles

Adding corner triangles to the facing is a quick and simple way to make it easy to hang small projects, like wall hangings. Wooden dowels, found at craft and hardware stores, can be cut to size.

- Measure the length and width of the quilt.
- Cut 2 strips of facing fabric, 2½" × the width of the wall hanging minus 2".
- Cut another 2 strips, 2½" × 2" *shorter* than the length of the wall hanging.
- For example, if your wall hanging measures 36" × 40", cut 2 strips that are 2½" × 34", and 2 strips that are 2½" × 38".
- Fold the strips in half *wrong* sides together with the long raw edges aligned.
- Cut 4 squares of facing fabric, 5" × 5".
- Fold the squares in half diagonally (corner to corner), *wrong* sides together.
- On the *front* of the wall hanging, align the triangles with the corners. (Fig. 1)
- Center the facing strips over the triangles on their corresponding edges of the wall hanging, aligning the raw edges. Each strip will be about 1" from the corners of the wall hanging.
- Secure the facing strips and the triangles to the wall hanging with binding clips. I use binding clips because the layers are thick and pins tend to distort the edges. (Fig. 2)

Fig. 1

Fig. 2

- Stitch the strips and triangles down around the perimeter of the wall hanging, using a ¼" seam allowance. Backstitch at the beginning and end of sewing.
- Sew a diagonal line at each corner to add stability; backstitch at the beginning and end. Trim outside the diagonal stitch line to reduce bulk. (Fig. 3)
- Turn the strips and triangles to the back of the wall hanging precisely on the seamline. The goal is that they don't show at all on the front.
- Push out the corners using a point turner or a chopstick.
- Press with a hot, steam iron.
- Stitch the strips down by hand with a blind stitch, using a matching thread color. Leave the triangles open so a dowel can be inserted for hanging. (Fig. 4)

Fig. 3

Fig. 4

SELF BINDING

This self-binding technique (also known as "backing-as-binding") folds extra backing fabric to the front of the quilt and creates a binding with it. This gives you the look of binding on the front of the quilt only, not on the back. The downside is there won't be any binding strips to cover the edges of the back of the quilt. This means any quilting that meets the edge will be visible on the backing, including heavier stitches like tie-offs and backstitching that you'd rather hide.

Projects like coasters, placemats, or potholders are perfect candidates for self binding. Joining binding tails is difficult for small projects so this method works wonders. Using the backing as binding works great with tied quilts, too, or when the quilting doesn't go all the way to the edge of the project. Leave ½"–¾" unquilted around the edges of the quilt to ensure that the quilting won't be compromised. Bury the tails of the quilting thread to have a polished finish.

- Start with the top and batting trimmed to exactly the same size and the backing trimmed to 1" *larger on all sides*. Use the techniques in *But First . . . Trimming*, page 234.
- Place the quilt *right* side up on an ironing board.
- Working on one edge of the quilt at a time, fold the backing fabric *wrong* sides together toward the edge of the quilt top. Butt the raw edge of the backing with the raw edge of the top. Press to crease.
- Apply a small bead of glue to the backing about ¼" from the edge of the top.
- Fold the backing fabric over onto the quilt top. (Fig. 1)
- Press to attach the folded fabric to the top. Pins or binding clips can be used but I find the glue to be accurate, especially on small projects where the fabric can distort easily.
- At each corner, fold the next edge of the backing at a 45-degree angle before continuing to fold, and glue it to the quilt top. This gives a mitered corner. (Figs. 2 and 3)
- Continue all the way around the quilt.
- Hand or machine stitch the backing to the quilt top. If you choose to machine stitch, use a walking foot and sew about ⅛" from the folded edge. Both straight and decorative stitches work well. (Fig. 4)

Fig. 1

Fig. 2

Fig. 3

Fig. 4

HANGING SLEEVES

A hanging sleeve is just what it sounds like: a sleeve on the back of the quilt for a wooden dowel or curtain rod to hang your project for decorative purposes. You might want to add a sleeve to every quilt you make. It seems that whenever I don't, the person I give the quilt to wants to know how to hang it. So back it comes for me to add a sleeve!

HANGING LARGE QUILTS

For a large, heavy quilt, divide the sleeve width by 2 and make two shorter sleeves. This allows you to support the quilt in the middle when hanging it. Otherwise, the dowel and quilt will eventually start to sag.

- Measure the width of the quilt and subtract 1½". This leaves room at each side to hide the dowel or rod behind the quilt when it's hanging.
- Cut a piece of fabric 9" × WOF. Trim to the width you need. For example, for a 36" × 40" quilt, cut a piece 34½" × 9" for a 4" sleeve sewn with a ½" seam allowance. (Most quilt shows ask for a 4" sleeve. A small project can do with a smaller sleeve.)
- Fold the fabric in half *right* sides together, aligning the long raw edges, and sew the raw edges together using a ½" seam allowance.
- Press to one side, not open, to give the seam more strength. (Fig. 1)
- Double fold the openings of the sleeve (the short edges) to the *wrong* side, ¼" for each fold.
- Topstitch along the edge of the folds. (Fig. 2)
- Turn the sleeve *right* side out.
- Center the seam on one side of the sleeve and press to crease the top and bottom edges of the sleeve. (Fig. 3)
- Place one long edge of the sleeve straight across the back of the quilt about ½" below the binding.
- Hand stitch the top edge of the sleeve to the backing. Use a blind stitch. Do not go through to the top of the quilt. You don't want your stitches to show on the front.
- Fold the sewn edge of the sleeve up ½" towards the top of the quilt and press the bottom edge to add a new crease.
- Smooth the sleeve and hand stitch the bottom edge to the backing, along the new crease. (Fig. 4)
- Hand stitch the bottom layer of the sleeve's side openings to the backing. Leave the top layer of the openings free to insert the dowel.

Fig. 1

Fig. 2

Fig. 3

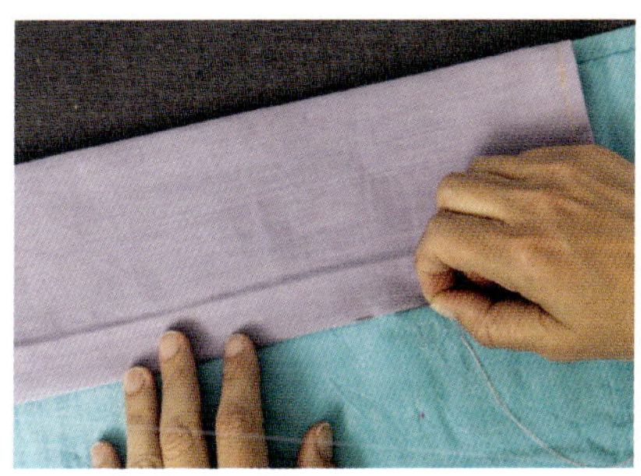
Fig. 4

QUILT LABELS

Whenever you make a quilt, you should label it. Why? Quilts often outlive the recipients. Some even last generations. Knowing where a quilt comes from adds special significance to it.

Labels are a place for adding special notes, quotes, inside jokes, or a welcome to a new baby with their birth date. They personalize a gift and show thoughtfulness.

Information to Include

What information should go on a quilt label? Really, that's up to you, but in my opinion, more is better. Load that label up with all the details you can! Labels don't take a lot of room, so it's no big deal to add information.

- *Your name and the names of other people who worked on the quilt, including the quilter if it wasn't you*
- *The name of the quilt*
- *Where and when the quilt was made*
- *The reason the quilt was made. A guild challenge or sew-along? A graduation or a new baby?*
- *Anything special about how the quilt was made or the fabrics used: hand appliqué or the silk ties from your favorite uncle when he retired*
- *The recipient's name*
- *A poem, prayer, wish, or special phrase*
- *Washing and care instructions*

PRE-WASH If you make a label with your own fabric, pre-washing is important. It removes finishing agents that weaken the bond between the fabric and the ink and make the ink more likely to fade.

Label Options

Labels can be simple or complex. I lean toward simplicity because, honestly, I just want to be done with the quilt at this point. Some folks make a-maaaaaaay-zing labels that are works of art; some purchase custom-made ones.

- Print a label onto a fusible fabric sheet using an ink-jet (not laser) printer. I prefer 100% cotton June Tailor Quilt Label Fabric Sheets. You can print whatever you want (even photos)! After printing, peel off the backing.

- Print a label on your own pre-washed fabric. Adhere the fabric to an 8½" × 11" piece of freezer paper and run it through your ink-jet printer. After printing, peel off the freezer paper.

- Hand write and/or draw the label. Use your own pre-washed fabric, an extra quilt block, or a pre-made fabric sheet. If you use your own fabric or block, stabilize it with ironed-on freezer paper or on a sandpaper board to keep it from shifting under your pen. Take short strokes, especially around curves, to avoid distortion.

- Use your sewing machine's text stitches to embroider a label. Back your fabric with wash- or tear-away stabilizer so the fabric doesn't pucker. Remove the stabilizer when you're done.

- Purchase a custom-made label. Look for vendors online (try Etsy) who create them. Have one made specifically for a quilt with that quilt's information or buy labels in bulk with just your name or signature.

Corner Labels

This technique is secure and saves a little time. Note: The label must be prepped before the binding is attached. It is sewn on *with* the binding.

1. Cut a 5" × 5" square of fabric. Fold it in half diagonally, from corner to corner, to create a triangle.

2. Write and draw the label information on the triangle. Stay about ⅓" away from the edges.

3. Heat-set the ink with a dry iron.

4. Place a few dots of glue on the back of the triangle and inside the 2 layers of the triangle.

5. Align the raw edges of the triangle with the raw edges of a corner on the back of the quilt.

6. Dry iron the label to set the glue and attach both layers of the label to the backing.

7. Sew the corner label down with the binding.

8. Hand stitch the fold of the triangle to the backing using an invisible or decorative stitch.

Adding the Label to the Quilt

For all except corner labels, the technique to attach it to your quilt back is the same. Finish this step . . . and you're done!

1. Make the label and set the ink with a dry iron.

2. Trim the label to ¼" larger than its finished size, on all sides. This is the extra "turn-under allowance".

3. Fold ¼" to the back of the label, on all sides, and press. Use a hot, dry iron for a good crease.

4. If folding the turn-under is too fussy for your fingers, cut freezer paper to the finished size and shape of the label. Fold and press the fabric around the freezer paper. Remove the paper and iron again to set the crease.

5. Put a couple of dots of glue on the back of the label and place it on the backing fabric. Dry iron to set the glue and hold the label in place.

6. Hand stitch the label to the backing using an invisible or a decorative stitch. Just be sure the stitching doesn't show on the quilt top.

PERMANENT MARKERS Use a permanent marker for hand-written and hand-drawn labels. But first test it on a scrap of fabric! Check that it doesn't bleed. Then heat set it with a dry iron and wash it to see if it fades too quickly. Once you've found a marker brand you like, stick with it.

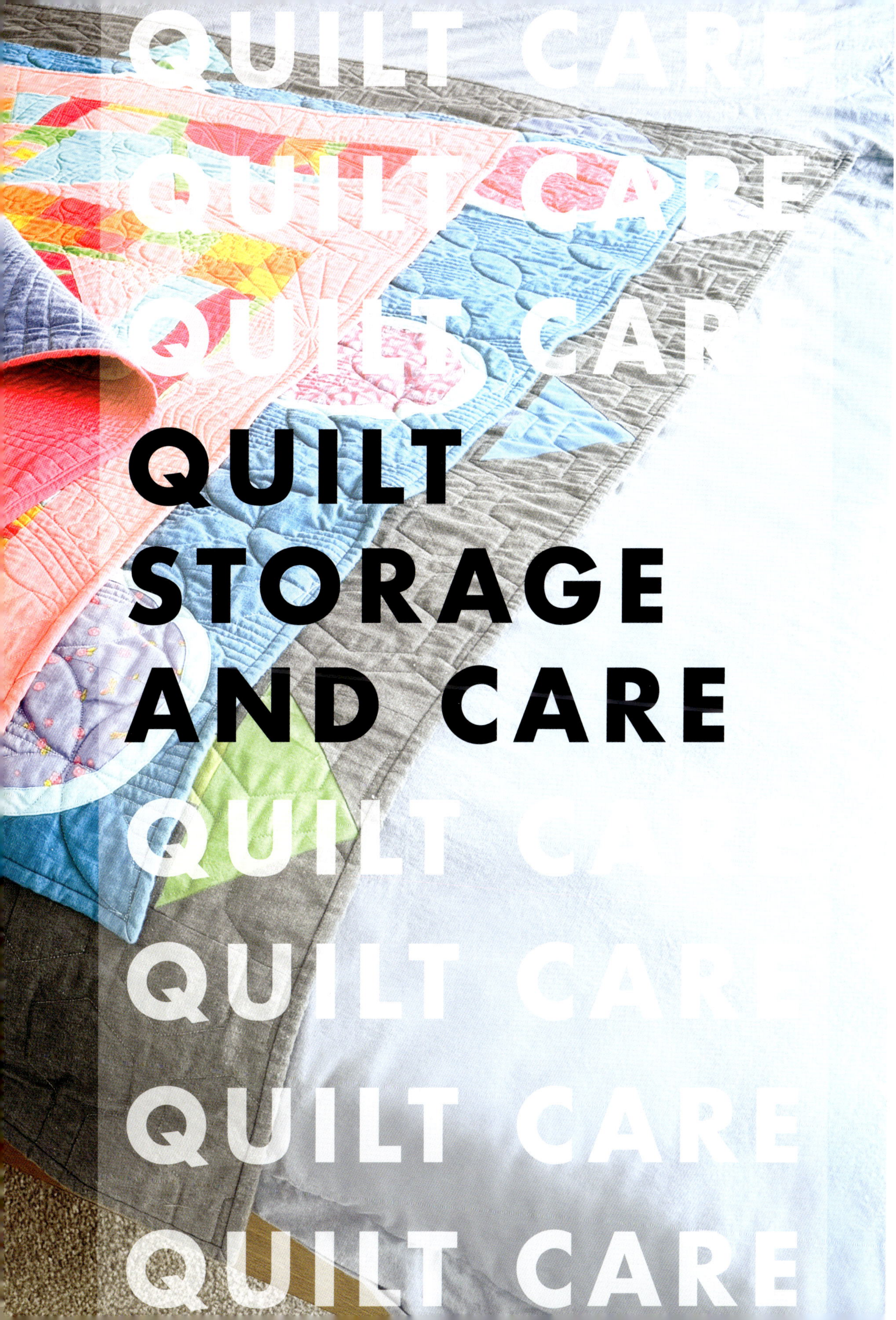

QUILT STORAGE AND CARE

QUILT STORAGE AND CARE

You've put a lot of time, money and effort into finishing your quilt, and you want to make sure it is well taken care of. There are ways to store and care for quilts that will keep them in tip-top shape for years (generations!). In my opinion, quilts are made to be used, so I keep stacks of folded quilts next to my couch. Over time, these quilts develop creases. For most of the quilts I make, this is ok, but some quilts deserve a little more care. If you are trying to store your quilt to keep it in perfect shape, these tips can help.

BEST PRACTICES FOR STORING QUILTS

- Store quilts flat. If you are able, store your quilts on a bed or other flat surface. Flat quilts won't wrinkle.
- If you don't have an unused bed for all your extra quilts, roll the quilts up with the right side in. Rolled quilts can be easily stored *under* a bed. Wrap them in a sheet to keep dust out.
- Roll a quilt around a pool noodle for rigidity and stand the quilts up in a closet. Place a sheet between the noodle and the quilt to prevent any chemical transfer. Wrap the rolled quilt in a sheet.
- Keep quilts out of the sun. Sunlight will discolor, fade, and weaken fabric.
- Regulate the temperature and humidity. Don't store quilts in areas with large temperature or humidity swings. Keep them inside the house, not the attic or garage.
- Don't store quilts in airtight bags. Cotton will deteriorate more quickly this way. Fabric needs to breathe. A cotton pillowcase or sheet is a great substitute for a plastic bag.
- Re-fold quilts periodically. If you keep your quilts folded, unfold them every now and then. Re-fold them with the creases going the opposite way. This discourages permanent wrinkles from forming.
- Keep quilts away from surfaces that might have chemicals. For instance, if you're storing a quilt in a wooden cabinet, the wood was likely treated with chemicals that can discolor it. Be aware of the surfaces your quilt will be in contact with.

WASHING QUILTS

The techniques and the fabrics used to make a quilt determine the methods used for washing it. Some quilts are more delicate than others.

Machine-Pieced Quilts

I'm fairly relaxed when it comes to washing quilts made on a sewing machine. I'm a busy mom, and I just don't have the time to hand wash my quilts. As I machine piece, quilt, and bind, I make an effort to ensure that my quilt is put together well, so it won't fall apart with machine washing. That way, hand washing won't be necessary.

Each time I make a quilt I hope that it will be used. Lots of people don't use their quilts because they don't want to get them dirty. To me, an unused quilt is a sad quilt, so USE THOSE QUILTS, PEOPLE! In this spirit, I make quilts that can stand up to regular use and washing in my home washing machine.

- This is my basic routine: Inspect the quilt. Open or loose seams and broken quilting threads get worse when the quilt is being tumbled in a washing machine. Fix any issues before washing.
- Pre-treat problem areas. If there are any stains that need extra attention, spot clean them before washing. I love OxiClean™ for this. (Test any product on a fabric scrap first.)
- Select the Gentle or Delicates cycle. A quilt doesn't need unnecessary wear and tear.
- Use a gentle, unscented laundry detergent or soap.
- Don't use fabric softener. Instead, add a few tablespoons of distilled white vinegar to the rinse cycle. This removes detergent residue, reduces odors, softens the fabric, and keeps colors bright.
- Throw dye-trapping sheets, like Shout Color Catchers, in the wash with the quilt. These absorb excess fabric dye released when washing. If you aren't a fabric pre-washer (I'm not), dye might be released when you wash your quilt, especially with saturated colors like red, black, and navy blue. If you have made a quilt that has white fabric as well as colored fabric, it is even more important that you throw a couple of Color Catchers in with the quilt. They really do work wonders!
- Remove the quilt right away once the wash cycle is done. (I once left a quilt in the washing machine for a couple of hours after the cycle ended, and some of the dye from the darker fabric transferred onto the lighter fabric it was touching.)
- Dry on low or normal heat. This one is a personal preference. (If you have pre-washed your fabrics, shrinkage will be minimal either way.) I usually dry on *normal* heat. Some might call this aggressive drying, but I like the crinkly look that happens when you dry on normal. If you prefer fewer of those crinkles, dry on low. If you really want to get meticulous about it, dry on low for 15 minutes. Then spread the quilt out on a flat surface to dry. What method you choose depends on the amount of time you want to spend drying a quilt and how you'd like said quilt to look after the process. Me? I'm all for easy, let's get this done!

Quilts with Hand Work or Delicate Fabrics

Some quilts merit the care of hand washing. These include ones with hand appliqué, hand quilting, antique fabrics, or delicate fabrics like silk. After spending all of that time on hand stitching a quilt, it seems crazy to just toss it in the washing machine. I couldn't do it. Heirloom-quality quilts need special treatment. Hand washing takes time and some elbow grease, but it is completely worth it.

Here is the method I use. I Inspect the quilt to make sure there aren't any issues. Just as when machine washing a quilt, loose or open seams and broken quilting threads can get worse when the quilt is washed. Fix any issues before washing.

- Pre-treat any dirty spots that need extra attention.
- Fill a clean bathtub or laundry sink with enough cold water to submerge the quilt. Add an appropriate amount of fragrance-free liquid laundry detergent to the water. Agitate the water to mix it in.
- Submerge the quilt in the water, and gently agitate the quilt for a few minutes with your hands.
- Leave the quilt in the water for 10 minutes, then agitate it gently again for a few minutes to loosen any dirt.
- Drain the water and refill the tub with clean, cold water. Agitate the quilt gently and repeat this process a few times until no soap bubbles are present.
- On the last rinse, add a few tablespoons of distilled white vinegar to the water. This helps remove any detergent residue, reduces odors, softens the fabric, and keeps colors bright.
- Let water run out of the quilt for a few minutes, then lightly press the water out. Start at the section furthest away from the drain and work toward it along the quilt. It is very important not to stress or twist the quilt, as threads can easily break.
- Cover a flat surface, larger than the quilt, with towels.
- Using a sling made from a sheet or a towel, remove the quilt from the bathtub and spread it out on the towels. Wet quilts can be very heavy, so make sure no part of the quilt is being pulled or stressed while it is being moved.
- Spread more towels on top of the quilt and gently roll the quilt and the towels together, squeezing excess water out of the quilt.
- Transfer the quilt to a flat sheet, out of direct sunlight, to air dry. If your only option for drying is in direct sunlight (out in the yard), place another flat sheet over the quilt while it dries.

HEAVY WHEN WET Never hang a wet quilt to dry. It is way too easy to distort the fabric or break threads when a quilt is heavy with water.

QUILTING TERMINOLOGY

Appliqué—Adhering a piece of fabric to a base piece of fabric by stitching

Appliqué needles—Hand-sewing needles used for appliqué

Backing—The back fabric of the quilt

Backstitch—Sewing in reverse, over previously sewn stitches, to secure them

Basting—Securing layers of the quilt sandwich together, with thread or pins to prepare for quilting

Basting stitch—A long stitch, used both by hand and on machines, to secure layers of fabric before stitching; intended to be removed after stitching

Batting/wadding—The layer between the quilt top and the quilt backing fabric

Bearding—When batting fibers pull through the quilt top or backing after quilting; they are visible on the front or back of a quilt

Between—Hand-sewing needle that is short, sharp, and thin with a round eye; allows for quick, easy, and small stitches through the quilt sandwich

Bias grain—Warp and weft threads are woven together at 90-degree angles to create fabric; bias is the 45-degree angle that intersects them

Bias binding—Binding made from fabric cut on the bias

Binding—Fabric used to cover the raw edges of a quilt; most often a folded band of fabric called "double-fold" binding

Binding tails—Pieces of binding not sewn down during the first part of the binding process; joined together and sewn down to finish attaching the binding

Bleeding—Color/dye migrating from one fabric to another when wet

Blind stitch/invisible stitch—Used when hand sewing a binding down; almost invisible on the quilt backing and not visible on the quilt top

Blocks—Pieces of sewn fabric joined to make a quilt

Bobbin—Small spool of thread on which the lower thread is wound; for use in a sewing machine

Bobbin case—Holds the bobbin; can be integrated into the sewing machine or be removable

Bolt—Holds fabric yardage; fabric is cut and sold from bolts in fabric shops

Border—Strips of fabric that "frame" the quilt; can be used as a design detail or to make the quilt larger

Bundles—Precut collections of fabric sold together

Chain piecing—Sewing in assembly-line fashion, without backstitching or cutting thread between blocks

Charm pack—A precut bundle of forty-two 5" × 5" squares of coordinating fabrics

Comic book boards—Lightweight, acid-free cardboard used as a "mini bolt" for easy, organized fabric storage

Concave curve—Inward bending curve, like the shape of the inside of a bowl or a cave

Convex curve—Outward bending curve, like the outside of a bowl or a dome

Cornerstones/posts—Fabric squares dividing sashing strips, usually at the intersection of quilt blocks; also used in borders at the corners of the quilt

Crosswise grain (Weft)—runs perpendicular to the selvage; has a little more give than lengthwise grain, but doesn't stretch like bias grain

Design wall—A blank wall where fabric can be placed to design your quilt; often covered with flannel

Directional print—Fabric that has a defined direction in the pattern, such as stripes

Dog ears—Small triangles of seam allowance fabric protruding over the edge of a quilt block when triangles are sewn together

Domestic machine—A home sewing machine

Easing in—Distributing excess fabric as you sew; often used around curves

Echo quilting—Quilting stitched at a repeating constant distance around a pieced or appliquéd design

Embellishment—Design elements added to the quilt after quilting is complete, such as buttons, crystals, and beads

Embroidery—Decorative designs with thread, added either by hand or machine

Embroidery needle—Long, sharp needle with a big eye; for thick thread or embroidery floss

English paper piecing (EPP)—Technique where fabric is wrapped around heavy paper templates and secured with glue or thread; the wrapped pieces are sewn together by hand to create a complex design

Facing—Finishing a quilt with no visible binding around its edges; the facing fabric is turned entirely to the back of the quilt; often used for modern quilts or wall hangings where a visible binding is undesirable

Fat Eighth (FE)—Piece of fabric measuring approximately 9" x 22"

Fat Quarter (FQ)—Piece of fabric measuring approximately 18" × 22"

Feed dogs—Metal teeth protruding from under the throat plate of a sewing machine; they move the fabric under the needle, as the needle stitches

Finger pressing—Using pressure from your fingers to press a seam open or to the side

Floating blocks—Quilt blocks surrounded by matching fabric to make them look as if they are floating on the quilt

Flying geese—Common quilt design of triangles stacked next to one another

Foundation paper piecing (FPP)—Sewing fabric to paper printed with a pattern, for detailed and accurate designs

Free motion quilting—Quilting by moving the quilt under the needle, in any direction

Freezer paper—Thick paper coated with plastic on one side; adheres to fabric by ironing; leaves no residue; is easily removed and re-used; used for appliqué, foundation paper piecing, and label making

Fusible adhesive—A polyester fiber that melts when ironed to bond together two fabrics; makes fabric less likely to ravel or fray

Fussy cutting—Cutting a specific image from a piece of fabric to isolate and use as part of the quilt design

Glue basting—Using washable glue to hold fabrics together for greater accuracy while sewing

Grain—Direction of the weave in fabric

Guide bar—An attachment for a walking foot; used to stitch lines at a uniform distance without marking

Half-square triangle block (HST)— Two triangles pieced together to make a square; one of the most common quilt blocks, HSTs can be arranged many ways to create designs

Hand appliqué—Using a needle and thread to attach a decorative shape of fabric to a base piece of fabric

Hand piecing—Piecing quilt blocks by hand

Hand quilting—Stitching by hand with a needle and thread to join the layers of the quilt sandwich

Handwork—Any part of the quilting process done by hand, such as needle-turn appliqué, hand embroidery, hand quilting, and embellishment

Hanging sleeve—A fabric tube sewn to the back of a quilt; for hanging a quilt for display

Hawaiian quilting—Symmetric designs sewn with needle-turn appliqué and hand quilted; patterns showcase the natural beauty of Hawaii and often include native plants, flowers, and fruit

Hera marker—Hand-held tool to make indentations in fabric

Hue—Color

Improvisational quilting—Piecing without a planned outcome

Interfacing—Used to stabilize fabric; available in a variety of thicknesses

Ironing—Using an iron in a sweeping motion to flatten fabric; may cause fabric or piecing to be distorted (see Pressing)

Jelly roll—A precut collection of 2½" × 42" coordinating fabric strips; typically includes forty strips

Label—A small piece of fabric attached to the back of the quilt to provide information

Layer cake—A precut collection of forty-two 10" × 10" squares of coordinating fabric

Lengthwise grain (Warp)—runs parallel to the selvage; has no stretch

Local quilt shop (LQS)—Your best resource for fabric, notions, machines and more!

Loft—Batting thickness

Longarm—A large sewing machine used for quilting; the machine moves over the quilt on both horizontal and vertical axes to create stitching patterns; longarms are both hand- and computer-"driven"

Longarm quilting—Joining the layers of the quilt sandwich with a longarm machine

Machine appliqué—Attaching a decorative piece of fabric to a base piece with a sewing machine

Machine piecing—Piecing quilt blocks using a sewing machine

Machine quilting—Joining the layers of the quilt sandwich with a sewing machine

Marking tools—Items used to mark quilts for sewing or quilting, such as Hera markers, chalk, and fabric markers

Matchstick quilting—Straight line quilting about a matchstick's width apart

Milliners/straw needle—Long, thin and delicate; creates a very small hole in fabric; used for basting, English paper piecing, and needle-turn appliqué

Mini charm pack—A precut bundle of forty-two 2½" × 2½" squares of coordinating fabrics

Mini quilt—A small quilt usually made to hang on a wall

Mitered border corner—Formed by joining two pieces of border fabric at a 45-degree angle

Mug rug—A fabric coaster, often oversized to allow room for a snack

Needle-punched—A type of batting; thousands of needles "punch" small holes, compressing and securing the fibers for stability

Needle-turn appliqué—Hand stitching a decorative piece of fabric to a base fabric by turning the edge of the decorative piece under itself, with the needle

Nesting seams—Pressing seam allowances in opposite directions to make the seams "nest" when sewn together; reduces bulk on your quilt top; makes matching points and corners easier

Non-directional print—A fabric that does not have a defined direction

Notions—Sewing accessories, such as needles, thread, scissors, thimbles, and rulers

On point—Placing (setting) square quilt blocks on a 45-degree angle, to appear as diamonds rather than squares. Side and corner triangles give the quilt straight sides.

Pattern matching—Matching the fabric pattern perfectly from one piece of fabric to another and sewing together

Perle cotton—Thick 100% cotton thread used for embroidery, hand quilting, and tying quilts

Piecing—Assembling and sewing together pieces of fabric to make a quilt

Pin basting—Using quilting pins to temporarily join the layers of the quilt sandwich prior to quilting

Point turner—A hand tool useful for turning points in sewing projects

Posts—See "Cornerstones"

Precuts—Fabric that is cut to a specific size and bundled for sale

Presser foot—Part of the sewing machine that presses fabric down as the needle is moving so the fabric does not shift

Pressing—Using an iron to press a seam; the iron is pressed on the fabric, held stationary, then removed

Pre-wash—To wash fabrics before using them

Quarter inch (¼″) foot—A sewing machine foot with a guide for sewing consistent ¼" seam allowances; mostly used for piecing quilts

Quilt-along—A group of quilters making the same quilt on a schedule determined ahead of time; quilt-alongs can be held in person or virtually with an online group

Quilter's knot—Simple, easy knot used for the thread on a needle for hand sewing

Quilt guild—A group of quilters who meet to talk about quilting, share projects, support each other, and learn

Quilt swap—An organized event where quilters sign up to participate; each quilter makes a quilt for another participant, and receives one in return

Quilt top—What will be seen when the quilt is right side up

Quilt sandwich—The three fabric layers of a quilt: the quilt top, the batting, and the quilt backing

Raw edge—The unfinished edge of fabric

Raw-edge appliqué—Sewing pieces of fabric with unfinished edges onto a base fabric, usually by machine

Relief quilting—Using blank spaces in dense quilting to create a design

Reverse appliqué—Fabric with cut-out design windows is layered on another; stitching around the windows and/or fusible adhesive between the layers secures them.

Right sides together (RST)—Placing together the printed sides of two fabrics in preparation for sewing

Rotary cutter—A circular, rotating cutting blade with a handle; used on a cutting mat with an acrylic ruler to cut straight, precise lines

Sashiko—Traditional Japanese embroidery using indigo blue fabric and white embroidery thread; used for decorative pieces or to repair clothing

Sashiko needle—Long, inflexible, and sharp; has a large eye to accommodate thicker thread

Sashing—Strips of fabric between quilt blocks to provide separation

Sashing border—Replicates the sashing between the quilt blocks; is added around the outermost quilt blocks

Scale—How large or small a print is on fabric

Scant quarter inch—Stitching that is one or two threads narrower than a quarter inch

Scraps—Small pieces of fabric left over from a project

Scrap quilt—Quilt made entirely of pieces of fabric left over from other projects

Scrappy binding—Binding made entirely of pieces of fabric left over from other projects

Scrim—Thin layer of polyester needle-punched or fused to batting for added stability

Seam allowance—Area between the edge of fabric and the stitch line

Seam ripper—Tool used to easily cut sewn stitching

Seam roller—Wooden tool used to flatten seams without heat

Selvage—The thick woven edge of fabric which prevents raveling; usually provides information about the fabric including brand, designer, colors used, production date, and location of printing

Sew-along—See "Quilt-along"

Shaft—Long, narrow section of the needle between the eye and the shank

Shank—Wide upper section of the needle inserted into a sewing machine

Sharps—General-purpose hand sewing needles; medium length, thin, delicate with sharp point

Solids—Fabric with one color; no pattern or print

Spray basting—Adhering layers of the quilt sandwich together using a light, fabric adhesive spray

Square up—Trim the sides of your quilt or quilt blocks straight with 90-degree corners

Stabilizer—Adhesive backing applied to fabric to stabilize it during embroidery or sewing; may be tear-away, wash-away, or permanent

Starch—Applied before ironing to stiffen fabric, making it easier to work with

Stash—The fabric you keep on hand; "I have a huge fabric stash!"

Stitch in the ditch—Stitching in the seam line where two pieces of fabric or blocks meet; used as a way to hide the stitching or to define areas of a quilt block; sometimes used to stabilize the quilt sandwich before free motion quilting

Stitch length—Number of stitches per inch

Stitch regulator—Feature of a sewing machine that regulates the number of stitches your machine sews relative to how fast you are moving the fabric; used for free motion quilting

Straight-line quilting—Sewing straight lines usually with a walking foot; one of the easiest ways to quilt on a domestic sewing machine

Strip piecing—Piecing strips of fabric together, then sub-cutting to make simple blocks

Synthetic thread—Thread made from synthetic material, like polyester, nylon or rayon

Tailor's clapper—Wooden tool used to press seams after ironing; creates a very flat seam

Tension—The balance between the top thread and bobbin thread while sewing on a machine

Thimble—Metal, leather, or synthetic finger cover used to protect the skin while hand sewing

Thread basting—Hand sewing large stitches with a needle and thread to temporarily join the layers of the quilt sandwich before quilting

Thread count—Number of threads woven into one square inch of fabric

Thread weight—How heavy or light a thread is; lower thread weight means thicker thread and higher thread weight means thinner thread; determined by how much length of thread it takes to reach a certain weight

Throat—Open window of space to the right of the needle on a sewing machine; more throat space can make it easier to work with larger projects

Tying—Using a heavy thread to tie the layers of a quilt sandwich together; an alternative to quilting

UFO (UnFinished Object)—Any project you've started and not finished

Value—Relative lightness or darkness of a color

Variegated thread—Thread containing multiple colors

Walking/dual-feed foot—Sewing machine foot with metal grabbers that move the top fabric under the needle at the same rate as the feed dogs move the bottom fabric; ideal for piecing and a *must* for straight-line machine quilting

Warp (lengthwise grain)—Threads running parallel to the selvage; during production; these threads are held stationary while weft threads are woven under and over them

Wavy borders—Borders that haven't been attached correctly resulting in undulating fabric around the perimeter of the quilt

Weft (crosswise grain)—Threads running perpendicular to the selvage; during production, these threads are woven over and under the warp threads

WIP (Work In Progress)—Any project that hasn't been finished

Whole cloth quilt—Quilt made from a single piece of fabric; the quilting stitches create the design of the quilt

Wideback—Fabric measuring 108" to 120" in width; often used for quilt backings

Width of Fabric (WOF)—Measurement from one selvage edge to the other, typically 42"–44"

Wrong sides together (WST)—Placing the unprinted sides of two fabrics together in preparation for sewing

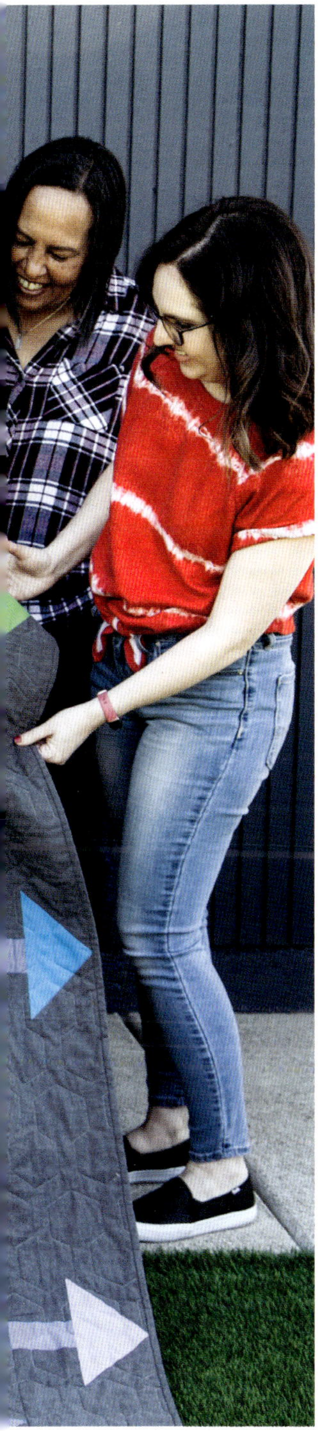

RESOURCES

Janome sewing machines and presser feet: Janome.com

Schmetz sewing machine needles: FatQuarterShop.com or Amazon.com

Tulip hand sewing needles: FatQuarterShop.com

Aurifil thread: FatQuarterShop.com

Quilters Dream batting: FatQuarterShop.com or Amazon.com

Kai Scissors: KaiScissors.com

Olfa rotary cutters: Joann.com

Quilters Select rulers: MissouriQuiltCo.com

U.S. Art Supply self-healing cutting mat: Amazon.com

Fabric markers: Amazon.com

HeatnBond Lite: Joann.com

Bias tape maker: Amazon.com

Oliso SmartIron: Oliso.com

Glue stick precision tip: Krebsbachhuber-crafts.square.site

Sue Daley rotating cutting mat: PinkDoorFabrics.com

EPP papers and templates: BrimfieldAwakening.com

SewTites: Sewtites.com

Pellon SF101 fusible interfacing: Joann.com

Fineline glue tip: PenAndPaperPatterns.com

June Tailor quilt label fabric sheets: Joann.com

WALK and WALK 2.0 by Jacquie Gering: LuckySpool.com

IRON MAN
EXTRA
CHEESE